Beyond
Marginality

SUNY Series on Modern Jewish Literature and Culture
Sarah Blacher Cohen, Editor

Beyond Marginality

ANGLO-JEWISH LITERATURE
AFTER THE HOLOCAUST

EFRAIM SICHER

State University of New York Press

Published by
State University of New York Press, Albany

Printed in the United States of America

For information, address State University of New York
Press, State University Plaza, Albany, N.Y., 12246

Library of Congress Cataloging in Publication Data

Sicher, Efraim.
  Beyond marginality.

  (SUNY series on modern Jewish literature & culture)
  Bibliography: p. 189.
  Includes index.
  1. English literature—Jewish authors—History and
criticism. 2. English literature—20th century—History
and criticism. 3. Jews in literature. I. Title.
II. Series: SUNY series on modern Jewish literature
and culture.
PR120.J48S53 1985   820'.9'8924   84-15266
ISBN 0-87395-976-0
ISBN 0-87395-975-2 (pbk.)

10 9 8 7 6 5 4 3 2 1

Contents

North–West

After

Acknowledgments

I WOULD LIKE to express my deep gratitude to my colleague, Dr. David M. Roskies, for invaluable bibliographical assistance; to Professor Harold Fisch, to whom I am indebted more than he might admit; to Professor Richard E. Sherwin for his encouragement; to Professor Sarah Blacher Cohen, for her confidence that the project was worthwhile; and, not least, to Borey Hoolom, without whom this book would not have been written.

Ben-Gurion University of the Negev
Beer Sheva

Adar 5743

CREDITS

2 lines from "Surprise! Surprise!" and 4 lines from "After the Release of Ezra Pound" by Dannie Abse, in his *Collected Poems*, London: Hutchinson, and Pittsburgh: University of Pittsburgh Press, 1977. Reprinted by permission of the author. © Dannie Abse, 1970, 1977.

12 lines from "I Was Not There" by Karen Gershon, in her *Selected Poems*, London: Gollancz, 1966. Reprinted by permission of the author. © Karen Gershon, 1966.

3 lines from "In a Cold Season" and 9 lines from "Treblinka" by Michael Hamburger, in his *Collected Poems*, Manchester: Carcanet Press, 1984. Reprinted by permission of the author. © Michael Hamburger, 1973, 1984.

3 lines from "This Time" by Bernard Kops. Reprinted by permission of the Editor of *European Judaism*. © European Judaism, 1982.

7 lines from "To T.S. Eliot" by Emanuel Litvinoff, in his *Notes for a Survivor*, Newcastle: Northern House, 1973. Reprinted by permission of the publishers. © Emanuel Litvinoff, 1973.

4 lines from "Struma" by Emanuel Litvinoff, in his *The Untried Soldier*, London: Routledge, 1942. Reprinted by permission of Routledge & Kegan Paul PLC, London, Henley & Boston. © Emanuel Litvinoff, 1942.

9 lines from "Returning, We Hear the Larks" by Isaac Rosenberg, in *The Collected Works of Isaac Rosenberg*, edited by Ian Parsons, London: Chatto & Windus, 1979. Reprinted by permission of the publishers. © The Author's Literary Estate and Chatto & Windus, 1979.

2 lines from "Job" by Nelly Sachs, translated by Michael Roloff, in Sachs' *Selected Poems*, London: Cape, 1968. Reprinted by permission of Suhrkamp Verlag, Frankfurt-am-Main, Jonathan Cape PLC, London, and Farrar, Straus & Giroux Inc., New York. © Suhrkamp Verlag, 1961; © Farrar, Straus & Giroux Inc., 1967.

8 lines from "Milkmaids," 4 lines from "Nature with Man," 4 lines from "Death of a Son," 3 lines from "The Coldness," 2 lines from "The People," 4 lines from "Isaiah's Thread," 3 lines from "A Word about Freedom and Identity in Tel-Aviv" and 3 lines from "To My Friends" by Jon Silkin, in his *Selected Poems*, London: Routledge & Kegan Paul, 1980. Reprinted by permission of Routledge & Kegan Paul PLC, London, Henley and Boston. © Jon Silkin, 1965, 1966, 1967, 1976, 1977, 1980.

3 lines from "A Prayer Cup" by Jon Silkin, in his *Selected Poems*, London: Routledge & Kegan Paul, 1980. Reprinted by permission of Norton & Co., New York, MidNAG Publications, and Routledge & Kegan Paul PLC, London, Henley and Boston. © Jon Silkin, 1976, 1980.

4 lines from "Into Praising," 2 lines from "The Lapidary Style," and 3 lines from "Lapidary Words" by Jon Silkin, in his *The Psalms with their Spoils*, London: Routledge & Kegan Paul, 1980. Reprinted by permission of Routledge & Kegan Paul PLC, London, Henley & Boston. © Jon Silkin, 1980.

5 lines from "Portrait of a Modern Jew" by Nathaniel Tarn, in his *Old Savage/Young City*, London: Cape, and New York: Random House, 1964. Reprinted by permission of Jonathan Cape PLC and the author. © Nathaniel Tarn, 1964.

Introduction

I N SOME WAYS this is a personal book. For one thing, any selection of literary material out of a wide variety of talents and genres is going to be subjective. Among the Jews writing in Britain in the three decades from 1953 are recognized major literary personalities (Arnold Wesker, Harold Pinter, Frederic Raphael, Jon Silkin, Peter Shaffer), while others are not always as well-known (the novelists Brian Glanville, Bernice Rubens, Gerda Charles; the poets Dannie Abse, Michael Hamburger, Karen Gershon; the East Enders Emanuel Litvinoff, Bernard Kops, Wolf Mankowitz). Yet all of these writers deal with problems of identity and community, reflected in their treatment of roots and alienation, menace and derangement, guilt and suffering. These are universal motifs, but their particular significance for Jewish writers relates both to their dissatisfaction with an inherited marginal status and to their critical portrayal of the Anglo-Jewish community.

The question of dual allegiance establishes a relationship with the Jewish community whether the writer wills it or not, while the Holocaust and the outside forces of History make inevitable the existential quest for literary and socioethnic selfhood. To accuse the modern Jewish writer, as Philip Roth and Brian Glanville have been accused, of anti-Semitism or self-hate is to deny the possibility of being a Jew and a writer, for the protest against the Jewish family so evident in contemporary literature is a protest against social and cultural marginality; it is a cry of pain, a pain from within which requires examination and treatment, not condemnation.[1]

Is there such a thing as Jewish poetry, or the Jewish novel, or a Jewish drama? Richard Fein thinks it is like the joke about the Elephant and the Jewish Problem: the Jew can make even the elephant relevant to his Jewishness, but the metaphor also says something about the universal terms in which the Jew must address the host society in order to express a sense of apartness and insecurity created by the modern world.[2] I believe poetry does come out of the Jew's dilemma because poetry of the most intense kind can be the only option for the serious writer under such immense social and emotional tension who wishes to reach a wide, predominantly non-Jewish audience. Whether that kind of writing can be considered part of Jewish culture is the subject of a recent debate between Robert Alter and Harold Bloom on the existence of a culture that is both culture and Jewish.[3] When the Jew has got as far from Jewishness as the elephant, when (as Harav Soloveitchik says) like Jonah fleeing to Tarshish he has fled his identity and communal responsibility, the search for Jewishness begins. Kafka's groping towards Judaism and Zionism is an example of how lost is the modern Jewish writer; out of this agonized searching is born, in lucky cases, the most passionate art.

In order to concentrate on works of lasting literary importance a number of popular novelists (Lionel Davidson, Rosemary Friedman, Maurice Edelman) and humorists (Cyril Kersh, George Mikes) have been passed over, as have been writers who are in no way troubled by their Jewish origins, either because it means little to them or because there is no conflict, as well as Commonwealth writers, who have problems of their own (Dan Jacobson, Adele Wiseman, Mordecai Richler),[4] and those poets who have left Britain for the richer pastures of the United States (Nathaniel Tarn, Denise Levertov) or for the resown fields of Zion (Dennis Silk).[5] Limitation of space and necessity of selection have rendered impossible discussion of poets Laurence Lerner, Philip Hobsbaum and Michael Horovitz, though the works of these and other Anglo-Jewish authors who deal at least partly with the problematics of Jewishness will be found in the bibliography. The accent on living writers regrettably discounts Lazarus Aaronson, as well as the great precursors of Anglo-Jewish literature, Israel Zangwill and Isaac Rosenberg, whose importance for the post-Holocaust generation will be discussed in the first chapter.

The writers who figure in this study have publicly identified themselves as Jews (even if not born of a Jewish mother, as in at least one case), but they are Jews outside the organized Jewish

community and distant from traditional Jewish life. They would deny they are writers who may be classified as "Jewish" and their responses to identity and community are distinctly individual in style and politics. To class them under any one heading would be to seriously misrepresent their work and to obscure individual merit, as well as to fail to see the hopelessness of grouping together many postwar British authors. Not only do they share certain influences with their non-Jewish colleagues, but their contribution to English literature was not initially a specifically Jewish one. If some burst onto the literary scene as Angry Young Men, they were not exclusively Angry Young Jews; if some were among the first in Britain to experiment with television and film, this has not necessarily to do with the prominence of Jewish television tycoons (Sidney Bernstein and Lew Grade to name but two) or Jewish film producers in Ealing and Hollywood. Nor were they made by Jewish publishers and critics, even the few publishers and critics with avowedly Jewish interests.

On the other hand, they grew up in the thirties and forties, just old enough to remember Hitler and Spain, evacuation and Blitz, and entered literature in the fifties, when new voices were being heard in drama, prose and verse. Beyond these circumstantial similarities, they record the social actualities and the aspirations of Anglo-Jewry both because this is an environment that has affected them personally and out of a desire to attack general social ills by describing a milieu they know only too well.[6] Sometimes Jewish heroes bear a disguised identity, at other times specific Jewish references are translated into poetic metaphor and fable, but the imaging of society reveals perceived values and self-images of the Jew. Lucien Goldmann insists on literary excellence as a criterion of coherence of social consciousness and his sociological approach to the novel is relevant here:

> An imaginary universe, apparently completely removed from any specific experience—that of a fairy tale, for instance,—may, in its structure, be strictly homologous with the experience of a particular social group or, at the very least, linked in a significant manner, with that experience.[7]

The artistic conceptualization of fictional actuality can assist an understanding of social problems in the real world far more effectively than statistical tables and "scientific" investigations (as if they were guarantees of objectivity and precision!). The hierarchical *values* of the fictionalized world are common to a wide thematic range of texts and to different generic forms among a writing population which can be defined as "Jewish" only by a complex and contradictory socioethnic formulation, yet which is responsive in terms of that group to similar historical and socioeconomic factors in the years 1953–1983. This was a period which opened with a new Elizabethan age, the death of Stalin, and the founding of the London *Jewish Quarterly* and which closed with economic Recession, the brief ascension of Andropov and a hard-line regime in the Soviet Union, and renewed anti-Semitism.

At the same time, Anglo-Jewish writing looks back to immigrant origins in the East End of London in order to examine the sociological process of upward mobility and suburbanization, with the attendant emotional and ideological crises for the Jewish child or adolescent. For this reason it is convenient to follow the geographical progression from the poorer East London postal districts (the East End), through North-East London (Hackney, Stamford Hill) to the affluent suburbs of North-West London (Golders Green, Hampstead, Finchley, Hendon); a not dissimilar pattern is observable in provincial centers of Jewish population (Manchester, Liverpool, Cardiff, Glasgow), except that for provincials, too, the outer London suburbs became the final stage of arrival. (As in James Boswell's day the sons of Scotland looked south for prospects.)

This survey aims to provide a useful comparison with the situation of Jewish writers in other countries of the Diaspora, in particular the United States, but there is no intention to represent an overall picture of Anglo-Jewish life, nor do I pretend to definitive evaluations of the total work of each author. The themes which shall be explored are characteristically, but not exclusively, Jewish, yet the inclusion of them does not in itself make the author Jewish. An author is a Jew or isn't, and if there is reference to being a Jew it is a way of giving meaning to an inescapable reality. Rather it is the writing which is made Jewish, even if its Jewishness is not unqualified or absolute. Nor is "Jewish writing" merely an expression of autobiographical obsession (however helpful may be Freudian interpretations of the literary text). To quote Rosenzweig on being a Jewish person, one lives Jewishness, one *is* it, and writing is a means to becoming, although the process must be understood within the complex relationship of writer to writing environment and to text. The problematic writing experience and the experience of being a Jew are locked in mutual catalysis and mortal conflict. Edmond Jabès has spoken of the "difficulté d'être Juif, qui se confond avec la difficulté d'écrire; car le judaïsme et l'écriture ne sont qu'une même attente, un même espoir, une même usure." And if there is relevance in the dictum of the Russian poetess Marina Tsvetaeva that all poets are Jews, this does not deny the uniqueness of being a writer who is a Jew, but, to paraphrase Jacques Derrida, the situation of the Jew has become paradigmatic of the situation of the poet and paradigmatic of the writing act.

There are of course many precedents for the involvement of Jews in non-Jewish and secular cultures, of which one example is Isaac Deutscher's claim for the place of the "non-Jewish Jew" in a Jewish tradition going back to Rabbi Meir and Elisha ben Abuyah in the Midrash. Deutscher's marginal Jew on the borders of the surrounding culture, yet not of it, was an iconoclast who, having broken out of the taboos and institutions of the Jewish community, was not tied down by the rigid categories of thinking in the adopted culture. Uriel Acosta, Spinoza, Heine, Marx, Rosa Luxemburg, Trotsky and Freud each in their own way strove for a universal *Weltanschauung* because they could not reconcile themselves to the kind of categories which defined them, too, in nationalist or religious terms. Yet how perverse a mockery the solidarity of man sounds even to Deutscher this side of the Holocaust! Perhaps, as Deutscher says, only Heine guessed at the tragic destiny of the modern Jew. Nevertheless, distrust in the nineteenth-century nation-state doesn't always endear the Jewish intellectual to Israel (Deutscher and George Steiner are two examples) and it makes the Jew even more wary of the value systems of the West European democracies.[8]

The excesses of Fascism and Communism affected the post-Holocaust Jew no less than the general disillusion with Socialism following the war, but at the same time the secular Yiddish culture that was the culture of the Jewish labor movement had been decimated by the Nazis and negated by the assimilating, socially mobile children of the post–1881 immigrants. All that remained to fall back on and hand down to the next generation was what Steiner has termed the dread inheritance of remembering the six million. It is from this vacuous position that the modern Jewish writer must seek a way back to Judaism, as well as to the Yiddish culture of the East European *shtetl*[9] and the Hebrew culture of modern Israel, in order to confront renewed threats to the Jew's moral stance and existence.

Inevitably, the writing is secular even in its biblical themes, though it should be remembered that Torah literature does not always refer ostensibly to Jews or God, for example the so-called wisdom literature, so attractive to secularists, which is intrinsically Torah-

Jewish: the Book of Esther provides a classic example of the "absence" or "hiddeness" of God. Several generations of medieval Jewish poets or the Israeli poetess Zelda (1914–1984), moreover, testify that there need be no intrinsic contradiction between Torah Judaism and secular literature, inasmuch as morality and aesthetics are defined in terms compatible with Judaism. Recently Yiddish folklore and Jewish concepts have been fashionable, whether it is the return to the old Hellenism versus Hebraism rift with a new confidence of cultural identity, as in the stories of Cynthia Ozick in the United States, or the conflict of sex and violence with Judaism, as in the stories of Clive Sinclair, recipient of the 1981 Somerset Maugham Award, who has been much influenced by Isaac Bashevis Singer, an influence present also in Elaine Feinstein's fantasy novel, *The Shadow Master* (1978). A most striking example of a reevaluation of the English literary tradition and particularly the modernism of T. S. Eliot and Ezra Pound from the point of view of the Jewish historical experience is the poetry of Jon Silkin in the collection *The Psalms with their Spoils* (1980); his most ambitious attempt to give a Jewish focus to the nature of man and history is the long *Footsteps on a Downcast Path*, begun in Israel in 1980 but published too late to be considered here, whose language and idea of God owe something to both Isaac Rosenberg and Yehuda Amichai.

The Jewishness of writing in non-Jewish languages which does not directly draw on Jewish literary traditions poses a problem not of definition but description. Jewishness, as distinct from Judaism, is a question not so much of biographies as of the writers' search for a writing identity and for a language, in the sense of a moral as well as a cultural code. One attempt to describe contemporary Jewish writing has adopted the term *mentshlikhkeyt* for such a code to which, consciously or subconsciously, Jewish writers turn in their rebellion against the older generation. The ethic of *mentshlikhkeyt* presumes man's basic ability to choose between good and evil and it involves a will to good as the prime aim of existence. This is, of course, to deny the concept of an absurd universe and to prefer belief in the moral significance of one's actions and in responsibility for the suffering of others (Ernie Levy doesn't in the end choose the existentialist way out in André Schwarz-Bart's *The Last of the Just*).[10] Such an affirmation, against all odds, of the humanitarian ideal calls into question any justification for evil and suffering in this world. It requires of God, too, to rise to the moral standards of *mentshlikhkeyt*. Indictment of the apparent lack of mercy balancing Divine justice is typical of much post-Holocaust writing, although there is a long Jewish tradition of patiently reminding the Creator of the Divine promises to man in the covenant with the Patriarchs that goes back to Moses defending the Jewish people against the wrath of the Almighty, Job's contentions in his personal tribulations and Jeremiah's laments over the troubles of Israel. Calling God to trial, as it were, is also found in the stories of the Khasidic masters, most notably in tales of Yitskhak-Lev of Berdichev, who in his advocacy for the Jewish people went as far as to bring a lawsuit before the Holy One in his famous *Kaddish* prayer.

What another Khasidic master, Nakhman of Bratslav, once said about telling a story to wake people up instead of telling stories to send them to sleep is probably one of the more apt statements of the aims of Jewish writing.[11] How post-Holocaust Jewish authors reacted against the sleepy complacency of the Jewish community, its spiritual and cultural poverty, yet have come back to Jewish sources and values in the attempt to combat the indifference of the world, to wake people up, is one of the central subjects explored in this book.

Writers in the Isles

Chapter One
Assimilators and Assimilated: From Israel Zangwill to Louis Golding

The Jews who came to England after the Norman conquest in the eleventh century were Norman French speakers who wrote Latin and Hebrew. Jewish writing in English is quite recent and Jews can be spoken of as English writers in Britain only in the decades following the Second World War. There exist precedents, such as Israel Zangwill (1864–1926) or the poet Isaac Rosenberg (1890–1918), and some of the ways in which they may be important for the post-Holocaust generation will be discussed in this chapter. (Benjamin Disraeli does not figure here if only because his preoccupation with Young England and presentation of the Jewish question in *Coningsby* and *Tancred* did not match his more serious reputation as a statesman.[1])

Anglo-Jewish literature nevertheless continues a tradition that goes back to *Mishlei Shu'alim*, the "Fox Fables" of Berekhiah ben Natronai ha-Nakdan, probably identical with Benedict le Pointur, known to be living in Oxford in 1194, not to mention such illustrious authors of *Tosaphot* (later commentaries on the Talmud, the Jewish legal code) as Jacob of Orleans, who perished in the London massacre of 1189, and the *paytan* (liturgical poet) Yom-Tov of Joigny, the central figure in the martyrdom of York Jewry in 1190.[2] After the expulsion of the Jews from England in 1290 there was to be no organized Jewish settlement in England for the best part of four hundred years and there was no significant Jewish contribution to

English literature until the nineteenth century. The Jew lingered mythically in the Christian reception of the Hebrew Bible and in the image of the Jew as Devil and Judas, the Antichrist responsible for ritual murder, which was handed down the ages as a mythical representation of the Jew's alien, parasitical role in society as usurer, poisoner and so forth, a tradition continued by Chaucer, Marlowe, Shakespeare, Dickens, T. S. Eliot and Graham Greene.[3]

One could start the story of Anglo-Jewish literature with Grace Aguilar (1816–1847) and a long line of literary ladies who composed edifying tales of Jewish heroism and ghetto life for domestic consumption. The first Anglo-Jewish novel, in the sense of a critical model of contemporary Jewish society, was *Reuben Sachs* (1889) by Amy Levy (1861–1889), who committed suicide at the age of twenty-eight. On the whole, however, the Anglo-Jewish novel of 1881–1920 bears little comparison with modern Jewish writing in Britian and modern Jewish authors look back rarely if ever to their Victorian predecessors. Yet there remains in *Reuben Sachs* some interest "in the extraordinary similarity of the monied, Bayswater Jewish society it depicts, at a time when the East Europe immigrants had yet to emerge from the East End—and their descendants in London today. There is the same ostentation, the same social intolerance, the same overt materialism, the same breach with Jewish traditions, uncompensated by a real identification with those of England."[4]

Even Zangwill fell into neglect until around 1964[5] and was virtually ignored by modern Jewish writers, with the exception of a few sparse tributes. Zangwill, like the regional realists Eden Philpotts, Arnold Bennett and others, uncovered an unknown aspect of English life, the Jewish East End, but, as Harold Fisch has made so admirably clear,[6] Zangwill imbued his realism with an idealism that rose above sordid facts towards the epic. Zangwill is perhaps more of a socio-cultural precedent than the modern Jewish writer might think, touching, as he does, on the problem of Anglicization and the dilemma of the Anglo-Jewish novelist. His protagonist in *Children of the Ghetto* (1892), Esther Ansell, is not just a poor Jewish girl, not just an autobiographical extension of Zangwill himself, but "She is ultimately a symbol of the Jew in an alien environment: she carries upon herself, consciously even, the burden of Jewish destiny . . ."[7] Esther presents the true Judaism of the East End pauper which does not withstand the passage westward, to the homes of the *nouveaux riches* "semi-divine" philanthropists and ministers of Anglican Judaism. The choice facing Esther of apostasy or return to the Ghetto is reflected in a number of protagonists and in the duality which the author had to work out in so much of his fiction. Esther Ansell, a living lesson of Jewish poverty and suffering, has written a novel, pseudonymously of course, which castigates the double standards and insincerity of Anglican Judaism. The reactions of Esther's shocked benefactors, who little suspect the viper is in their midst, are not so far removed from the storm of "defense mechanisms" which met Brian Glanville's controversial novel *The Bankrupts* (1958) and which may well have been introduced here to preempt Zangwill's own critics.

Mrs. Henry Goldsmith, Esther's wealthy benefactor, who has, out of magnaminous philanthropy, salvaged her from the poverty of the Ghetto, brings that favorite "defense mechanism" into play whenever a picture of Jewish life is less than flattering: what will the Gentiles think? There may well be some unrepresentative family that thinks of nothing except dress, money and solo-whist, but why should all Jews be tarred with the same brush? It doesn't occur to Mrs. Henry Goldsmith that the opprobrious and elusive Edward Armitage (Esther's pen name) might be saying something applicable to her circle. Certainly her circle could not admit Mr. Armitage now. One of the distinguished guests assembled at the Goldsmiths', Miss Cissy Levine, speaks for the genteel Jewish authoress who "believed in the mission of Israel, and wrote domestic novels to prove that she had no sense of humor,"[8] when she declares that criticism of one's own people is definitely not cricket. Montagu Samuels, the "narrow-minded and narrow-chested" City magnate, decides "the rascal has only written it to make money," deliberately exaggerating and distorting because "anything spicy pays nowadays."[9] No one denies the author's talent nor the element of truth in the descriptions of Jewish society, but these ostriches of West London seek to deflect criticism by attributing scurrilous motives to the author:

> 'The whole book's written with gall,' went on Percy Saville emphatically. 'I suppose the man couldn't get into good Jewish houses, and he's revenged himself by slandering them.'[10]

The guests at the Goldsmiths' Chanukamas celebration take turns guessing the real identities of some of the scandalous portraits in the book but immediately deny they have read the book themselves— there are actually jargon words in it, vulgar Yiddish! Criticism is condemned as anti-Semitism by these "poor rich Jews" whose "national literature" comprises what is called today the "hatched, matched and dispatched" (social and personal) columns of the *Jewish Chronicle*.

The task of the Jewish author to Zangwill/Esther's way of thinking is to depict Jewish society truthfully, with all the snobbery, hypocrisy and vulgarity it shares with English society. Leon Raphael warns her, however, that the author must not forget the true Jewish poetry of the Bible and of medieval Spain, and must not forget the spiritual potentiality of Judaism.

The Children of the Ghetto is a bittersweet satire of London Jewry in the decade of the Russian pogroms which crowded the poorest streets of the East End with waves of penniless Ashkenazic East European laborers; their ghetto Judaism and alien jargon embarrassed the monied, cultured, emancipated, Anglicized Sephardic Jewish aristocracy. Far from indulging in nostalgia for an ideal traditional-minded community—and the East End was never totally or overwhelmingly religious—Zangwill saw the signs of disintegration, although for the next assimilated and reformed generation, who had segregated their Race from their Religion, this was a bastion of orthodoxy. None is spared Zangwill's caustic eye, and extravagant space is allocated to polemical bones of contention between Orthodoxy and Higher Biblical Criticism (Zangwill's 1889 contribution to the *Jewish Quarterly Review* on English Judaism is relevant here). Yet oddly enough Zangwill, a promising English humorist, was at first reluctant to take on the job of doing a Jewish *Robert Elsmere*, a commission offered by the Anglo-Jewish journalist Lucien Wolf at the instigation of the American cofounder of the Jewish Publication Society, Judge Mayer Sulzberger. There was a Jewish novel in him struggling to get out, but Zangwill wanted to go beyond the "Jewish details" and make of it a story of human interest that would be "that cosmopolitan thing, a work of art;"[11] later he tried to resist editors' attempts to tie him to exclusively Jewish themes.

The married women of the East End maintain a pious respect for the Torah and wouldn't dream of mixing milk with meat, while the men relax quite naturally in their synagogues and prayer houses. But Zangwill's alienated prejudice is soon evident: in the social clubs that were the synagogues the men chat between needlessly overlong prayers, which not all of them could understand anyway. For Zangwill ritual amounts to so many outward signs and motions which do not answer to the poverty and squalor of everyday life. The poor literally have nothing to lose but their religion. It is as if the official fast days are just an extra burden to add to the other hungry days in the year. Unemployment is acute, but many a father's insistence on Sabbath observance ruins a young man's career.

Zangwill's castigation of ruthless sweatshop owners and Jewish commercial practice approaches something like George Eliot's deprecation of gaudiness and materialist vulgarity in the Cohen household in *Daniel Deronda* (in contrast to the idealization of Mordecai and Daniel). One of the tasks of the Anglo-Jewish novel, however, is to combat stereotypes without wincing from unpleasant truths.

> 'We have always been badly treated in literature,' said Raphael. We are made either angels or devils. On the one hand, Lessing and George Eliot; on the other, the stock dramatist and novelist, with their low-comedy villain.'[12]

The Jews are not all wealthy and the Jewish financier, while not exactly a positive figure, is not the sinister Machiavellian villain he is supposed to be. The Ghetto usurer is, in fact, a kindly Christian and the image of Jewish peddlars is corrective of the standard caricatures in *Punch* and Victorian English literature.

> For the despised three-hatted scarecrow of Christian caricature, who shambled along snuffling 'Old clo',' had a strenuous inner life, which might possibly have vied in intensity, elevation, and even sense of humour, with that of the best of the jeerers on the highway. To Moses 'travelling' meant straying forlornly in strange towns and villages, given over to the worship of an alien deity, and ever ready to avenge his crucifixion; in a land of whose tongue he scarce knew more than the Saracen damsel married by legend to A'Beckett's father. It meant praying brazenly in crowded railway trains, winding the phylacteries sevenfold round his left arm, and crowning his forehead with a huge leather bump of righteousness, to the bewilderment or irritation of unsympathetic fellow-passengers. It meant living chiefly on dry bread and drinking black tea out of his own cup, with meat and fish and the good things of life utterly banned by the traditional law, even if he were flush. It meant carrying the red rag of an obnoxious personality through a land of bulls.[13]

Here is the modern Jewish predicament, but persecution has not taught the Jews hate, for sufferance is the badge of their tribe (Zangwill appropriates the Shakespearian phrase), even though they are threatened by Christian missionaries who barter religion for bread.

The Jewish pauper is an uncultured, unwashed alien, but there is humanity in his heart and there is "the stuff of human life" in the Ansells' tiny drab garret at No. 1 Royal Street. Yet the family squabbles do not give the impression of the closeknit extended family modern writers associate with the East End, although the community, for all its cruel sectarian pride and its superstitious ignorance, does pull together in times of distress. There is no future in the folkways of the East End and one by one the children break away. They question the narrow rigidity of Jewish law and their unwary parents are unable to answer pertinent questions regarding the permissibility of organs in synagogue services, or to respond to scepticism about divine revelation and other topics then being raised by the Reform movement in Judaism. Like the pre–1881 Russian *maskilim* (proponents of the Jewish Enlightenment), Zangwill is ready "to defend and to attack" (to use an expression of L. Levanda), to defend the Jewish people against slander and prejudice and to attack whatever seemed primitive and backward in Jewish life. Zangwill picks a favorite example of an institution which causes real heartbreak, the marriage restrictions affecting *Kohanim* (priests), but he also points out the levity with which some young people treat the sanctity of marriage and he suggests that the antireligious anarchists do not carry the working-class Jews with them.

Esther Ansell thinks of herself unquestionably as English, although she has no real knowledge of the world outside the ghetto except for Victoria Park, the one local oasis of greenery and recreation amid slums and workshops. Esther discovers "heroic love" in the magazines she reads at Dutch Debbie's, the black sheep of the Ghetto, and she awakens to the meanness and ugliness around her. Like other children of her age she is terribly ashamed of her uncouth, shabby, Yiddish-speaking father. She goes to school to be Anglicized, as well as to qualify for charity clothes. She begins to read a brown-covered book, the New Testament. Within her she harbors an unfathomable sadness, born of despair and revolt, yet in the end she throws off her dependence on the rich Goldsmiths, abandons her false position in their house and returns home to the East End. Doing this, she "defies the universe," for she has abandoned traditional values in spite of her acknowledgment at heart of the goodness of Providence. Her pessimistic and critical outlook is presented as something quintessentially Jewish, for she is painfully aware of unpleasant self-truths, too, which prevent her losing her identity problem in an easy reconciliation with socialism or assimilation.

The move to the West End is a step up the social ladder and it is a step to Anglicization. The Goldsmiths observe the ancient rites mainly for fear of offending their devout Roman Catholic housekeeper

Mary O'Reilly, who knew more of these things than her masters cared to know, while they maintain the largely self-reciprocal exclusivity of their set. Henry Goldsmith has arrived, in more senses than one, from the provinces and with all the drive his wife can command he has built himself up as a pillar of the United Synagogue and a light to Anglo-Jewry. His wife would also like him to become a light to Parliament and persuades him to stand for the Whitechapel constituency in the East End.

Sydney Graham (né Abrahams) epitomizes the assimilated Jewish artist who justifies his change of name as conforming more truthfully to the image others would have of him. He nearly marries into a strict Wesleyan family who didn't dream he might be a Jew!

Leon Raphael embodies Intellectual Orthodoxy, his culture certified at Oxford, but he has little in common with the traditional Jewish way of life of the East End masses, whom he seeks to convert to his ideas on the symbolic function of Judaic practice through his editorship of the *Flag of Judah*, the organ of the Henry Goldsmith party. Leon is adequate neither in adapting to the harsh realities of human nature nor in countering the arguments of Esther or Striletski.

Joseph Striletski, the successful minister of Kensington Synagogue, is choked by the white tie and clerical collar he is paid to wear. Like Esther, he concludes that Jewish ritual is outmoded but, like her, he returns to the East End and attends a Day of Atonement service. He sails out on the same boat as Esther to America where a wide range of Jews develop their liberal beliefs. Only in the "land of the free" can Judaism be revived as a socioethnic model. Indeed, Zangwill's invective against all sectors of Anglo-Jewry allows for few redeeming qualities and the only hope for the future seems to reside in America. Zangwill's facetious, publicistic metaphors are directed to the outside world, to show how Jews embrace all shades, good and bad, and have their peculiarities like any other nation. But the author takes issue with George Eliot when he has Striletski argue that it is not enough to be like other nations with one's own homeland. The Jews' spiritual mission cannot be accomplished in Palestine. (This was written before Zangwill met Herzl and joined the Zionists, though he later split away after the Uganda Plan was defeated and formed the Jewish Territorial Organization.) The "Holy Land League" (*Hovevey Tsion*) is ridiculed as a feeble attempt to collect paltry sums for easing the hardships of the Sabbatical Year. The return to Zion is realized only in old Hyams' pious wish to die in Jerusalem. The modern Hebrew poet Pinchas Melchizedek, a caricature of Naphtali Herz Imber (1856–1909), author of the Zionist national athem, *Hatikvah*, is exposed as a fraud.

Jewish identity leaves none of the protagonists neutral, none can remain indifferent, one way or the other, to their unchosen religion, the Chosen race. The confrontation of Judaism with modern scepticism and Western culture is experienced as a personal crisis by the "Grandchildren of the Ghetto," as it was by Zangwill, and this is what enables Zangwill's use of real models and historical actuality to approach artistic truth.

Zangwill was one of several Jews in the fifty years after Jewish emancipation who were not primarily interested in purveying the expected exotica to the English reader and were not concerned solely with the light in which the Jew appeared to the Gentile.[14] The post–1881 persecution of Jews in the Tsarist Empire had in any case aroused a storm of sympathy in England where the Jews was now revealed as a pogrom victim. Some acquaintance was made with the East European *shtetl*, not least through Karl Emil Franzos, whose *Jews of Barnow* was translated in 1882. George Eliot's *Daniel Deronda* had also done something to change set attitudes and to invest the Jew with tragic dignity and national pride, though partly deriving from Romantic conceptions of the legendary Wandering Jew. But if George Eliot's aim was to criticize English society for its mediocrity and for the public image of the Jew, those who wrote and lived as Jews tended to write with the passion of one who knows Jewish life from the inside and who is ready to criticize its underside. The sociological documentation of immigrant life deals with the changing conditions of the Jew as a member of English society and, though not many Jewish novelists were remarkable in literary distinction, they are symptomatic of Jewish writers motivated by an inner questioning of identity for whom Yiddish and certainly Hebrew were not viable options. They are removed from the Jewish East End and its predominantly Yiddish culture of the early twentieth century, which they see as an imported, self-imposed ghetto in a free country, but they go back to immigrant roots to show how the younger, English-born generation can change and be changed, how acculturation can be achieved without succumbing to the vices of the West London Jewish bourgeoisie. The novel of social conscience tells us much about social mobility and aspirations, although the attempts to grapple with dilemmas resulting from social acceptance sometimes follow patterns which may specifically deny the possibility of a Jewish writing. Certainly not a few shared the attitude of the *Allgemeine*

Zeitung des Judenthums to the appearance in 1840 of Heine's *Der Rabbi von Bacharach,* that the Ghetto and what it represented was dead, buried and better forgotten. The chronicling of East End life in Zangwill's *Children of the Ghetto* or Samuel Gordon's *Sons of the Covenant* (1900), however more romanticized than Abraham Cahan's picture of New York's Lower East Side, was, it seems, for some too uncomfortable a reminder of their origins and identity.

CROSSING THE STREET

The interwar generation of Anglo-Jewish writers was to have fewer qualms about any allegiance owed to their Jewish brethren: the worst imaginable aspects of the East End came to represent all of Judaism and Jewishness in sum. The spiteful blaspheming of the Jewish religion is the reaction of the son of an East End immigrant family who is determined to change the world in Max Mundlak's indicative though hardly memorable *Journey into Morning* (1940). Gerald Kersh's *Thousand Deaths of Mr. Small,* published in 1951 though set in the interwar years, illustrates the social progress of the immigrants with a bitter attack on the monstrous Jewish mother, who sucks the soul out of her children, and the ne'er-do-well *shlemiel* of a father, whose religion is hypocrisy and self-deception in the worst taste.

Suburbanization in some sectors of Anglo-Jewry in the interwar years meant not only a break with the Jewish past, as can be seen in a paler version of Zangwill's epic, Louis Golding's *Magnolia Street* (1932), a novel of provincial Jewry in the northern city of Manchester in 1910–1930, the years of war and Depression. The Jews of "Doomington" have already begun to infiltrate Gentile quarters and mingle with non-Jews—the book starts with the premise of this hope—but on Magnolia Street Jews and Gentiles keep to their respective sides of the street. These are slum-Jews who go hungry in order to keep up with payments on mahogany sideboards, who turn a front parlor into a candy store (here is corroboration of the stereotype of Jewish commercialism), who get rich from manufacturing rainproof coats (Jewish war-profiteering). But there is also Rose Berman who supports her widowed mother by working for a Deansgate music store, Saturdays included (but tolerated). Her love for John Cooper, the sailor from across the wide ocean of the street, is filled with a secret spiritual harmony and reciprocity. War and Benny Edelman's rescue of little Tommie Wright from drowning unite Magnolia Street as one and boost Mr. Emmanuel's campaign for universal union: with a bit of courage and love the two sides of the street can come together, even if they feel more comfortable in their own places of worship.

Yet most of the time the two sides live together in mutual animosity, while their social aspirations mirror their history. The Jews push their children toward the professions and move to more wealthy middle-class districts; the Coopers have come down in the world. The Jews boast a transatlantic boxing champion, Mick Shulman, while Steve Townie on the other side plays for the city's football club. America is the Seigels' dream, though it's not in reality the *goldene medina*, the Promised Land where fortunes are made, and there are such illusions in the non-Jewish houses too. The men are like overgrown boys, though perhaps just a little more degenerate on the Gentile pavement. These types are quintessentially human (Max Emmanuel uses them in his paintings) and Magnolia Street comprises a microcosm of community relations. It's just the same in the Jewish quarter in Salonika, and the pattern is presumably repeated in London's East End or anywhere else. The novel has been called overrated, but the author does convey the nervous introspection of the characters, their prejudices and paranoia. Despite his simplistic conviction that Jew and Christian can overcome preconceived ideas of each other's strange ways, Golding recognizes the blind hate of anti-Semitism and actually shows that medieval accusations survive into the twentieth century. Yet he exploits the capacity of his characters for sympathy and pity to suggest that although these people don't comprehend the subtleties of the larger forces of history and ideology the strongest force for bringing them together is sex.

JEWISH POETRY OF THE TRENCHES

The hope of a harmonious union of Jew and Gentile was dashed by the rise of Hitler. Golding did deal with Jewish suffering in the Holocaust (in his *Hitler through the Ages* and *The Jewish Problem*, as well as in his novel *The Glory of Elsie Silver*, 1945), but the menace of fascism at home and abroad helped make Zangwill and Golding less relevant as models for the modern Jewish writer. If there was a model, however equivocal, it was Isaac Rosenberg (born in Bristol,

1890) the First World War poet/painter from the East End who was killed in the trenches. Rosenberg's work expresses for Dan Jacobson

> both his sense of estrangement from the world he was writing for—even his estrangement from the language he was learning to use with such power—and his radical dissatisfaction with that estrangement, his determination to find a way out of it.[15]

Sprung from Moses' loins, Rosenberg's Jew (in the poem "The Jew," 1916) has lit the world with a lamp of immutable ethics, a moon pulling the world's moral tide. This makes his alienation irrational, but it also turns the mythical Jew into a Leopold Bloom confronting (rather than celebrating) the human condition.

Rosenberg's images grow peculiarly from the Jewish Bible and historical experience; this, together with the poet's provocative social commitment, may explain why he was barely read by his generation. Yet Rosenberg's concerns anticipate and, in the case of Jon Silkin, precipitate those of the post-Holocaust generation. Jon Silkin has singled out Rosenberg's involvement

> as a Jew and as a human being with no ultimate allegiances other than those which make basic human demands . . . . He brilliantly projected this human struggle by speaking in personal terms of his experience of the Anglo-Jewish predicament, and by relating it to an ultimately human wrestling with divine demands.[16]

The struggle with the demands of God, like the struggle with the angel in Genesis which earned Jacob his name of Israel, perpetuated in the name carried by the Jewish people through the ages, is expressed by Rosenberg as a protest against a malign existence. Rosenberg's trench poems of 1916–1918 particularized the poet's protest and refined his language; the knot of his difficult and lonely thought was pulled tight into the long verse drama *Moses*, allusive, in the view of Dennis Silk, to contemporary Anglo-Jewry: Moses will utilize the trapped energies of the Israelite bondmen, "the manacled, sweaty horde," to redeem commercial vulgarity and pointless oversensitivity.[17]

Vulnerable, but open to experience, Rosenberg knew the risk of which T. S. Eliot spoke, that creativity is too near to suffering. That risk is realized by the modern, post-Holocaust Jewish writers, whose universe was incomprehensible to their parents, sometimes even to themselves.

Louis Golding may have been a best-selling author of popular fiction, journalist and man of letters, but the young Jewish writers who gathered at his house after the war had little in common with him, with the possible exception of Emmanuel Litvinoff, who wrote a stage version of *Magnolia Street* (1951).[18] Their sense of Jewish identity is more anguished, more uncertain, further from Jewish sources and from the Eastern Europe of their grandparents, yet at the same time more intense.

Chapter Two
Contemporary Anglo-Jewish Literature: A Political and Cultural Background

The end of the Second World War left Britain in a new balance of power, in European alliance with America against Russia. No adequate air cover could protect the British population against Communist attack—defense lay in the atomic deterrent. The prospect of a mad atomic war between the two emerging superpowers on European soil was a recurring motivation for political agitation when most other topics left the general population apathetic. The debt to the United States weighed heavily on the annual balance of payments; the standard of living had risen during the war years, yet the postwar years saw austerity: butter, fats, meat and bacon remained on the ration book until 1954. Exchange control in 1947, the fuel crisis of the bitter winter of 1946-7, food and clothes shortages—those were the ingredients of the British housewife's humble pie.

The socialist program of the Labour administration which replaced Churchill in July 1945 introduced nationalization as well as central planning of major industries and transportation, but effective results were slow in coming. Wartime aspirations and a certain radicalization among the armed forces in 1943-4 met with disillusion after the realization of the Welfare State. A National Health Service was set up and infant mortality was brought down, but the government introduced a 50% charge for spectacles and dentures; over the years the NHS became famous for inefficiency and long waiting lists.

When the Conservatives came back into office in October 1951, under an ageing Churchill, they did not dismember the socialist system or reverse political reforms. The narrowing electoral majority separating the two major parties in the early fifties discouraged the introduction of controversial legislation. Successive Cabinets continued muddling through and the electorate found there was little to choose between Labour and Conservatives. A vote for the Liberals or Communists was more or less a wasted ballot slip.

The Labor movement no longer seemed at the forefront of the political struggle. Many industrial disputes seemed to involve wage differentials and other minor issues. The Labour-controlled London County Council dealt with the acute housing shortage by building uniform blocks of functional unimaginative council flats. Ugly pre-fabricated dwellings, meant to last only ten years, adorned city bomb-sites.

The British Empire dissolved into the independent developing nations of the Third World, though several of them remained in the British Commonwealth, contributing non-dollar imports of food or resources and receiving overseas aid. Emigration to Rhodesia (Zimbabwe) and other white settlement areas reached the rate of about 100,000 a year, while immigration from Africa, Asia and the West Indies brought cheap labor and racial tension. Britain in the fifties was unused to its new image of an industrial, urbanized society; it was unsure of its social priorities and its role in the world.

The rich carried on as before—fee-paying private schools (the "Public Schools") educated the elite and annual balls resumed at Oxford and Cambridge—though some felt the pinch and turned over their stately homes to the public. It took some years for the new provincial universities to expand and to take in a rather different generation of undergraduates from the grammar schools and lower middle classes.

THE CULTURAL SCENE

The 1951 Festival of Britain did not especially outshine its Victorian predecessor, the Great Exhibition of 1851, but it did leave as a legacy on the South Bank of the Thames the National Film Theatre. London drama flourished on the usual high-quality Shakespeare productions, as well as on light-hearted successes such as

Sandy Wilson's *The Boy Friend* or *Salad Days* and slick American musicals beginning with *Oklahoma* (1947); Tennessee Williams and Arthur Miller also crossed the Atlantic.

The rage, however, soon became outrage. Anything "anti" was "in." The Teddy Boys affected middle-class Edwardian Styles in their protest cult of vandalism. Long-haired youth jived to LP discs (first introduced in 1950) and the overnight Cockney star Tommy Steele hit the charts. Sartre, Beckett and Brecht were discussed in expresso bars (continental style, as in the French films then in vogue). British society and culture had changed in many ways, although old vested interests didn't vanish and the class divide was not broken. There was a world of difference between "U" and non-"U," the quasi-humorous terms Nancy Mitford gave in the September 1955 issue of *Encounter* magazine to the snobbish distinction in language usage between Upper and non-Upper Classes, based on the findings of Professor Alan Ross. The common man could not articulate the social changes, while the spread of television and an improvement in living standards created a mass popular culture that fed on gossipy Sunday papers, Bingo halls and motoring holidays.

The year 1953 was in a sense a turning point in the British novel just as 1956 was for drama. In fall 1953 John Wain's *Hurry on Down* (U.S. title, *Born in Captivity*) appeared, followed the next year by Kingsley Amis's *Lucky Jim*, Iris Murdoch's *Under the Net* and, last but not least, William Golding's *Lord of the Flies*.

> In these years the new was being eagerly awaited, but the form it would take was not, of course, easily forseeable. All one could say was that there was a new generation of writing age that had been brought up during the war years and in the years of social change that followed.[1]

Whether any of the new authors of those years have much in common is, in retrospect, perhaps an academic point. But no one in Britain, soldier or civilian, could have gone through the war unscathed nor have escaped the changing social climate after 1945. *Lord of the Flies*, as Frank Kermode has shown, is a brilliant antidote to the schoolboy's classic *Coral Island* by R. M. Ballantyne (1858), a textbook of the civilizing spirit of Victorian imperialism. In *Lord of the Flies* the castaways are evacuees from a nuclear war, who set up "a world of active, proliferating evil which is seen, one feels, as the natural condition of man" but which recollects "the vilest manifestations of

Nazi regression."[2] William Golding has returned to an apocalyptic vision of wartime Britain in his recent *Darkness Visible*, but it would hardly be fair to say that most British authors in the two postwar decades were concerned with such serious issues. It is true, nevertheless, that the writer in postwar Britain had to deal with a blitzed world, in which the usual conventions of humanity and morality were bombed out, a world that had grudgingly accepted a greater degree of permissiveness without totally understanding the "angry young men" or rock-and-rollers on their motorbikes who were fed up with the Establishment.[3]

THE JEWISH SCENE

Jewish writers were no less affected by these developments, but, as will be seen in the course of this study, they responded in a particular manner that partly grew out of the Jewish experience of the Second World War, and partly out of a love-hate relationship with the Jewish community.

The Holocaust disfigured Jewish historical geography until it was unrecognizable. British Jewry was left the largest single Jewish community in Europe, outside the USSR, and, before the influx of North African Jews into France in the 1960s the fourth largest in the world. British Jewry held the tricky responsibility of being closest to influence the government, if any Jewish body could, in its handling of Palestine. Yet the immediate emotion aroused by the tragedy of European Jewry and the establishment of the State of Israel subsided into unthinking apathy and routine indifference.

This was a community transformed by the 1881–1920 mass immigration from Eastern Europe whose links were now cut with the spiritual center of Jewry in Poland. From long hours for little pay in workshops many Jews had risen to become independent in tailoring, shoe and boot making, ready-made clothing or cabinet making; some were instrumental in the organization of mass production and modern techniques of consumer goods distribution: Michael Marks' little stall in Leeds market from 1884 grew into the nationwide Marks & Spencer chain; Montague Burton's ready-made clothing store in Chesterfield, opened 1900, likewise branched out around the country.[4] The refugees who fled Nazi Germany or who survived the Holocaust introduced further enterprise, though the stereotyped image of the Jew as crooked financier and schemer was hardly enhanced by such cases as the Rachman scandal or the proceedings at the end of the 1970s for tax avoidance against Lord Kagan, maker of Harold Wilson's raincoat.[5] The dream was independence—hence the popularity of hairdressing and taxi driving after the war—and middle-class prosperity. The professions developed slowly and the arts were never seriously respected by the Anglo-Jewish community. The descendants of those East European immigrants were more easily integrated into Britain than their parents, as were the newcomers from Hitler's Germany who were culturally secular and European and who were no less alienated than their British-born peers from the religion of their forefathers.

The London-based *Jewish Quarterly*, established in 1953 under the stalwart editorship of Jacob Sonntag (1905–1984), after a number of desultory attempts over the years to set up a Jewish cultural medium, set out to tackle the whole question of Jewish identity in Britain without, on the one hand, giving in to "accommodation" or, on the other hand, returning to the "exclusiveness" and "isolation" of the ghetto, by which several contributors meant observance of "Orthodox" Judaism.[6] The meaning of diaspora Jewish life and culture had to be redefined and Sonntag saw as one of the *Jewish Quarterly's* main tasks the introduction of the lost Yiddish heritage to Anglo-Jewry in English translation, at about the same time as Irving Howe and Eliezer Greenberg were helping American Jewry rediscover Sholom Aleichem and other classics of East European Jewish literature. Sonntag clearly hoped for an important role for Yiddish in a postwar Jewish culture that need not be centered on Israel. The Yiddish revival, however, was slow in coming, despite the lone stand of Avram Stencl (1897–1983), the East End Yiddish poet. The issues discussed so vociferously in the pages of the *Jewish Quarterly* were important in the formation not of any ideology or concensus but of a moral standpoint and self-definition. These questions included German rearmament which affected British Jews in a particular way because their historical emotions colored their moral and political feelings, but at the same time their concerns were larger, humanitarian ones for the safety of Europe endangered by the atomic arms race between the superpowers.

These discussions gave the younger generation food for thought at a time when intellectual Jews had no voice in the community and little sense of separate ethnic existence, but also no satisfactory substitute for the assimilatory position debunked by Hitler's history lesson. The *Jewish Quarterly* did not create the "new wave" of Anglo-Jewish writing and one shouldn't overstate its influence, but it did offer a uniquely and specifically Jewish forum for the young writers among its contributors—Wolf Mankowitz, Dannie Abse, Emanuel Litvinoff, Frederic Raphael, A. C. Jacobs and Jon Silkin—as well as giving first publication of several works by Arnold Wesker. The *Jewish Quarterly* was a haven for refugee poets (Karen Gershon, Michael Hamburger); it reevaluated "Germany's stepchildren" and German-Jewish culture (Heine, Zweig, Walter Benjamin, Feuchtwanger, Brod, Kafka) and promoted Yiddish as well as modern Hebrew poetry for the majority who knew little of either. Regular sections covered historiography and art. At quarterly intervals (more or less, it not always being easy to guarantee donors!) the magazine weathered soaring printing costs and a highly uneconomic market. There is no Jewish readership in Britain as there is in America and the uncultured philistinism of Anglo-Jewry was the very thing the *Jewish Quarterly* had pledged to fight.

The death of Stalin in 1953 removed an idol whom Jews on the left had shared with fellow Communists. Communism offered an answer to fascism that appeared to "solve" the "Jewish problem" by making anti-Semitism one aspect of the global class conflict. Khrushchev's secret speech at the XX Party Congress came, therefore, as an especial eye-opener to Jewish Communists who had tried to maintain faith in the Soviet Union as a model of socialism. The murder of Mikhoels in 1948 and the execution of the Yiddish writers in August 1952 came as a cruel blow in addition to the Slánský trial; the 1956 Soviet invasion of Hungary brought many to break with the Party.

Israel, too, was something of a disappointment as a socialist secular state. The Arab refugees remained homeless. The 1956 Suez Crisis did much to discredit British foreign policy and put Israel in a bad light as a "tool of imperialism," while stirring up all over again the "dual allegiance" of British Jews. And doubts over Israel's moral position were to be articulated after Hannah Arendt's account of the 1961 Eichmann trial, although that occasion in particular awakened consciousness of Jewish suffering.

Jewish resistance to Nazi oppression was particularly stressed in the *Jewish Quarterly* (a number of contributors were Holocaust survivors), and space was also given to the Trevor-Roper/Hilberg debate. Jewishness was not to be regarded as a *shmaltzy shtetl* creed that acquiesced in its own death. But what sort of culture could the

Diaspora offer? And who was to create it? The literary critic David Daiches gave his own answer when he rejected out of hand the Hebrew scholar Chaim Rabin's plea for a Hebrew-language culture as "utopian" and dismissed the Yiddishist Dr. Roback's hope for a resurrected Yiddish culture as "unrealistic"; Hebrew, argued Daiches, was an ecclesiastical tongue that enabled the Jew to read the Bible or a book from Israel, while Yiddish had not outlived the *shtetl*. Daiches espouses the concept of the Jew as a native minority in a pluralistic culture, with little attachment to Israel and unrestricted by a ghetto, and therefore believes that

> the Jewish writer who writes in English on Jewish themes or who exploits some aspect of his Jewish heritage effectively in English is writing for more than his own people. And is not that a challenge and a responsibility?[7]

The community, however, shut out the new young writers and when Brian Glanville did a series of interviews for the *Jewish Chronicle* in December 1958–January 1959 with Wolf Mankowitz, Alexander Baron, Peter Shaffer, Dannie Abse, Bernard Kops and Arnold Wesker it reacted with shock and abuse instead of realizing that the interviewees' lack of identification with Judaism was something to be concerned about and might indicate a failure on the part of the community. Chaim Bermant claims a causal connection between this intolerance of secular culture and the "Jacobs affair;"[8] both the writers and Jacobs did seem to threaten the stability (or rather the stagnation) of certain sectors of the community who were wary of modern scholarship and the kind of attitude which could be potentially appealing to the young drifting away from the community.

Nevertheless, the truth of the matter is that the much-maligned religiosity of the intolerant members of the community was more imagined than real and resembled polemical stereotypes of the *Haskalah* (the nineteenth-century Jewish Enlightenment), for similarly bigoted protests were in later years to be voiced in the *Jewish Chronicle* against so-called religious fanaticism. It is also a fact that while the community remained largely insensitive to the criticisms of Anglo-Jewish writers (who were accused of self-hatred and anti-Semitism, à la Philip Roth), they were quite prepared (typically perhaps) to applaud their success as a Jewish achievement! Bernice Rubens and Chaim Bermant defended their critical standpoint as having the community at heart, yet there were others, like Brian Glanville, who echoed Arthur Koestler's thesis that the diaspora Jew must assimilate or go to Israel; Glanville saw no values in diaspora society worth preserving and presumably therefore saw no harm that negative portrayals might do to Jewish youth because he could think of no reason to oppose assimilation.[9]

On the 1956 Tercentenary of the Resettlement of Jews in England, Anglo-Jewry lacked dynamic leadership and suffered a widening polarity between secularism, or "dropping out", and "Orthodoxy," or strict observance of the Torah, the Reform movement trying to pull in the "middle of the road" Jews between the two extremes. Far from widespread devotion to the Torah, many practised the sham of candle-lighting and might even attend both the synagogue and the football ground on a Saturday. Jewish education had obviously failed, despite a few good day-schools in the big cities (wartime evacuation hadn't helped any), and it should not be surprizing that children should think of their parents' Judaism in terms of an intolerable and intolerant religion of exacting but meaningless rituals, not a living faith.[10] On his induction in 1967 Chief Rabbi Jakobovits noted that there had never been as much reason for anxiety "about Jewish survival as . . . in this age of unequalled freedom, affluence and opportunity."[11]

Anglo-Jewish intellectuals became increasingly critical of Israel's policies after the rallying-round and euphoria of June 1967. The threat of genocide and destruction of the Jewish State receded and Israel was maligned by the Left as an "imperialist aggressor" and "neo-colonialist occupier." Even Jews for whom anti-Zionism was not a convenient form of self-hatred started searching their consciences—after all, weren't the Jews supposed to act more morally than any other nation and as Jews weren't they supposed to be morally hypercritical? The Arab refugees became the "Jews' Jews," based on the reasoning that the Jews, being human, must be capable of Nazi-type atrocities and must not be allowed to escape judgment for injustices.[12] In the Jewish and international press, as well as in the *Jewish Quarterly*, letters from Israel talked of *yerida* (emigration from Israel) and, after Begin's election victory, complained of right-wing extremism. The socialist ideal in Israel seemed no longer to shine so brightly, just as it seemed to be fading in Britain, while the hope for liberalization in the USSR, embodied by the appearance of the Soviet Yiddish journal *Sovietish heymland* and the memoirs of Ehrenburg, could hardly survive the 1968 Soviet invasion of Czechoslovakia, repression in Poland, and Soviet intervention in Afghanistan. PLO terrorism and neo-fascist outbursts reminded European Jews they were still vulnerable, while the struggle on behalf of Soviet Jewry occasioned reexamination and recommitment to Jewishness among the campaigners.

Growing evidence for the complicity of the Allies in the fate of European Jewry (the conspiracy of silence, the refusal to bomb Auschwitz or to absorb refugees, documented by Bernard Wasserstein, Martin Gilbert and others) and a reassessment of the Christian roots of anti-Semitism by Hyam Maccoby and others reinforced the conviction that the Holocaust could happen again and it "could happen here." The Jew was obviously best placed to warn of the coming, final nuclear holocaust; Arnold Wesker and Bernard Kops marched with Bertrand Russell in the Campaign for Nuclear Disarmament. The Holocaust and the dubious position of the European Jew as resident alien afforded the Jewish intellectual the opportunity to put forward a universal moral view learned from centuries of suffering.

Bernard Malamud and Philip Roth never had to constantly question their place as Jews in society and literature in the same way. England was no cosmopolitan melting-pot in which a distinctive and separate Jewish ethnicity could function. There was no Anglo-Jewish lobby as such and no Jewish intelligentsia; there were no more than 450,000 Jews after the war in England, or less than one percent of the total population. Yet an extraordinary number of talented Jews became prominent in literature and the arts, several of them major figures in modern British culture.

Anglo-Jewish Writing Beyond Marginality

The breakthrough of the Anglo-Jewish novelists, playwrights and poets in the 1950s has been compared with that of the German-Jewish writers of the Weimar Republic or the American-Jewish writers of the 1930s,[13] but with the difference that they wrote within the new discovery of ethnicity, working-class roots and social commitment. Also they did not have any separate cultural role or identifiable group voice, something inimical to the English tradition.[14] Their success depended on their ability to appeal to a wide reading public and in a culture unused to hearing a Jewish voice. It was with surprise that American Jews discovered the same Jewishness in English literature that they habitually assumed belonged exclusively to New York.

. . . for me it never quite registered that in the British Isles, those very British Isles that were the college-English-course territory of Shakespeare and Dickens and kings and queens, . . . there could be places and people as redolent of the real thing as the front-page format of the *Forward*, which were forever Yiddish: or as forever Yiddish as our parts of New York itself will remain.[15]

Actually, it was the Anglo-Jewish community itself which helped to form the young Jewish writers' self-definition as Jews belonging to English literature and not as specifically Jewish writers. The novelist Brian Glanville declared that there were Anglo-Jewish writers but "no such thing as Anglo-Jewish writing."[16] Anglo-Jewry fostered no cultural life, its middle-class materialism and possessive love alienated the Jewish writer who wrote one protest novel and left the community when it reacted with wounded pride and indignation at the unflattering picture. The English literary environment, by comparison, did not exert as much pressure to conform.[17] Philip Hobsbaum, in fact, saw the Anglo-Jewish writer as a transition to assimilation.[18]

Looking back in retrospect, it was the problem of dual allegiance, together with a realization that attitudes toward Jews had not changed substantially, which made the alienated Jewish writer confront Jewish identity and explore Jewishness critically. Cut loose from Jewish roots, yet unaccepted as Jews in English society, the young writer had no option but to go beyond a shaky marginal status. This entailed examining the causes of alienation in order to work out a creative self. Negation of any identification with other Jews or denial of any interest in Judaism so often disguise a declaration of uneasiness, as shown by repeated direct and oblique references to the subject in the authors' books. After the Holocaust it was not a meaningful inheritance to be the kind of marginal young Jewish intellectual once characterized by Irving Howe as a cultural *luftmentsh:*

Usually born into an immigrant Jewish family, he teeters between an origin he can no longer accept and a desired status he cannot attain. . . . He suffers, of course, from the same sense of alienation that besets Jews as a group. Even when he succeeds in detaching himself fairly completely from Jewish life, he continues to exhibit all of the restless, agonizing rootlessness that is the Jew's birthmark.[19]

The first to emerge from the aftermath of reaction to immigrant experience in America included those New York intellectuals "who did not define themselves through either a nostalgic or a hostile memory of Jewishness." Because the "Jewish immigrant milieu had branded on its children marks of separatism while inciting fantasies of universalism" they were taught to become universal before they could be national writers. Their values were cosmopolitan and secular, with overlays of European culture: "strategic maneuvers of the vanguard had first been mapped out on gray immigrant streets."[20]

In England this process was doubly painful as there was no cosmopolitan safety-net. The sheltered parental home indoctrinated its children in bourgeois materialist aspirations which denied the traditions of immigrant roots (except their sentimental value) and denied the right to be different. The very acculturation of Anglo-Jewry pressurized the young into the British Public School (a fee-paying elite establishment) and the golf-club, where they were not infrequently ostracized as Jews, yet were not equipped with an adequate knowledge of what Jewishness meant nor adequate defenses to combat anti-Semitism. The radicalism natural to the grandparents' immigrant experience disappeared with bourgeois prosperity. The demographic move to the comfortable suburbs of North-West London from the poor quarters of East London incited a generational protest that looked back at the East End which was no more and which contrasted with the hypocrisy and philistinism of their parents.[21] The loss of community in the East End and the loss of six million because they were Jews do much to explain the ethnicity of modern Anglo-Jewish writers.

East

Chapter Three
East End Writers I:
Litvinoff, Mankowitz, Kops

The East End is, strictly speaking, a couple of square miles on the north bank of the Thames, hard by the London Docks. From the ships downtrodden, destitute Jews directed their weary footsteps, or found themselves directed, to the narrow streets around Aldgate, just outside the City of London. They made up some two-thirds of the annual immigration flow of between two to five thousand in the years 1881–1905; others disembarked at coastal ports and settled in the provinces or also made their way to the East End. Not a few stayed because their voyage for America took them no further; anyone who thought England was the *goldene medina* soon found out their mistake. The Jewish population took over street after street, but not all streets: some areas of the East End were always more Jewish in character than others. The new settlement grew faster than the continuous flow since 1860 of upward-moving Jews to West London and the northern suburbs, although the Anglo-Jewish establishment and its charity institutions tried to disperse the moral influence and the cultural threat of these East European Jews to Notting Hill and eastwards to Poplar, as well as to Walthamstow, West Ham and East Ham (outside London's boundaries).[1] There the process of acculturation was much faster than in the East End which thrived no less vigorously and for a somewhat longer period than New York's Lower East Side.

The overcrowded tenements of the East End teemed with life but the insanitary conditions, exorbitant key-money and high rents added to the poverty and the squalor. As in America, but not at all on the same scale, the new life weaned Jews very quickly from traditional ways and the radical movements of Eastern Europe found fertile ground. Among the Yiddish newspapers of the turn of the century the *Arbeter Fraynt* reflected a Bundist stand, though from 1892 it was anarchist, while *Der Veker* took an anti-anarchist social-democratic line; Zionism and tradeunionism activated the East End Jewish workers but the political sectarianism and overall religious conservatism proved as divisive as the old rivalries between "Litvaks" (Lithuanian Jews) and "Polaks" (Polish Jews), to which was now added contempt for Dutch Jews (as portrayed by Zangwill in *Children of the Ghetto*). There were also social distinctions of class and oc-cupation, as well as of neighborhood as the Jewish settlement spread from Aldgate and Whitechapel and eventually extended outside the East End proper to Bethnal Green, Stepney Green, eventually to true Cockney land, Bow, all the time looking ever northwards and up-wards—to Dalston, Hackney, Clapton, Stoke Newington, Stamford Hill and, at last, to Willesden, Hampstead and Golders Green.

However, at the turn of the century the concentration of such a large number of immigrants in so small an area inevitably invited charges of cheap labor, criminality, anarchism, immorality, disease, parasitism and even interference, by their very presence, with ob-servance of the Christian Sunday! Here the Anglo-Jewish establish-ment, several of whom were in influential positions (such as Baron Ferdinand de Rothschild and Samuel Montagu), championed the right of refuge of Jews fleeing Russia and Poland in the debates leading up to the 1905 Aliens Act, which restricted (but did not in fact seriously curtail) Jewish immigration.

The intervention of Anglo-Jewish leaders in the Aliens Question did not conflict with their desire to have the new community integrate into Anglo-Jewry through anglicization. English and "English habits of thought and character" were acquired in the local non-denomi-national schools but also in the Jews' Free School in Bell Lane (where Zangwill was a pupil-teacher for some time). So rigidly enforced was the process of anglicization that one candidate for the school headship was turned down on the grounds of foreign parentage! There were also the Jewish clubs where conversation and sports were English. Of the children born in the East End only a minority had a command of Yiddish and it was even considered a stigma to be heard using Yiddish words. (As an example of what the anglicizers were eradi-cating we may recall the hilarity when Solomon Ansell in *Children of the Ghetto* describes Travel in a school composition as peddling, which is all his father ever knew of travelling the wide world!)[2]

Another aspect of anglicization was patriotism. As friendly aliens the East End immigrants could not be conscripted into the First World War and many of them were not exactly eager to fight on the same side as the Russians, their recent tormentors. The idea of the non-Jewish way of life in the army was not appealing either, not to mention the possibility of getting killed. Some did rally to the colors, but the *Jewish Chronicle* had to voice its embarrassment at the large number who had accepted English sanctuary from persecution but were not willing to accept loyalties and duties to England. The anti-Semitic component in the agitation against the twenty thousand or so Jewish alien draftdodgers and shirkers was particularly disturbing. The government decided in early 1917 that those who did not volunteer for service in the British Army would be deported to Russia. There was much bitter debate within the Jewish community, but the Anglo-Jewish establishment stood by King and Country. However, the 1917 Balfour Declaration and the formation of a Jewish Battalion, the 38th Royal Fusiliers, at the beginning of 1918, helped to strengthen the East End children's education in Patriotism so that they came to think of themselves first and foremost as British and as Empire-builders.

Anglicization disaffected the children from parental norms, but the Anglo-Jewish establishment did not intend to disaffect them from Judaism, although it was hoped traditional Orthodoxy would follow English models. It should not be surprizing, however, that the children tended naturally to realize Anglo-Jewish social aspirations outside the community, even to totally assimilate. Yet not all conformed, and the harsh lessons learned on East End streets found expression in creative talent.

THE GOOD OLD EAST END

East End novels were numerous, including Zangwill's *Children of the Ghetto* (1892), Samuel Gordon's *Children of the Covenant* (1900), Izak Goller's *Five Books of Mr. Moses* (1929), Simon Blumenfeld's *Jew Boy* (1935) and *Phineas Kahn: Portrait of an Immigrant* (1937), as well as the bitter satires of Gerald Kersh and Willy Goldman. Typical of the second-generation novel is resistance to pressure to get on and out of the East End, resistance to the high prestige accorded a place in a grammar school and a "respectable" profession. If the father did not rise to have his own workshop he hoped at least his children would be manufacturers and entrepreneurs and would move West. The hero of, for example, Blumenfeld's *Jew Boy* typically leaves home early on and renounces Jewishness, East and West, involving himself with the problems of the non-Jewish world: strikes, unemployment, politics and sex. The father is usually a failure, a *shlemazl* or *shlemiel*, the mother self-sacrificing. The closeknit family allows no privacy, its possessive love stifles and the hero usually disappoints the family's obsessive ambition to live through its children and to become "respectable" or "classy." On the streets of the East End the boy learns hard lessons and turns to the worst of apostasies—to art and artistic awareness.

William Goldman's *East End My Cradle* (1940) is a good illustration of the interwar mood (the book was revised in 1947 in consequence of the events during the Second World War). Welk Street, like Magnolia Street, has its Jewish and Gentile sides, with the children making a game of the rivalry between them. The Nazis, however, have made the street battles more relevant and menacing. An invasion of Jewish areas could happen here. True, the street pulls together as one when it comes to a challenge from outside and plays as one loyal team in soccer matches. But the children don't share their parents' memories of pogroms and when locals hurl drunken abuse on the way home from the pub, instead of cowering resignedly, they feel themselves "English and outraged." As for the heroes of Magnolia Street and several East End novels, the favorite sport is boxing and the Jewish boys are quite ready to break the windows of the anti-Semites who question their Englishness.

The restrictions hemming in the slum kids on all sides are bound up in many ways with religion and class. The *kheder* (Jewish Sunday School) employs sadism to inculcate a catechism of mumbling and forces them into a militant atheism. The local school is run on reformatory principles and gives no preparation for life. At fourteen the child is turned out into a rough sort of growing-up in the sweatshop with as much idea of adulthood as could be got from the adored stars of the big screen at the weekly Saturday matinées. The parents aren't much more religious—they're in bed sleeping instead of praying in the synagogue on Saturday morning.

Parental aspirations for a marriage partner center on a steady business (Aunt Beyla considers a fish shop sufficiently respectable);

however, the narrator's girlfriend, the consumptive Minka, lives in a "dangerous" area on the edge of the Jewish East End, in one room with her widowed mother (her status is low socially and ethnically), and the narrator's prospects are nil, bar his claim to "manliness." "Manliness" is picked up in the billiard halls where the razor boys hang out. The Jewish gangsters live up to *mentshlikhkeyt* in their reverence for the aged and these latterday Benya Kriks are moved to tears by the plight of the poor. But this is a rough world of gambling, football and sex.

In the 1929 Depression the seasonal slack characteristic of the tailoring trade slumps into chronic unemployment. Casual labor becomes scarce, especially for the narrator, because the docks are not "safe" Jewish territory. As the week stretches out aimlessly the East End becomes stifling with the heat and the bugs. The fortunes of the narrator's father deteriorate even further and the narrator curses his father's failures. Although he doesn't believe in the synagogue, his father trusts implicitly in divine munificence, but can't hold down a job and gives away his last penny to beggars. When the four horses are stolen he takes a stall in the market; market traders are characterized as mutually envious of the respectable, home-loving master tailors, they are coarse and irreligious, and prefer the rough talk of Yiddish cafés to being at home with the family. The narrator is ashamed of his father, of his shabbiness and his Yiddish, but he himself is made to feel guilty when his elder brother gets married and settles down.

Weirdos were not uncommon in the East End, they were social misfits or thwarted artists. The narrator dropped out because he was constantly harassed at home and deprived of all privacy. He illustrates his humiliating attempts to live on his own with the story of a fellow outcast, Ephraim Wise, an incorrigibly impractical and selfless artist whose family take out their frustrations and disappointment on him. Are they millionaires to throw away money on art school? (They clearly haven't heard of Isaac Rosenberg!) Prejudiced officials and rich benefactors "up West" deny his talent and destroy him. He ends up in a psychiatric hospital, a not unique tragedy of a frustrated artist.

The bullying which made his childhood miserable and the experience of poverty make the narrator want to put the East End down on paper. "It would be the history of a poor Jewish family, but in some of its deeper implications it would also be a sort of history of the human family."[3] This is a Marxist analysis of the

Jewish East End and it shares with Zangwill's *Children of the Ghetto* certain critical assumptions, for example the Dickensian satire of the Anglo-Jewish charitable institutions. But some of the "deeper implications" were becoming anachronistic by the time the book appeared. Britain and Russia were at war with Nazi Germany, while six million Jews were on the way to their mass graves regardless of their class origin or religious belief, and the East End was changing forever. Nevertheless, *East End My Cradle* offers a typical example of East End attitudes, even if the writing is not yet distanced from the immediate experience of destitution and a despair that sometimes reaches the point of madness or suicide. Writing brings a *raison d'être*, if not money, and it also functions as a bitter retribution against an unjust, unfeeling society responsible for the death of a consumptive young woman and a promising artist. Neither of them had a chance.

EMANUEL LITVINOFF'S SMALL PLANET

The same impulse fired Emanuel Litvinoff (born 1915) to set down the East End on paper.

> The vitality compressed into that one square mile of overcrowded slums generated explosive tensions. We were all dreamers, each convinced it was his destiny to grow rich, or famous, or change the world into a marvellous place of freedom and justice. No wonder so many of us were haunted by bitterness, failure, despair.[4]

Litvinoff's old elementary school headmaster criticized his novel's preoccupation with sex and squalor and when Litvinoff returned in 1946 from six years military service in West Africa and the Middle East he burned the cheap exercise books in the backyard. The East End as he had known it had been bombed into rubble.

> Those of us who survived and were still young were moving eagerly into the universe of the future and had no wish to look back at the retreating past.[5]

That nothing could be the same again was the conclusion which hit with equal driving force Emanuel Litvinoff, Arnold Wesker, Bernard Kops and Harold Pinter. In his appraisal of Litvinoff's two collections of verse *The Untried Soldier* (1942) and *A Crown for Cain* (1946),

Dannie Abse claims Litvinoff as the first avowedly Jewish poet in England, a war poet's voice full of protest, death, frustration and the pity of it all, but addressed to the Jewish predicament. He writes out of a conflict of dual allegiance, torn between the "Jerusalem" of childhood innocence, of Jewish roots, and the temptation of Christianity and mixed marriage. The poet cannot forget that the civilization which sent him to war, which he is risking his neck to save, inflicted so much pain and suffering on his race over the centuries.[6] After the sinking of the *Struma* with its load of Jewish refugees in 1942, he invokes Jesus

> To come down from the mountain and the sun
> And walk into my lonely dwelling-place,
> My house of mourning, to seek out and bless
> Me for my dead, my dead for peace.[7]

Having been brought up to think of oneself as more English than the English, having started writing in English for the English, the postwar Jewish writer eager to move into "the universe of the future" was pained to read T. S. Eliot's "Burbank with a Baedaker: Bleistein with a Cigar" (1920). Litvinoff's reply "To T. S. Eliot" was a proud rebuke read at a London poetry evening in the 1950s chaired by Herbert Read before an audience that included T. S. Eliot and Stephen Spender; Spender rose to make an irate defense of T. S. Eliot, though the author of *The Wasteland* commented that Litvinoff's was a good poem. Litvinoff accords the great poet all his moral stature but demands an apology for sniggering at the Jew as a subhuman monster, a traditional anti-Semitic image, and complains his eminence should have risen to protest the crimes committed against the Jews.

> . . . walking with Cohen when the sun exploded
> and darkness choked our nostrils,
> and the smoke drifting over Treblinka
> reeked of the smouldering ashes of children,
> I thought what an angry poem
> you would have made of it, given the pity.[8]

The pride with which the Jew wears the badge of sufferance ("Bleistein is my relative and I share the protozoic slime of Shylock"[9]) makes all the difference between the Anglo-Jewish writer after the Holocaust and his predecessors or English contemporaries. Being "Chicago Semite Viennese" must be turned to advantage.

Litvinoff admits to being wholly concerned with the destruction of European Jewry[10] and his novel *The Lost Europeans* (1959) describes the experience of a Jew in sleazy postwar Berlin, while *The Man Next Door* (1968) probes the workings of the anti-Semitic mind. A 1956 visit to Moscow marked the beginning of Litvinoff's involvement on behalf of Soviet Jews (he edits the campaign newsletter *Insight*) and when he turned to the revolutionary connections of the Jewish East End in *A Death Out of Season* (1973), a novel about the 1911 anarchist siege of Sidney Street, it was with the perspective that the Revolution had not solved the problems of the world's poor nor of the Jews and that the postwar promise of socialism had not lived up to expectations. *A Death Out of Season* was the first in a trilogy which takes Jewish revolutionaries through the Russian Revolution and Civil War to final disillusion in the purges. There is no hope of salvation in a socialist Russia as in Blumenfeld's *Phineas Kahn*.

On revisiting the East End from his comfortable country home, Litvinoff convinced himself he had to write a book about growing up in the East End where coming to terms with adolescence meant coming to terms with being a Jew. This reminder of a lost world explains the writer's Jewishness and his social commitment; it is a timely memorial when the East End has passed into the hands of new immigrants from India and Pakistan. The parallel between the two waves of immigrants was also made by Wesker in the television documentary based upon his memoir *Say Goodbye, You May Never See Them Again* (with John Allin, 1974). The social occupations and aspirations are strikingly similar (tailoring workshops and retail trade, thrift, hard-working effort to climb the social distance to Ilford and Golders Green), but here Litvinoff is impressed by the deadness of what was his past, by the irrevocable change.

> Clumps of Muslim men stood aimlessly on corners and there was a curious absence of women. Shrill, eerie music wailed in the heat of the afternoon. The odour of spices mingled with the stench of drains. Skinny little girls with enormous, solemn black eyes sat on doorsteps nursing babies. Outside a cinema crudely painted posters of veiled ladies and jewelled rajahs advertised a film from the sub-continent of India.[11]

Litvinoff's autobiographical *Journey Through a Small Planet* (1972) comes across as real and even poetic. The boy's father is one of those who went or was sent back to Russia during the First World War and arrived in time for the Bolshevik Revolution, never to be heard of again. In the absence of a father the boy develops a jealous oedipal relationship with his mother, while the claustrophobic closeness of the home and the intrusion of an unsympathetic stepfather suggest a similar Hamlet theme to the one in Bernard Kops' *Hamlet of Stepney Green* (1956), which actually continues Gordin's and other adaptations of Shakespeare in the early New York Yiddish theater in terms of the rebellion of Jewish youth against their elders' adherence to bourgeois and religious values, and which is here coupled with the modern adolescent's difficulty in coming to terms with his own precocious sexuality and confused identity.

In Litvinoff's tour of the East End, *Hamlet* is played in Yiddish, in the dying Yiddish theater, a truly plebeian theater which cannot, however, compete with the picture palace. Orphaned Fanya is adopted out of charity and enters the adolescent narrator's life the summer his mother is pregnant with his stepfather's third child. Under the darkened arches of a railway bridge smelling of industrial grime and gloom, where danger lurks like the spirit of Jack the Ripper, the boy anticipates sexual maturity and comes away confused by the depressing burden of male lust. Fanya is apprenticed as a dressmaker in the West End and dresses herself up according to the latest fashions "up West." Called in to help with the wardrobe of the New York Yiddish Theater, Fanya falls head over heels for Hershel Rosenheim, the star, but he is an actor, not someone with his own business, and what kind of respectable match is that?

The theater in fact turns out to be as unromantic and filthy as the boy's tenement building, yet a Goldfaden comedy can make the audience believe in good old days and escape the monotony of daily misery. Fanya believes in her Hamlet's promises, that he will bring her over to America, to a nice apartment with wall-to-wall carpeting and "a good air-conditioning so summer and winter would always be the same," maybe even a colored maid. Fanya ends up with an abortion and moves to Manchester where no one would know her disgrace. The boy is left marooned on the small planet of the East End with dreams of being Hamlet but has to live with being fourteen, specs on his nose and a failed scholarship.

> The choices were few and gruesome. I could boil a glue-pot and sweep up wood shavings, carry a tailor's sack from workshop to retailer, learn to baste a hem, press out a seam, nail a fur, lather a chin, weigh sugar into one-pound bags, or diss a stick of lead type with average competence. . . . At the end of the

week I'd buy my first packet of fags and have nothing to hope
for but the Revolution.[12]

Reprieve comes with entrance to Cordwainers' Technical College but
it is an entrée to the boot and shoe trade, not to the cloisters of the
elite.

The ancestors whom the narrator presents in the first chapter
are anarchists who argue over the use of violence, their ideological
differences finding expression in the different subversive messages
which the tailor Golombek slips into the khaki tunics destined for
the Western Front. The boy's inherited idealism takes him from
anarchism to the Communist Youth to sex mania; however bad the
squalor and deprivation the Jews are natural optimists and find
salvation in ideology. Communism is learned by the boy not from
Marx but from daily misery: his were hunger politics, like Michael
Gold's in *Jews Without Money*. His education is an extracurricular
maturation into violence that serves as a lesson in identity not so
different from the one in Isaac Babel's stories. When his name is
called (mutilated to "Pissoffsky") he has the sensation of taking up
a long-rehearsed role. The humiliation breeds a thirst for revenge
and martyrdom, so that he begins to wish the headmaster would
make him convert or eat pork!

Strangely enough it is the Italian fascist Leoni, another foreigner
but one who, unlike him, does not feel English, who supports the
boy against the Jew-hating Grindle. He "was fighting them all," but
"in some deep recess" of his being he knew violence was not his
way. The dreamy *shlemazl's* curse of tactless indiscretion and plain
bad timing turns revenge into farce. An inner toughening nevertheless
comes to him through cockiness and the "cleverness" he picks up
in Bethnal Green Public Library. He knows real fear only when he
is outside Jewish territory, where "some deep racial memory stirred
the sediment of disquiet and fear of the uncircumcised."

Actually, the boy's heresy is nowhere seen as a break from the
Jewish people. The mother sends him to the Talmud Torah Hebrew
Bible classes only because, being a Jewish mother, she exaggerates
her fears that without a father he may not grow up to be a *mentsh*.
The boy, being a Jewish son, is never understood when he hopes
to become something better. In the end he is caught by the System
he is fighting and he calls out to the Jewish mother to save him.
Yet he has awakened to sensuality and to art. When he writes a

poem, he does not understand its significance except that "things would never be the same again."

WOLF MANKOWITZ: THE BESPOKE GOGOL OR "LAUGHTER THROUGH TEARS"

One of the most funny and folksy East End authors is Wolf Mankowitz (born 1924), though educated outside the East End, in East Ham. His father dealt in second-hand books and he himself sold in the street market before winning an Exhibition to Downing College, Cambridge. He became an Oscar-winning film scriptwriter and was also successful in the pottery business, recognized as an authority on Wedgwood and the Portland Vase. His books are filled with East End *luftmentshen* who scratch a living from trading and whose self-taught philosophy is that the trader is the ultimate human being. He cares that his customers should care, whether it's for eighteenth-century English pottery or their religion or the happiness of their children. You do business to keep alive, to feed your family, but you do it with loving affection. Mankowitz's villains are the kind of people who calculate their transactions coldly and are out for each other's blood, like the antique dealers in *Make Me an Offer* (1952) going down by train to break up a country house. They're not like Charlie. Ever since he was a boy Charlie has dreamed of the Portland Vase. It's a passion that makes his life purposeful. Everyone should have a passion like that. His father taught him to specialize and he chose Wedgwood. Now he has a hunch he is in luck. There is a room full of Wedgwood but it's fake. What he has his eye on is a Portland vase in the old groundsman's lodge, an early copy, white cameo on a deep sea green, a work of genius. The story is told simply yet with a working knowledge of life and people and a conviction that beauty is rare and worth love. Charlie can articulate his practical metaphysics more competently than Malamud's store-keeper in *The Assistant* but his attachment to family and life is similarly down-to-earth; his story is told with irony and affection, but without sentimentality. Mankowitz is a masterful storyteller in the tradition of the Yiddish anecdote and his language is artistically attuned to the Yiddish tones in the talk of his East Enders, as well as in his parables and tales of the Old Country. But the moral is neither the bittersweet insight of Sholom Aleichem, nor the spiritual-ethical message of the Khasidim. This is a cynical voice that trusts neither in God nor man, yet affirms the possibility of good in human nature.

A good example of this is *A Kid for Two Farthings* (1953), modelled superficially on the Aramaic Passover folksong *Khad gadyah* ("A kid for two zuzim"). One mystical interpretation (by the eighteenth-century Rabbi Yaakov Emden) has it that the kid-goat represents the soul which is sent down to earth to undergo all the tribulations of human life. Each stanza follows the "House that Jack Built" pattern, each stanza adding a further element which devours its predecessor, until finally

> The Holy One, blessed be He, came and slew the angel of death,
> who killed the slaughterer,
> who killed the ox,
> that drank the water,
> that quenched the fire,
> that burnt the stick,
> that beat the dog,
> that bit the cat,
> that devoured the kid,
> that father bought for two zuzim,
> one kid, one kid.

In the end everyone must meet their Maker, must account for all the wasted opportunities during a lifetime on earth, but there is a sustaining hope for redemption. So too in Fashion Street, in the East End, which is about as far as you can get from fashion and where Kandinsky is coughing over an old-fashioned goose iron as he presses trousers. Above his workbench in the basement is a picture of Hope blindfold. Her eyes are bandaged so that she doesn't see what's going on in the world, because if she did she'd lose hope. The other picture in the workshop is also a form of hope blindfold, a pious *shtetl* Jew, Kandinsky's father, who dreamed of setting up business with his son in bespoke tailoring. It was not to be. But then that's life, all dreams and work.

Joe is nine and lives upstairs with his mother. His father has gone away to South Africa to make money buying and selling, like other East End Jews who had despaired of the long slack periods in the tailoring trade. Kandinsky is Joe's spiritual mentor and teaches him a great deal about the world. Joe finds out all about unicorns from Kandinsky and unicorns become an obsessive passion, rather like Charlie's Portland Vase. The unicorn has something in common with the Jews in the East End: almost extinct, ragged and tattered from poverty, dying in a bottomless pit, not unlike Isaac Rosenberg's emblematic unicorn in his draft of a legend of a dying race. There is something pitiful in their lost beauty and they symbolize an almost lost hope that is the more precious for its rarity. Joe believes Kandinsky who assures him that there really are unicorns in Africa, flickering symbols of hope like his father's letters. So Joe goes to the animal market in Club Row to buy a small unicorn which he could keep at home. He finds a pathetic creature with one horn and buys it with the sixpences he has saved up from helping Kandinsky in the workshop. The unicorn is a dream that makes life worth living. They give it a name, Africana, because after all, it's "also human." Shmule, Kandinsky's assistant, has a dream too, to be a champion wrestler and buy his fiancée Sonia a proper diamond ring with the prize money. But the prize money could also buy Kandinsky his dreamt-of patent steam presser. That means jobbing and steady work. So Kandinsky persuades Sonia that a ring doesn't really count for as much respect and security as Shmule in the role of guv'nor, coming into the business as a partner, on the condition he brings with him one secondhand patent steam presser. Dreams seem to be fulfilled, only the orphaned unicorn has disappeared and with it the promise of Joe's father returning from Africa. Kandinsky says the unicorn has gone to Africa to be with other unicorns, but has generously left a golden sovereign which more than any magical horn can help with a passage home. After all unicorns can't live on Fashion Street, but little boys have to.

Bespoke tailoring, the dream of Kandinsky's father, turns a workman into an artist, and the typically whimsical, witty East End tailor in the one-act play *The Bespoke Overcoat* (1955) imparts a sad but compassionate philosophy of life and art learnt the hard way, on East End streets. This is Gogol's *Overcoat* resown and retailed as a long Jewish joke. The ghost of Fender, a warehouse clerk, appears in the room of Morry the drunken tailor. Morry remembers Fender coming to him with his coat in shreds, but miracles are against Union rules. The coat is beyond repair. It's freezing in the clothing warehouse and Fender's boss Mr. Ranting is getting fed up with the old man complaining about the cold. But he won't let him take a sheepskin coat off the racks on account. Soon Ranting takes on a younger clerk and fires Fender after over forty-two years with the firm. Morry offers to finish the coat all the same but Fender is dead before he can hand it over. Fender has gone to the hotel that is heaven where he doesn't want for anything. Yet he can't get Ranting's sheepskin out of his head. He gives the staff a headache with it until they send him back to get the overcoat. That's how he turns up in Morry's room posthumously. Morry and Fender go to the warehouse to get the coat which Ranting owes him for nearly forty-three years labor. The coat isn't made with the workmanship Morry puts into a garment (Ranting himself wouldn't wear one of his own coats), there's no love sown into it, but Fender's sense of justice, his claim on *mentshlikhkeyt*, is satisfied and he returns to heaven with the sheepskin. The play closes as Morry recites the *Kaddish*, the Jewish prayer for the dead.

Love is a commodity the very poor can afford but which doesn't enter the account books of employers like Ranting. He has seen a machine at an exhibition which

> can add up how much you made last year, take away your overheads, knock off your income tax, and show you if you got anything left. By my life. It has a dictation machine a suspended filing system, a place special for telephone directories, and a permutator for working out football pools so they should win. And I worry myself to nothing, worrying, worrying the whole time over an old clerk's mistakes. What you say? Can a machine laugh like a man? Can it cry like a man? What difference? So long as a clerk clerks good, what difference he's laughing or crying?[13]

His belly full with good chopped liver, Ranting can't see that it does matter whether Fender laughs and cries over the beigel he eats without even a drop of soup to go with it. With a humility reminiscent of Bontshe the Silent in the story by Peretz, Fender swallows the deprivations he suffers because he accepts life. Morry, too, is a "connoisseur," and not just of brandy, for he knows life with an affection but also a conscience that makes him love someone even poorer than himself. Ranting can understand this even less than Gogol's Important Person. The East End wholesalers and master tailors spare little mercy (more fitting here is the Yiddish term *rakhmones* because it includes love). The only irony that Mankowitz doesn't mention is that every hardworked, underpaid little tailor dreamt of owning a sweatshop himself, just as his hard-hearted slavemaster had probably worked his way up from near-starvation. Only now tailoring is a dying trade and Morry is a dying breed.

This East End message of humility and *rakhmones* very nicely fits Mankowitz' universalization of the theme in fables or parables as in "Laugh Till You Cry" (1955), a Jobian parable about a salesman cast away on some Caribbean island with the Ditt tribe. The Ditts acquire power over the tribe through buying each other out. He who throws the most assets on the fire is chief. The narrator becomes chief himself when he throws a dazzling display of his stock—of practical jokes: itching powder, stink bombs, exploding cigars, the lot. The company motto is "laugh till you cry" and well one might cry as the practical jokes backfire in the customers' faces, humiliatingly exposing their corruption and meanness. It's just like the East End, or any human society. The priest is the purveyor of wealth-magic, a tycoon controlling the people's purchasing power and bankrupting his enemies into mortified shame and exile. The religious rites of material accumulation are part of an age-old tradition which embodies the characteristics of those who practise them; to deny tradition is to deny one's true nature. Ecclesiastes would say that there is nothing new under the sun; when the narrator succeeds in defeating his enemies he soon tires of absolute power, irritated by the puny vanity of the boastful men and the ogling women, by the hypocrisy of "this accursed people" (the label usually applied to the Jews), and then can say in the words of a Rantz Joke Company Cracker taken from *Ethics of the Fathers* 2,8:

The more flesh, the more worms.
The more property, the more anxiety.
The more servants, the more dishonesty.
The more women, the more witchcraft.

He despairs of human existence and he retires from "business", but he must first learn to despise material success, the golden calf of a disguised Jewish tribe, in a Jobian trial of secular faith. He joins a group of exiled bankrupts, society's rebels and discontents, who lead an idyllic existence which revolves around a ritual of entertainment, Jewish humor put to philosophical purpose. By making contact via a passing ship, continual supplies are obtained from the Rantz Company of perhaps the most valuable goods of all—laughter.

A fable in a similar vein is *The Biggest Pig in Barbados* (1965), a racy story of the Batchford pig spirited away by a wild magic man. The Creole English narration makes the West Indies as close to home as the East End, with its homeliness, its crazy characters and its sense of communal identity. The magic boundaries (protective amulets like those on Jewish doorposts?) keep strangers out of the wild man's territory, but they are surmounted by the boy cricketer Belgrave who rescues the wonder pig after a match of wits. The magic is broken and, vanity of vanities, the Wild Man's palatial grounds and forbidding colonial mansion are revealed as a tin shack. This tale of bogeymen and black magic is nevertheless as real as the simple community life it describes. The supreme triumph is to go on living and affirming life.

Fables such as *The Biggest Pig in Barbados* are part of what Mankowitz calls his "entertainments"[14] in which he writes from a Jewish point of view but sometimes writes the Jewish aspect out of the text; in his direct use of Jewish sources, as in the use of Cockney Yiddish dialogue or biblical motifs, he confronts directly the problems and conflicts of being a Jew, but the message is universal. An example is a dramatization of the Book of Jonah called *It Should Happen to a Dog* (1955) in which the author is saying that by sparing Nineveh God is more tolerant of man than man is of himself. Mankowitz wants to seek the divine through knowing and living life, like Leo Botvinnik in *The Mendelman Fire* (1957), who carries round his Jewishness cheerfully with his hump and shares all the joys and trials of dying Morris Mendelman, a typical East End *luftmentsh* turned tycoon, whose dream is to transfer his company funds to his daughter Rosa before his assets are liquidated. Mendelman dies on the point of telling Botvinnik the truth about life. He must work it out for himself, but he forgets the point and just cries instead. Real laughter through tears. Mankowitz puts this universal "truth about life" like this:

> I believe if one reaches "God," one does it through the enlargement of life and the pleasure of the senses: through the amazement of looking, and hearing, and tasting, and touching, and smelling; or through certain pleasureful activities—like making love when one is in love, or like singing and congenial working. And writing poetry, by the way, is a kind of singing and a kind of beautiful work that names things. And the naming of things, itself, ultimately—a country or a star, a flower or a baby—is a kind of worship.[15]

This conclusion comes directly out of the intense living of the East End, out of an intrinsically Jewish experience which made the writer what he is, even though he doesn't attach importance to the rituals of Judaism, "a meaningless hindrance to a true appreciation of basic philosophical truths.''[16] Mankowitz, then, illustrates well the distillation of that compound of direct childhood experience of Jewish life, anti-Semitism, the Yiddish heritage and Jewish ethics into more universal writing approaches.

BERNARD KOPS: OEDIPUS' END OR HAMLET IN TOWER HAMLETS

Like Litvinoff, Wesker and other East End writers, Bernard Kops (born 1926) learned his art on East End streets. He was a docker, chef, salesman, waiter, elevator operator and barrow-boy before he settled down to be an unsettled writer. His autobiographical *The World is a Wedding* (1963) is the cry of pain which Philip Roth diagnosed six years later as *Portnoy's Complaint*.

The World is a Wedding follows an archetypal pattern. The immigrant father, a poor Dutch Jew, does well out of the First World War as a "clicker" supplying the army with leather jerkins. He is a "trier" but in the postwar slump he can only give the family more children. The seven children share two single beds in a dingy attic in Stepney Green. It's a noisy attic because everyone is talking at once, pulling and pinching to make the others listen, and even though they subsist on relief money and pawning their shoes, the family maintains its self-respect.

> It was a self-imposed ghetto, but a happy world. And there was a spirit of community as in a village. People were involved in each other's lives, and not for the wrong reasons. Now, looking back, I see it was a desperate time—but then it meant security, and happiness.[17]

The boy doesn't know anything outside poverty or outside the East End. His father says they are too poor to afford religion, but the candles are lit on Friday night and the religious rites of passage are observed. In fact his father is "a strange atheist" and the boy cannot stop himself rocking and shaking as if really praying. Their religion is the family, the family shares and it cares, but it also devours. When an aunt coos "You're so lovely I could eat you," cannibalism has been made Kosher.

The boy comes to hate his father, especially for the heritage of exploitation which he would bequeath. The relationship with the mother has all the obvious Freudian associations—the boy loves the smell of her hair and he clings to her in a tunnel—while she is so obsessed by fear and anxiety, so convinced of impending disaster, that she dare not leave her family for a moment. This possessive love consumes the boy so that he must either yield to belief in imminent death and pressure to marry a "nice Yiddishe girl" or flee the Jewish home. To flee is not so simple, because the narrator doesn't know where he is going. His urge to become is to discover the self, but in a sense he has become his mother and killed his father. He can't just walk out. The inner desire of the alienated Jew is to be thrown out of the Jewish home. But the Yiddishe Mama doesn't willingly cut the umbilical cord.

He can't get anywhere with a morally-minded Jewish girl, but he is unexcited by an Irish chambermaid and he doesn't take up with the ATS girl. He ends up as a sex-starved anarchist writing poems: "There I was, full of pimples and dreams."[18] Writing affords the only freedom that doesn't tie him down, it is the only way he can become himself. All other options are no more than retreats and temporary escapes.

Walking the streets of Whitechapel with a carrier bag of manuscripts he journeys into himself to cancel out his mother's suffering. His is a private, silent war against conformity to maternal aspirations and faith in social norms. He leads a suicidal half-life in Soho to prove his refusal to become a "wage-slave" like the zombies of the suburbs. As soon as he manages to earn a simple penny he moves on. He is constantly on the run, from himself and from marriage with a Jewish woman (of both respectable and unrespectable types). He sinks lower into the abyss of depraved bestiality and deprivation, but can't help feeling guilty for the anguish he causes his mother. In the end the typical hero of modern Jewish writing must always return home and if the death of his mother frees him physically and artistically, he is not free from guilt, from the knowledge that "a child needs his parents dead."[19] The irony, as always, is that he settles down to become a *mentsh*, stealing his girlfriend Erica from a relatively comfortable bourgeois Jewish home and setting up a market stall selling books (traditional Jewish graft!).

The return to the urban Jewish trap is nevertheless not quite a defeat. He has come back torn by doubts and conflicts. He has come back from the brink, after finding refuge from the breakdown of the world in mental breakdown. Love and human kindness are discovered in the psychiatric ward. Out of complete desperation and disorientation he finds a moral purpose, though no less painful:

I considered that the achievements of mankind would be swamped by the horror we had perpetrated. We would not be able to outweigh our crimes against ourselves. Hitler was not the end of something; he was the beginning. Man was alone without faith or God; terribly alone. I was outraged by my visions of the weeping children of Warsaw; by my mother's tears and by my indifference.[20]

Zionism and Christianity each offer no solution. He tries the cross as well as a priest and wishes it could be that simple, that he could believe. Fortunately for him, Erica thinks on the same wavelength; together they flaunt convention and tread on Jewish family values, yet, like many of their generation, they relive them through sexual and social accomplishment.

I was a Jew, therefore I was a man. It is only by accepting I am Jewish that I am able to accept it. I, who spent my years running away, was taking a journey into myself, through myself, all the time. I, who wanted to get away from the family, wanted only to create a new family.[21]

The hope for the future is that the children of ex-drop-outs will be saved from blindness to morality, from mindless servitude to work, from a life controlled by others. Marriage with Erica bridges a classic class bridge between East and North-West London. The penniless East End boy with nothing to offer challenges the illusions of bourgeois suburbia and subverts the parents' aspirations of living through their children, their consuming love, by taking their daughter to a doss-house in bohemian Soho. They get married in a synagogue and in the East End, turning the revenge into a return, and they call their son Adam. Adam is born into a world of the Hungarian and Suez crises, just as his father was born thirty years earlier during the General Strike. Nevertheless, the lesson of his father is that it is worth living because, as the Yiddish saying goes, the world is a wedding.

Kops' treatment of disillusioned socialists in his books and plays is not black and white. He shows the aberrations of the human mind which lend his fantasies that absurd quality so characteristic of Ionesco, Beckett and Pinter. Everyone is capable of killing love, of Nazi excesses, we are all guilty, we all wish to be victims. Search for identity as a Jew breaks down into a universal search that goes beyond the frontiers of the East End, beyond England, where, in the words of *The World is a Wedding*, everyone is a "yes-man" in a "no-man's land."

In *Yes from No-man's Land* (1965) a dying old man, Joe Levene, meditates in his delirium on similar questions of being and identity in bed in a hospital for terminal cases in Hackney. His family has fallen apart and gone its separate ways—to Hampstead Garden Suburb and Tottenham; one son, Barry, has espoused the cause of mankind and is marrying a non-Jewish CND protester, while another son has abandoned socialism and mankind to go to Israel. The old man is a cause of unhappiness to his family in their settled bourgeois lives. Yet despite his cold-heartedness, Barry secretly envies his father his illusions, his family love and his indestructible faith which enables him to noisily eat a salmon sandwich and conduct invisible radio orchestras on his death bed. The old man's cancer is the pain of the Jewish people, a portable Wailing Wall. Barry hates what he sees of his fat sister and the noisy old people, he hates their clinging to distress, to history. Yet Barry, the architect who dreamt of building the new world, cannot replace this community of feeling with anything except some empty socialist phrases, a vacuum he cannot hide from himself.

Poking into the cavities of strange bodies may express the New Morality, but it isn't satisfying. It merely accentuates loneliness. Fully reciprocal union with the one person capable of giving and taking is the sole relief from loneliness and estrangement. Barry thinks his union with Susan will finally take him away from the Jewish family, but it doesn't solve the problem because Susan wants a child, whereas Barry refuses to burden another being with family and death. Susan wants to comprehend and come to terms with that eccentric tribe, the Jewish family, who bring everything into the open. To Barry's surprise his dying father doesn't make too much of a fuss about Susan not being Jewish and he must be disappointed if he expects to be liberated by the family's rejection. In an article about his own mixed marriage, Emanuel Litvinoff has described what is probably a typical East End attitude towards exogamy as something shameful and to be discouraged but not the end of the world. Hostility to prospective (or consummated) gentile marriage partnerships was based on socioethnic, not religious, scruples: the Jews felt themselves superior, cleaner and more caring for their children, while anti-Semitism pressed home the moral that one was best off among one's own people.[22] Outside the security of the Jewish East End these socioethnic scruples are not so big a deterrent to assimilation. But without obtaining complete rejection from the family there is no letting go.

The rite of passage into the Gentile world—usually sexual—so often results in that inner vacuum Barry feels and the way forward leads directly into the past. The drop-out from the North-West London Jewish community in *The Dissent of Dominick Shapiro* (1966) proclaims that "the one religion he didn't subscribe to was ancestral worship," but running away to Cornwall with a *shiksa* still leaves an aching need for spiritual fulfilment, for genuine religion. This sense of need symbolizes the loss of belonging, the loss of family, a loss catalyzed first and foremost by the dissolution of the Jewish East End. Kops has a gifted way of articulating the philosophical and moral implications of despair through the eyes of these confused, lonely people and nowhere more humorously than in *By the Waters of Whitechapel* (1969). Set in the postwar dying East End, it describes one of the remaining Jewish families, or rather all that's left of one. The East End is thick with ghosts—the Jews have gone to Golders Green, Israel or the cemetery. But Leah will never leave her candy store where she doles out promises of plastic eternity to Pakistani children standing in line for a taste of Mecca; there are also "doomtubes" (cigarettes) for anyone seeking a quicker way out of this foggy damnation. While the cash register rings up the sweet profits of Jewish commercialism, Aubrey fantasizes putting his mother out of her misery—out of pure love, of course,—yet his body can't do without the sweet-and-sour Jewish delicatessen. The candy store is a permanent Peter Pan childhood and he lives in dreams of himself as a child watching his father march off to help Trotsky organize the Red Army. Leah Feld holds the door open and offers the train fare (change at Charing Cross for Golders Green, Hendon, Edgware), but Aubrey stays. It's raining outside anyway. And his mother wouldn't let him go without something to eat.

Aubrey is ashamed of what he is and where he's from, he is ashamed he is not a barrister, that he has not traversed the Northwest Passage from the East End, and suicide seems the only way of resolving the contradiction between daydreams and the nightmare of reality. Until he meets Zena, *femme fatale* of Stamford Hill. Then for a brief moment he is a St. John's Wood barrister driving a Lotus Elan. With a few lies and a little embezzlement he almost pulls it off. But Leah has hired a private detective to track her son down and he is brought safely home.

Leah does die one day, so Aubrey packs her into the candy store safe and dispatches her to the depths of the Thames, where she disembarked so many years ago from Odessa. Aubrey is free of nagging and can love her without hate; but to keep up appearances he dresses in her clothes and acts her part, retiring to the security of the past that will never fade. Aubrey's incestuous fantasies are realized when he reproduces his mother.

It may be that Freud's own rebellion against Judaism can be explained by oedipal complexes,[23] but Kops' obscene Freudian imagery is also telling sociologically: the Yiddishe Mama's crippling delay of the child's emotional emancipation is motivated by a strategy of socialization.[24] On the one hand status competition among the immigrant community makes her want the child to excel academically *(nakhus)*, to earn her peers' respect by getting on and stabilizing at a higher social level *(yikhus)*; on the other hand she wishes to enforce retention of ethnic identity and maintain the close ties with the womb. Because of this excessive identification with the child and moral concern for it, her feelings of anxiety and guilt are internalized in her behavioral patterns: she coaxes, she cries, she coos, she frets, she threatens, she thinks of every Yiddish endearment and every Yiddish curse. The threat of anti-Semitism makes her overprotective to the point that the child becomes in effect emasculated and thus unable to leave home and fulfill the Yiddishe Mama's most ardent aspirations! In the end the child's rejection of enforced ethnic identity contradicts self-hood. Outside the home-womb the grown-up child must conform and become its mother or find itself socially and ethnically maladjusted, both structurally and culturally marginal.[25]

Bernard Kops' reputation was made with his drama *The Hamlet of Stepney Green* (1956). It laments the dying East End, but it's a comedy that affirms life, for in the battle to survive poverty "every day was a holiday from the dark." A dying East End stallholder, Sam Levy, the king of *shmalts* herring, insists on dying in his bed in the middle of his garden, an oasis of grass and flowers in middle of bombsites. He is just beginning to realize that he has nothing to show for his life. He didn't retire, he didn't move to Golders Green: "Life slipped through my fingers and as it was slipping, that was life."[26] His marriage went sour and it's too late to solve problems:

> Oh, God, life was a mistake, it shouldn't have been given to us, we didn't deserve it. The cockroaches deserve life more than human beings.[27]

Everything good in his life is dead. His life is poisoned. His wife was his life, so it was she who poisoned him, he declares on his deathbed. His son David overhears this and gets the idea he should avenge his father's death by murdering his mother. David is the prince of song—the play has several song and dance routines reminiscent of the Yiddish theater as well as modern dramatic improvization—but he is a drifter getting nowhere, unsure of tomorrow. His mother is slowly killing him with her love and his father nags him to marry a nice steady girl like Hava Segal and settle down. Yet David forces him to admit he wants his son to do better than stand behind a market stall, he doesn't want his son to make the same mistakes.

After his funeral Sam comes back home to sort out his son, who won't get the idea out of his head that his father the fish king really was poisoned. The mother, Bessie, is marrying Sam's old friend Solly Segal, and Hamlet determines to avenge his father's death. Now he has a meaning in his life and a way of waking people up— he has a ghost of which only he is aware, for to them these are the soliloquies of a madman. It is they who are dead and unaware of what is happening around them, unaware of poetry or even the Bible. Now, dressed up as a Teddy Boy, the angry young Jew plots revenge with his ghostly father. Sam is interested in avenging his life not his death (like Fender in *The Bespoke Overcoat*), but goes along with his son. Instead of a death potion, Sam gets David to administer a love potion, and although David doesn't drink it he wakes up to Hava who has been waiting for him all the time. She even went to Israel to get away from him and came back when she didn't find him there. The lovers come together and look forward to settling down happily in Golders Green. Hamlet's role is at an end and Sam is avenged on life. Before he is finally exorcized, though, Sam reminds David that the way to put meaning into life is to be aware of the question of the meaning of life. His parting advice is to

> . . . commit arson every day in your imagination, burn down the previous day's lies, have a little revolution now and again in your heart; . . .[28]

David has decided to leave home for good, to grow up as Jew and man, to do exactly what his father wanted—to break out of the ghetto. He also learns to break out of the ghetto of his mind, though it should be noted it's his father who has to help him do this!

David will leave the East End which is dead and populated by ghosts, but the kind of community that the East End was does not exist in the North-West London suburb of *Enter Solly Gold* (1961). There Solly Gold, an East End conman, finds that people are dead to the world, engaged in exchanging meaningless clichés and just waiting to be relieved of the burden of their money, waiting to be swindled. It takes a Tartuffe to wake up Mr. Swarz to the truth. Swarz lets himself be persuaded for a while that he is the messiah and finds blissful peace. The daughter, Romaine, is supposed to lure Solly into a confession of the swindle but lets him kidnap her instead, thus escaping respectable marriage with a Jewish accountant or heir to a business. Solly fails in the end because he can't choose between the ransom money and the woman, but he has woken up the wedding guests to the meaning of life. The theme was later reused in a novel *Settle Down Simon Katz* (1973), where it is the father who refuses to leave the East End and conform to the humdrum mediocrity of North-West London. He gives his children such aggravation, that they are prepared to pay fabulous sums never to hear from their father again. In both cases, the conman's dishonesty with others and with himself questions identity; the symbolic role-playing and the surreal absurdity of the situations make Kops seem almost close to what Pinter is doing.

As in *The World is a Wedding*, the author writes out of a personal need to come to terms with community and self. "All my plays are concerned with family relationships. These are the themes that obsess me."[29] The Stepney Green Hamlet's oedipal complex is a desperate critique of conventional Jewish family life which the family dismisses as insanity. This is not just the all-out attack on the Yiddishe Mama which Professor Fisch has described in his remarks on Anglo-American Jewish writers,[30] it is a complaint in both Portnoyan senses of emotional blackmail: maternal love denies psychological and sexual independence and claims possession as payment for "the things I did for you," "everything I sacrificed to make you happy and safe," to quote Kops' play *The Dream of Peter Mann* (1960). But the reaction against the archetypal monstrous bullying Jewish mother does bear more significance than the breakdown of Jewish communal structures: it "functions as part of a Brechtian analysis of society and its imminent decay."[31] As in *The Lemmings* (1963), Kops places his characters in a nuclear apocalypse and the parents want their children to share their senseless deathwish: in *The Lemmings* suicide is not merely symbolic and the children are tempted to the brink of the sea that is to claim them in a final mass baptism of salvation by suicide (suicide is a recurrent image in Kops' works). *The Lemmings* links the fate of a Jewish refugee family (Lemmings by name and by nature) with their English middle-class counterparts; they preserve to the last racial apartness, prejudice, adulterous lust and meek male obedience to female whims. The young Jew and the young English-woman break away from their families' unthinking obedience to a society manufacturing its own destruction and set up an interracial commune for two in a cove. But the end of the play holds out little hope of a new start for mankind as the waves lap over the heads of the last survivors.

The dying of a community, specifically the East End, ends in the dying of the human race, a message repeated in *Home Sweet Honeycomb* (1963), a dystopic fantasy of the near future. An East London working-class family hands over each of its sons as one after the other they "go to the bad" and are executed by the borough council, the local arm of totalitarian authority. Yet the security of the confining council flat is paper-thin, making escape possible by literally breaking out through the walls into the street. After the break-out, however, where to? The London Underground (subway system) is crowded with morons going nowhere, living dead. Suicide offers a tempting security, but false, like the council flat walls. Conformity, Kops is saying, is a form of death, and mankind is not interested in the future, in survival, in escape from the numbing, regimentalized routine run by fascists from the local council.

The self-alienated Jewish adolescents of Bernard Kops and Eman-uel Litvinoff have much in them of the modernity of *Hamlet*, not just the obvious parallel with the Oedipus complex, but also the self-negation arising from inability to act. The heroic act looms ridiculous and parodic in the face of the adolescent's impotence; indeed, there seems little possibility of action in the postwar at-mosphere of disillusion and in the ontological void following Ausch-witz. Isadore Traschen has noted that

> There is no doctrinal, religious consolation in [Hamlet's] tragic, dying declaration that 'The rest is silence'.[32]

Wolf Mankowitz's early writings (among them *My Old Man's a Dustman*, 1956) are touched by this existential dilemma; however, the East End experience in general suggested a Brechtian approach rather than the perspective of Beckett.

Kops belongs to the working-class revolution in British theater—the so-called kitchen sink drama—which shoved the drawing-room off stage. Writing in 1961, he said he subscribed to the shared belief in socialism, but it is a hope tinged with the Brechtian realism that "he who is an optimist obviously hasn't heard the bad news."[33] Kops felt then that people from different origins could communicate through a common humanity, and it is as a Jew that he warns of the danger to humanity from the final, universal, nuclear holocaust:

> This time there will be no more time;
> Time itself will be in the box-car.
> This time we are all on our way to the fire.[34]

Chapter Four
East End Writers II:
Arnold Wesker

The Jewish East End which Emanuel Litvinoff, Wolf Mankowitz, Bernard Kops and Arnold Wesker write about has long been a graveyard. Their works are social documents but their primary meaning is universal; they claim merit today on grounds of literary and not ethnographical appeal. Anglo-Jewish writing has reached that "symbolistic stage" which David Daiches saw as succeeding the documentation of Jewish immigrant life, as in Zangwill's record of that historical transition from *shtetl* Jewishness to Englishness, or in the partly angry, partly affectionate autobiographical accounts of committed Leftists in the 1930s.[1] Anglo-Jewish writing has come of age in the same way that Walter Allen sees American Jewish writing coming of age with Bellow and Malamud, whose ethical concerns are American, but no less Jewish for that.[2] The East End writers are not chroniclers of the tough immigrant neighborhoods as were Daniel Fuchs, Nathaniel West or Meyer Levin in America; but the dying of the East End did teach them universal commitments that nevertheless were grounded in specifically Jewish concerns. The result is a plethora of novels and plays by authors who have salvaged from nostalgia for what was and is no more a commitment to present-day social issues, to moral awareness, because of what the East End and the dying of the East End meant to them.

The East End was, as we have seen, a world apart, and Jews grew up there sharing a common poverty and a collective identity. The problem of identity did not usually crop up until adolescence when one had to step out into the hostile Gentile world of job competition and fight to make ends meet. Whether one got a scholarship or entered a trade, it was outside the Jewish home that one suddenly became Jewish and had to deal directly with anti-Semitism. Having been brought up to believe one belonged in England, one suddenly found oneself unwanted. Of course anti-Semitism was felt to be endemic but when Oswald Mosley's blackshirts marched in a change came over the East End. Organized anti-Semitism presented a very real threat, a living menace that was no less sinister for the absurdity of snotty-nosed slum kids tramping around in black uniforms shouting "We gotta get rid of the Yids!" or Mosley playing Mussolini with a prissy upper-class accent. The attempt by the fascists to march through the East End in 1936 crystalized the commitment of many East End Jews to Communism and the proletarian revolution. When a seven-year-old girl is thrown through a plate-glass window in Wesker's *Chicken Soup with Barley* a stand has to be made.

The Second World War blended conscripts into the anonymity of a uniformed mass dedicated to fighting a war against the Germans, and if news of Nazi genocide leaked through it did not penetrate the consciousness of the majority, except that they knew they would have it rougher than their mates if they fell into German hands. During the Blitz sirens wailed and sent East Enders scampering for shelter in Underground railway stations where they would spend the night, each feathering his own nest. The mass evacuation of children had been eerie enough, but the sight of the bombed-out ruins of the East End was certainly macabre. Hitler was bringing the threat against the Jews into the heart of the East End. The knowledge that the bombs did not discriminate between Jew and non-Jew was little consolation, although it no doubt brought the two indigenous populations together in common suffering.

The 1940s also brought more opportunities, encouraging the Jews to move out of the East End in far greater numbers than before. The crumbling of the communal infrastructure and the gradual dispersal of close relatives or life-long neighbors were the background to postwar reconstruction and the move northwards to Hackney, Dalston and Stamford Hill, the steppingstone to the bourgeois, semi-detached, semi-rural utopia of Golders Green and beyond.

EAT CHICKEN SOUP OR YOU'LL DIE

The dissolution of the East End was to be a point of departure and a point of return for the East End writers as they overcame their marginality and tried to find a way back to roots. Personal associations of the East End recur because they are important in tracing what went wrong with the Jewish community, with the revolution, with the world. In a way it's like Kops' Yiddishe Mama problem: the adolescent anti-hero can only love her devotedly when she's dead; so too the East Enders always wanted to leave the ghetto that bore them, but it was never easy to separate from that womb. Litvinoff recreated an East End childhood before the war and Kops showed what happened to the East Enders who stayed after the war. Mankowitz' pessimistic idylls are timeless, though set against a remembrance of the East End at its poorest. The most direct account of the actual dissolution of the East End is given in Act I of Arnold Wesker's *Chicken Soup with Barley* (1958), the first part of his *Trilogy*. By the beginning of Act II the Kahns have moved to a London County Council apartment block in Hackney, "the 1930 kind, with railings," the year is 1946 and the working-class is that bit more respectable. The *Trilogy* is a look back in anger at the ideals of an East End family and what became of them from October 1936 through 1959. The long timespan allows for the clearest analogy of personal associations of the East End with universal preoccupations; *Roots* fits into the middle of the *Trilogy* as a brief and abortive excursion by the East End Jewish intellectual into a rural working-class Norfolk family before the final, frustrated attempt to break with the past.

Arnold Wesker was born in Stepney in 1932, which makes him the youngest of the East End writers. The family moved to Clapton Common during the war, so that Wesker's education was divided between Stepney and Hackney and was completed with a book-keeping, shorthand and typing course at Upton House Central School in Hackney. His mother worked in kitchens to support the family; his father was a Russian-born tailor and often out of work. After leaving school Arnold Wesker worked as a furniture maker's apprentice, plumber's mate, farm laborer, seed sorter, kitchen porter and pastry-cook.

What was a "smashing time" for Wesker as a child was sheer misery for his family: "It's a trap, the East End, to be sentimental

and full of cosy longing for 'the good old days' . . . I mean, *I* may
have loved it . . . written about it with love, but my family remember
it with misery. *I* may be riddled with nostalgia, hoarding the past
as though it were food for a time of famine, but not them, not them
. . ."[3] Elsewhere Wesker has warned about making the easy equation
of a slum childhood and commitment to socialism: "It amuses me
when people say to me, 'O but you're a socialist because you come
from the East End and suffered poverty.' It's not true—we experienced
poverty, but we nevertheless had a marvelous time. I loved it."[4]
Rather socialism was in the family, it was something breathed in
with a mother's milk. Sarah Wesker was in real life one of the
Rothschild Building tenants and Garment Union activists who led a
struggle for improved social conditions; the Charlotte de Rothschild
Buildings were put up by the philanthropic magnates of Anglo-Jewry
as model dwellings for the East European Jewish immigrants,[5] but
by the time of Wesker's childhood the model dwellings were no
smarter than any other local tenement and lacked basic amenities
like hot water. Standing up to authority was a lesson learned in
Eastern Europe where the majority had no say in their fate, while
the involvement and intensity of living in the Jewish East End made
"responding" to life as common and as natural as eating, when one
had food. There is for Wesker a basic difference between "responding"
and merely "reacting":

> To react is to behave out of a kind of fear [whereas] to respond
> is to open out one's whole being, in an act of recognition, is to
> be enthusiastic in an unashamed way . . . to react is to feel in
> a negative way, to respond is to affirm.[6]

In John Allin's primitivist paintings which accompany Allin's and
Wesker's childhood memories, *Say Goodbye—You May Never See Them
Again* (1974), the people stand out large against the mundane slum-
iness of the East End and Hackney. In the *Trilogy* Aunt Esther calls
Flower and Dean Street a prison from which she always wanted to
escape[7] and, despite the whimsical street names, it's the people who
lived in those streets (and the streets *were* lived in) that made the
East End at all bearable.

The war, however, made people hard. Evacuation meant the
first trip into the countryside, while the war changed the East End
completely. The bombed-out ruins and dilapidated, partly abandoned,
slums were gradually torn down and replaced by the sterile anonymity
of a concrete jungle. All that remained to look back on was the

neighborliness, the friends, the political arguments. These were Wesker's education, not school which taught only pig-headed discipline.

> . . . Ach it's obsessive, the past . . . something wrong . . . I keep thinking it saps your energy . . . but hell! What can you do? Places, buildings, names—they *do* carve strong images . . .[8]

There wasn't much religion in the Wesker household and the boy didn't have a *barmitzvah*, but at fourteen he did join the Zionist pioneer youth movement, *Habonim* ("The Builders"). He was churning out reams of adolescent poetry in imitation of Dylan Thomas, as well as in imitation of his brother-in-law who had left the East End with Wesker's sister to settle in a quiet country cottage, just like Dave and Ada in *I'm Talking About Jerusalem*. During his National Service in the Royal Air Force (1950–2) Wesker wrote a novel *The Reed That Bent*, which was a kind of Lawrentian evocation of the oneness experienced during squarebashing; this was later turned into the play *Chips With Everything* (1962), where the idea of group cohesiveness can be seen in the team effort that goes into stealing the coal. Amateur acting attracted Wesker to the theater and the stimulus of John Osborne's *Look Back in Anger* (1956) made him decide on a career as a playwright. Perhaps his lack of much grounding in the theater explains the raw, unconventional construction of his early plays for which he has been so often reprimanded, as has Bernard Kops, but he did save up enough money by working in Paris restaurants to take a short course at the London School of Film Technique, where he met Lindsay Anderson who helped bring Wesker to public attention.

In 1953 Wesker had begun working on a play *And After Today*, and parts were incorporated into *Chicken Soup with Barley*, which Wesker started writing in 1957; the same year his dramatic adaptation of those two years in Paris restaurants, *The Kitchen*, was disqualified as too short for the *Observer* play competition. The development of provincial repertory companies, together with the activities of the West End Royal Court Theatre and Joan Littlewood's Theatre Workshop in Stratford, East London, made possible the success of John Osborne and other so-called kitchen sink dramatists new to a theater that had seen nothing like them. *Chicken Soup with Barley* and *Roots* were first produced by the Belgrade Theatre in Coventry (as was *I'm Talking About Jerusalem*) before being transferred to the Royal Court, which also presented the premiere of *The Kitchen* and the first showing of the entire *Trilogy*, all under the direction of John Dexter. Being a working-class outsider, a Jew from the East End, Wesker fits into the general non-conformism of the new subversive kind of *théâtre maudit* which sought to *involve* the audience. The vitality and expressiveness of East Enders Wesker, Kops and Mankowitz suited the new kind of dramatic handling on the stage, while the iconoclastic, radical voice of the restless Wandering Jew, the eternal heretic unhappy with ready formulas and established authority, had something to say in the arena of the equally frustrated Angry Young Man. Not that the crazy dreamers of Kops and Wesker are identical with the Angry Young Man, but the cross-currents are there and they are important. Wesker thought he recognized in Beckett's *Waiting for Godot* and Pinter's *The Birthday Party* the same terrible lack of communication he is trying to convey in *Roots;*[9] in the Kahn family we see people ready to bridge that gulf by putting their craziest lunacies into effect, an existential revolt that comes from suffering centuries of persecution and injustice, as well as from looking to the ideals of Soviet communism, the result of over sixty years of revolutionary sympathies among Jews from Russia and their descendants in the East End. Sartre, in *Refléxions sur la question juive*, believed Jews got involved in political commitment rather than metaphysical interests as a natural consequence of the Jew's social handicaps and insecurity.

Wesker is didactic, though he warns in the author's note to the *Trilogy* that his characters are not meant to be masks; art and politics are one to him and this is what makes as well as strains his plays on the English stage. G. S. Fraser has urged us to rethink our conception of politics in order to appreciate Wesker's characters as more than walking caricatures; we should see them as part of a universal concern for humanity, something like R. H. Tawney's "cooperative action." Wesker is both more articulate and more naive than Osborne and other committed writers, but perhaps it is precisely Wesker's East End radicalism that is embarrassing to a non-working-class English audience unused to caring and having to care.

Wesker openly identifies his personal life with the characters in the *Trilogy*, and if we can hear the author speaking, this is because "to speak is to act" (Sartre); the acting out of action alerts the audience to the need for awareness and change. The author explains the weak position of Ronnie (an analgram of Arnold) as a device to allow the development of the other protagonists.[10] Wesker, unlike Ronnie, married his Norfolk working-class girlfriend, Doreen Bicker, in 1958, and wrote *Roots* after their marriage. Wesker has in fact written his East End origins into his plays in a rather obvious way. He felt the security of the social and political life at home despite the rows between his parents and that security comes across in *Chicken Soup with Barley*. The chicken soup with barley which keeps Ada alive and which Sarah brings with her at the beginning of *I'm Talking About Jerusalem* reflects a real anxiety about malnutrition, though it doesn't sustain ideals when they are put to the test in the big wide world; yet it does in many ways symbolize the warmth and caring of the Kahns' East End home: "if you don't care you'll die," shouts Sarah as the curtain comes down. Sarah exudes love and vitality, in complete contrast to her husband, Harry, who is amiable, but weak and work-shy. His desertion of family and principles is paralleled by the apathy of the Norfolk farming family in *Roots*, the Bryants, and their unwillingness to think about vital moral issues. The difference is that the Kahns learn new attitudes toward their ideals through caring, while the Bryants have never cared and the only live spark of their community is the alcoholic Stan Mann who drops down dead in the middle of the play.

Chicken Soup with Barley opens on 4 October 1936, the day of Mosley's historic attempt to march his fascist thugs through the East End. The Jews and workers of the East End turn out to stop them. Harry doesn't want to know and after timidly waving the hammer and sickle flag which Sarah has given him he runs away to his mother's—he is both failed Jewish father and the son tied to the Yiddishe Mama's apron strings. Sarah, however, cares for and cares about (even if she confuses what was to be known as the Battle of Cable Street with the Siege of Sidney Street, when the anarchist Peter the Painter held out against Churchill's men). Not only Jews want to stop the blackshirts—the Limehouse dockers come out in support together with other East End workers and Labour Party members. The reference to a dance in aid of a bereaved Roman Catholic girl stresses the ecumenical solidarity of the working classes. And it is a question of class: the Board of Deputies, the official representative body of Anglo-Jewry, has asked the Jewish population to keep away from the march. For Dave Simmonds, however, a stand has to be made. Mosley has to be stopped in the East End and Hitler has to be stopped in Spain. The cry that goes up is the watchword of the Spanish Republicans: "They shall not pass."[11] It looks like the revolution is coming.

Act II shows the Kahn Family after the war, in their Hackney flat. Harry is as much a failure as ever. When everyone else has been busy making money during the war Harry has been losing one tailoring job after another (a theme also of C. P. Taylor's *Bread and Butter*, 1967, set in the Gorbals, Glasgow's version of the East End). Harry retreats into himself, retreats into Yiddish and a childish dependence on Sarah which becomes total after he is incapacitated by heart failure.

Like other East Enders, Dave Simmonds fought in Spain, then in World War Two, and now Ada Kahn waits for him to be demobbed. There is a Labour administration; nationalization and a welfare state will change the nation. Ronnie, now an exuberant fifteen-year-old schoolboy, looks forward enthusiastically to a new, socialist, planned society. Yet Ada is not so sure. She is bitter after six years of clerical work, discovering office girls are morons, while Dave found out that his comrades-in-arms against Hitler behaved like animals and didn't know what they were fighting for (as Jimmy Beales doesn't know in *Roots*). Ada reacts against her mother's militancy. She sees modern industrial society as the enemy of individuality and of the family, as a jungle (perhaps it's no accident Harry reads Upton Sinclair's *The Jungle* instead of joining in the demonstration); she sees Communism as a struggle to transfer the means of production to the worker not in order to destroy the machine and the values of industrial capitalism, but in order to own them. Nor can Sarah's love for the world possibly embrace a billion people, it's a theory which is impractical and presumptuous. When Dave comes back they will move to the country, away from the ratrace and the stultifying routine of the city, so hated by Kops' drop-outs.

> That'll be our socialism. Remember this, Ronnie: the family should be a unit, and your work and your life should be part of one existence, not something hacked about by a bus queue and office hours. A man should see, know, and love his job.[12]

The homeliness and extended family of the East End is not the same thing as a happy family. Ada will be glad to get away from her bickering family, to make a family in her own image that will know and appreciate life and see things for what they are; David will be independent and a craftsman, making things with his own hands. The fight against estrangement brings Wesker close to Brecht's *Entfremdungseffekt*, but also relates to John Ruskin's ideal, later the initial aesthetic premise of William Morris, that the architect should combine art and craft; only in integrated, non-alienated work can the artist-craftsman achieve free expression of his art and pleasure in it.

Ada sees what Sarah doesn't see: the committed Communists have moved out and settled down as successful businessmen. Monty and Bessie have lost contact in more ways than one. By 1955 Monty has a shop, up north, in Manchester, and has left the Communist Party: the anti-Trotskyite purges extended as far as the frontline in Spain and the liquidation of the Jewish Anti-Fascist Committee makes it impossible to consider the USSR as "our" homeland of socialism. Monty is only concerned for his family, his home and an education for his child. He doesn't want anything to do with politics: "It's a big lousy world of mad politicians—I can't trust them, Sarah."[13] He won't accept the false black-and-white divisions he attributes to Sarah, but there's nothing he can do to stop an atom bomb dropping on his head. Nevertheless there's something missing in his life and he looks back to the East End for the lost comradeship, for the example of Sarah who was always fighting.

> It was a slum, there was misery, but we were going somewhere. The East End was a big mother.[14]

Sarah doesn't share this sentimentality ("Ach! Horrible times!"), but before she can give a full reply Harry has an attack of incontinence and she must demonstrate her philosophy of caring in action.

After the Soviet crushing of the Hungarian uprising in 1956 Sarah is still in the Party and can't comprehend her mistakes, just as she can't understand where she went wrong in the game of solo. She still believes that people can be happy if they have enough to eat. Ronnie comes home from working in a Paris kitchen to accuse her blind faith and all she can do is fuss over him with tea and cake. He has lost his enthusiasm:

> The family you always wanted has disintegrated, and the great ideal you always cherished has exploded in front of your eyes. But you won't face it.[15]

Yet Sarah won't give up:

> You want me to move to Hendon and forget who I am? If the electrician who comes to mend my fuse blows it instead, so I should stop having electricity? I should cut off my light? Socialism is my light, can you understand that?[16]

There will always be the idea of brotherhood and if philosophy tells us it all means nothing we still cannot afford to despair, because acceptance, apathy, means death. Sarah fulfills a traditional role of the East End Jewish mother; she would have liked Ronnie to settle down to a trade, she resents his leaving her to work in Paris, but her love is not something that kills and devours. She resists the North-West London syndrome "Hendon," preferring to remain in a block of council flats in Hackney, where nobody knows anyone else or cares, while she continues to believe that caring is important. Yet she has not equipped Ronnie with the tools to cope with the breakdown of ideals in the ugly world of reality.

What Ronnie has realised is the futility of struggling one's whole lifetime to earn money. He has almost come around to his father's position of giving up because he couldn't make sense of it all.[17] He no longer cares, because it makes no difference. "That's all we are—people terrified of old age, hoping for the football pools to come home."[18] The same sort of disappointed idealism is implicit in Wesker's short story "Pools" (1958) in which an old woman, Mrs. Hyams, dreams of winning the football pools—the sort of obsessive dream Mankowitz writes about (Mrs. Hyams also lives on Fashion Street). So why should Mrs. Hyams win? Who is she anyway? So nothing! Wesker's comment: "This woman represents millions in England."[19]

Yet Ronnie can't refute the urgent priority of caring, if only because he has nothing better to offer. He has been deeply hurt by the failure of people to live up to ideals and the play ends with his blubbering confusion. Once he wrote poetry and wanted to put his socialism into a novel. Now he is lost for words, the same Ronnie who has taught Beatie in *Roots* how to build bridges with words. At the end of *Roots* Beatie has become articulate, has found herself and no longer needs Ronnie who never appears in the play.

The bickering Bryant family in *Roots* is allegorical of any closed-in community, though their language is specific to an isolated rural Norfolk community, just as the language of the Kahns is specific to the East End. Their brutishness and the conviction that something must be done about it clarify the parallels with *Chicken Soup with Barley* and with the Jewish East End; this is why Wesker "always thought of *Roots* as a Jewish play."[20] The Jewish community abhors and fears the *Lumpenproletariat* because of its destructiveness and because of its coarseness and in expressing this Wesker teaches a Jewish moral.

The theme of the modern mass-production jungle is here, too, for country folk can be as brutalized as city workers. They seem immune to change, they instinctively stick to their outdated attitudes (Mr. Bryant begrudges his daughter the electricity to bake a sponge cake for Jenny; Mrs. Bryant would sentence hooligans to life imprisonment without much consideration), though sometimes their hypocritical bigotry can protect members of the community from the authorities or the outside world (there are two cases mentioned of extramarital cohabitation; Jenny's illegitimate child is accepted). But they don't see the meaning of the roots with which they work and live every day in their market-garden allotments:

> Roots! The things you come from, the things that feed you. The things that make you proud of yourself—roots![21]

Not only vegetables and corn need roots. People need them too, they need strong roots to know where they're "pushing up from," to give them a sense of direction. But the Bryant family doesn't care, they don't care if an atom bomb dropped on them tomorrow, because if they cared they would have to do something about it.

The message of the East End socialist "Jew-boy" Ronnie Kahn comes through in *Roots* by means of Beatie's repetition of her lover's favorite phrases. Socialism, quotes Ronnie's mouthpiece, is not talking, it's passing it on to someone near to you. If that's what socialism is, Ronnie has failed and by the end of the play he knows he has failed. He never really got through to Beatie, who doesn't understand all of what she repeats. She has been touched, made aware of something beyond her comprehension, but she has not been changed and she knows she can't change her family. As Harry once said to Ronnie, in *Chicken Soup with Barley*, you can't change people, you can only give them some love and hope they take it. Beatie is forced to admit,

> . . . Mother, you're right—the apple don't fall far from the tree do it? You're right, I'm like you. Stubborn, empty, wi' no tools for livin'. I got no roots in nothing. I come from a family o' farm labourers yet I ent got no roots—just like town people— just a mass o' nothin'.[22]

The failure goes deeper, however. The Bryants are typical of the working classes whom socialism is trying to reach. Yet despite a socialist administration in office they have no power and they acquiesce in the status quo. They don't respond to the call of trade union protest even when their own livelihoods are at stake. They reason there's nothing you can do about the sackings which follow every raise in pay and they are quite incapable of discussing basic moral issues—or any problems at all, including Mr. Bryant being put on casual labor after eighteen years on the farm. He doesn't want to read his union magazine and kowtows to his smooth-talking boss Mr. Healey. Jimmy Beales serves in the Territorial Army and is ready to come out against the striking London busmen. Farm laborers have it much harder but they don't think of fighting injustice because they don't have the East End family's sense of moral right or its tradition of vocal radicalism.

People in the East End walked around with Jerusalem in their heads, believing with complete faith in the possibility of universal salvation, but after the war there's no evidence of that class solidarity we saw in Act I of *Chicken Soup with Barley*. The Jewish intellectual must be disappointed if he expects to build Jerusalem on his own. The ensuing despair is captured in Norman's words in Kops' *The Lemmings:* the Jerusalem in "Next Year in Jerusalem is nowhere. It's next year. It's just a dream, I suppose. We're not connected to anything. We don't belong anywhere."[23]

Even the removal men in *I'm Talking About Jerusalem* can't understand what makes Ada and Dave move out to the country, far from basic modern comforts. Their dream of living socialism and not just talking about it means going back to primitive conditions, drawing water from the well and lighting Tilley Lamps (as the Bryant family are still doing a decade later), going back to Nature and learning what Dave learnt on active duty in Ceylon, "that a man is made to work and that when he works he's giving away something of himself, something very precious—."[24] In city factories the worker becomes brutalized, turning out the same article day in, day out, with no return for the energy put in. The city alienates the worker from family and from the means of production in Marxist and aesthetic terms (a comparison can be made here with the aesthetics of both Mankowitz and Brecht), yet to Sarah's way of thinking leaving the East End is a running away from both family and socialism, because she is prevented from living her ideals through her daughter, and because socialism is with people.

Dave and Ada renounce the "easy life," which Sarah never had but which she presumably hoped her children would enjoy, because city life has fragmented experience; they want to bring work and family together, to do things for themselves without relying on the labor of others, to do the things they want to do, to discover the world anew, without preconceptions (notice the way Wesker has characters *doing* things on the stage like washing dishes and preparing food). Their children will learn to deautomatize experience and that's the point of Daniel's "learning to live life" game however clumsy it may seem on the stage. The game is an exercise in awakening the senses to a life which has been made so familiar by bourgeois living that vital details are passed over unnoticed in the habitual routine of daily existence. The Russian formalist Viktor Shklovsky refers to this in his remarks on Tolstoy's aesthetics, in which Shklovsky defines art as an estrangement that makes strange in order to renew perception so that we are, in the words of Frederic Jameson, "reborn to the world in its existential freshness and horror."[25] Danny reemerges from the womb as clay, as a *golem*, and Dave, the *maker* of things, must breathe life into him to make him into a human being with the gift of sight who can see and talk without automatically thinking in stereotyped labels. He can now be Daniel the lionslayer.

Ronnie's talk about words as bridges is for them empty because impracticable; however, they in turn are accused by the cynical Libby Dobson of not seeing further than their own simple, inane phrases. Dobson too believes in Jerusalem but he got bruised and burnt-up putting his ideals into practice. To him their going back to nature is a lie and an outdated one because if every worker decided to follow suit and express his individuality, modern society would soon wind down. Moreover it ignores human nature, for people soon forget their ideals, they become possessive and insensitive and become like the Bryants, guzzling their food and not getting any enjoyment out of life. Dave himself has succumbed to the city factory mentality and steals a roll of lino from his employer Colonel Dewhurst. He is doubly caught—for petty thievery and lying—but he has also failed to understand the farmer-boss/tenant-worker relationship can't be brushed aside just like that. Ada wounds Dave deeply when she points out his ideals "have got some pretty big leaks in places."

Dreams of chicken runs, youth hostellers and self-sufficiency have to be dropped. Dave is fired and must stand the test now of his independent cooperative workshop. Yet though he picks up a rustic Norfolk slang, he can't infuse his apprentice Sammy with his vision. Chairs made by hand craftsmanship breathe poetry, more than that they are built with disinterested passion. Dave offers original design, trying to fulfill William Morris' ideal of not becoming a slave to machines; the machine is a labor saving device to help the worker and not to replace him in the process of production. He wants to make something he will enjoy making, not make what other people want (the theme of designing is commonplace in the Anglo-Jewish postwar visions of the new life). The workshop allows the two men freedom and independence. Sammy knows all this, but wants to "get on," he wants that baited trap, a nine-to-five factory job. Then Dave finds out he's not so free and independent after all: he depends on philistine, uncaring customers who let him down; notwithstanding their determination to stick it out, Ada and Dave pack up after six years and return to London. Dave will open a cabinet-making workshop in a basement; life will go on. Ronnie is the most disappointed. It is 1959, the year of the action in *Roots* (Ronnie has broken with Beatie). The Socialists are out of office and discredited by their record of going back on ideals and building the Bomb. Dave and Ada were the only two who seemed not to have sold out after the war. Now they, too, admit defeat. Dave was Ronnie's god who fought in Spain, but for Dave it was a useless war that didn't stop Hitler and didn't stop the extermination of six million Jews. The postwar perspective makes it impossible to recapture the glory of the workers' struggle of the 1930s. Dave (like David in Kops' *Hamlet of Stepney Green*) didn't want to be a stallholder handling coppers like his Aunt Esther and settle down in a jerrybuilt house. He wants to do something purposeful and shouts at her that he is a prophet, the second (Davidic) Jewish preacher of universal salvation after Jesus. More than once, Sarah and Esther shouted back that you can't change the world and now Dave no longer has pretensions to be a visionary. This leaves Ronnie in despair, for no one, including himself, has lived up to ideals. Like Monty Blatt before him (in *Chicken Soup with Barley*), Dave can only worry now about the day-to-day concerns of his family and his work. Visions don't work, Dave yells at Ronnie.[26] Yet Ronnie, the one character who is present, at least implicitly, in all three parts of the *Trilogy*, has the last word: "We must be bloody mad to cry."[27]

The bitterness of the ambiguity is Wesker's own, but he points out in the Author's Note that these are real people, not caricatures. "The picture I have drawn is a harsh one, yet my tone is not one of disgust . . . I am at one with these people: it is only that I am annoyed, with them and myself."[28] The tone of protest may at times strain the dramatic impact of Wesker's plays, but it's relieved by a typically Jewish bittersweet irony and only the crudest reading of Wesker's embarrassing sincerity can see in it a reduction to black-and-white issues. There is a desperate disappointment here, but it in no way negates Wesker's socialist *Ani ma'amin* ("I believe," the traditional Maimonedean declaration of messianic faith). For him the idealists may have failed, but not the ideals.

After the war the working-classes have lost sight of their aspirations, settling for the imitative illusions of suburban comfort with its third-rate pop culture and mass-produced consumer goods. In *Roots* Beatie tries to make her mother see that the recent pop song she sings doesn't *say* anything, it doesn't *do* anything to you (which doesn't stop Beatie singing it with some enthusiasm to the end). She plays Bizet's *L'Arlésienne* to bring some life and happiness into the Bryant house where the repetitious smalltalk demonstrates the boredom of a daily routine without books and paintings, without culture. Notice that Ravel's *La Valse* is on the radio in *Chicken Soup with Barley*, Act III; Ronnie Kahn is "conducting" Beethoven's Egmont Overture in *Chicken Soup with Barley* Act II, Scene 2 (though it annoys Aunt Cissie the trade union organizer) and his Ninth Symphony in *I'm Talking About Jerusalem* Act I, scene 1. Wesker wants to alert the audience to the confusion of bourgeois comfort with aesthetic pleasure, to awaken us to the deadening effect of the impersonal, mechanized society which encourages the tendency to elevate fragments of experience, partial truths, into total, absolute ideologies.

The workings of *The Kitchen* (1959) demonstrate how individual actions become mechanical, meaningless units of a larger, monstrous machine, which produces luxuries for bourgeois clients who do not appreciate the art of the pastry cook. Notice the way action is *mimed* in the play, unlike the film, the way the ovens are always there. Similarly, *Chips with Everything* studies the way the authorities subjugate the individual into unthinking, bestial obedience. Pip's primordial scream in scene 8 is eloquent in this respect. *The Kitchen* is an allegory of the human condition, though it and the author deny symbolism. The representatives of Europe's working classes employed in the kitchen include a sensitive Jew, Paul, who is a disillusioned idealist, another version of Ronnie. The long-suffering German, Peter, challenges his workmates to dream, to have big dreams, not just money, women and petty material things. None of them can really meet this challenge; they lack the means and the imagination to change their lives. Peter makes his big gesture and goes beserk, bringing the kitchen to a halt. The boss, Marango, can only protest at this sabotage, but he ends the play with the same question raised in the *Trilogy*: when you've stopped the world, what is there more?

Wesker's attempt to alert the audience to action was even less successful in his own frustrated attempts to bring culture to the masses, which he describes in the essays collected together as *Fears of Fragmentation* (1970). The flood of social protest unleashed by

Osborne, complains Wesker, did not result in the expected anti-philistine revolution because no one wished to overthrow the status quo. Nobody listened to the playwright because nothing had been done to bring down class barriers in culture as well as in industry. Wesker laid the responsibility at the door of the trade union movement. In the early sixties Wesker managed to excite some interest and the Trades Union Congress passed the famous Resolution Forty-two, setting up a committee of inquiry into the arts. Its findings were accepted and then shelved. However, Wesker, together with Bernard Kops and Doris Lessing, worked on plans to bridge the gap between artist and public, out of which grew the Center 42 project, named for the TUC resolution. The trades council festivals around the country in 1961–2 had been a success, but the project needed a permanent home. With the encouragement of Harold Wilson, then leader of the Labour Party, a disused Victorian engine-shed was acquired in London's Camden Town; the Roundhouse was converted by the French architect René Allio but the appeal for funds failed to reach its target. Even though Wesker's ideas had caught on as far afield as Tokyo, wide-scale support was lacking in England. The Roundhouse had to be hired out as a fringe theater outside the West End. In 1970 Wesker broke with the Roundhouse; in any case he was moving toward a broader view of art in relation to society, something closer to grass roots. Wesker tells the story in *Fears of Fragmentation* in a similar way to the procedure in the *Trilogy*—going back to beginnings, to his 1960 speech at Oxford "O Mother is it worth it?" (when Broadway was negotiating for *Roots* and success threatened to devour him) in order to trace the disintegration of the dreams. Wesker begs the same question we must ask Dave Simmonds and Ronnie Kahn: what happens to the ideals when the idealist fails? That question motivates Wesker's plays long after the hippies have settled down to respectability and beatniks are passé.

LOOKING BACK WITH SADNESS

Something of the disappointment Wesker experienced in the Center 42 Project is transmuted into *Their Very Own and Golden City* (1965). Andy Cobham's imagination is captured by Durham Cathedral in 1926, but the cathedral can both soar and imprison the spirit. When he becomes a self-taught architect he determines to build

Jerusalem in the form of six golden cities collectively owned and managed by their inhabitants. In the complicated series of flash-forwards over the years to 1990, the six utopias dwindle to one and the prophecy of William Morris in his 1886 lecture on socialism is fulfilled: the Trade Unions have become allies of Capital and part of the well-oiled machine which fragments experience, down to the food the workers eat, the clothes they wear and the houses they live in. By a stroke of irony Andy Cobham is knighted for his services to architecture and the factories of the Golden City are now owned by outside financiers. The betrayal of the ideal to mould habits of mind through a reintegration of environment and work sours personal relationships, and the breakdown of personal relationships becomes as relevant as the failure of profound social change in the argument of Wesker's next play *The Four Seasons* (1965). *The Four Seasons* gets away from the complex structure of Wesker's earlier plays and concentrates on two lovers who come into occupation of a deserted house. Wesker handles the Pinteresque setting most poetically but more heavily than the master of such betrayal situations: Wesker can't resist writing an Epilogue to explain his uncharacteristic meanness with information about the two characters in a room.

Adam and Beatrice start life again in a country retreat, discovering anew the pleasures of living. They are trying to break out of the familiar patterns of betrayal and their experience of disappointed love is very much equivalent to the disappointment of ideals in the *Trilogy*. Wesker argues forcibly in the Epilogue that private pain *is* relevant to a discussion of social issues and it must not be ignored if art is to function properly. This is also an attempt to redeem language from the well-worn catchphrases exploited by multimedia advertising, something Wesker does not find terribly easy to do, and to build on the kind of dialogue of everyday experience which has become commonplace since Osborne's *Look Back in Anger* and Wesker's own *Roots*.

Beatrice, the silent figure of suffering, shares with Sarah Kahn the belief that love is necessary if the brotherhood of man is to attain socialism. Adam puts his finger on the syndrome which threatens every effort towards an ideal: we use the same "tried gestures" of love that have been compromised by earlier betrayals when we try to reclaim passion. As in *Their Very Own and Golden City* the idealist knows that history is against him, he knows the mistakes he risks and the price of failure, yet he nevertheless tries to subvert history. There is something inevitably sad about the cycle of the four seasons, something almost pathetic about the psychosomatic fears, the ruthlessly exploited guilt. The breakdown of the relationship brings a confession of ultimate futility. Even after Jerusalem has been built there will be dissolution of relationships and lamenting of old age. The autumnal leaves will not catch fire and there seems little prospect of resurrecting the integration of fragmented experience or personal relationships.

Old age and obsession with past mistakes become the pessimistic themes of Wesker's plays *The Friends* (1970), *The Old Ones* (1972) and *Love Letters on Blue Paper* (1977, based on a short story of the same name). The "Friends" are between forty and forty-five, partners in an interior design business on the verge of bankruptcy, once again the theme of failure to affect public taste, to change ways of living. Only the dying Esther has achieved any consistent standard with which to judge her life and weigh up values and relationships. These are Wesker's bruised Jewish idealists of whom Crispin (a transformation of an older Andy Cobham) says that Jews alone arrive at sadness instead of despair on discovering that nothing makes sense. They are caught up in nostalgic regret for the past, revelling in the pain of self-immolation. Their fumbling for some kind of order ends with a macabre final scene when Esther's corpse is propped up in a chair facing the portrait of Lenin, fulfilling a life-long ambition which enables the others to carry on as before—the ambition to live.

The Old Ones (1972) delves more directly into old age and is more specifically a Jewish play about dying, rather than a play about dying Jews. Wesker is one of those "1967 Jews" who came back to a public commitment to Jewish identity when the tiny State of Israel seemed threatened by another Holocaust. It was only in the years after the Six Day War that Wesker awoke to the extent that he felt Jewish "in a *belonging* or a protective way."[29] *The Old Ones* is essentially the first play in which Wesker deals directly with Jewish sources and symbols, as distinct from his constant drawing on the experience of the social situation of growing up Jewish. The action revolves around the building of a *sukah*, a temporary wooden booth covered with leaves put up to celebrate the festival of Tabernacles, the festival of joy, but also an autumnal harvest festival, appropriate for reaping the intellectual fruits of one's life. The *sukah* represents the transitoriness and frailty of man's sojourn on earth and his dependence on Divine Providence, just as the Jews who left Egypt had no shelter but these rickety dwellings. The lesson of the Master of Khasidism, the Baal Shem Tov, is to serve God with joy, because joy brings love for all mankind, so that Wesker's tabernacle is dedicated not just to the glory of God but also to mankind and socialist ideals. This makes it meaningful even to the atheist Sarah who wishes to remember her family through a ritual otherwise meaningless to her. Wesker's understanding of Khasidism is peculiarly that transmitted by Buber; the dialogue in *Four Seasons* could even be a striving for an I-thou relationship between the protagonists to replace their obstinate refusal to recognize the difference between them.

The shouting matches in *The Trilogy* are preserved by the two brothers Manny and Boomy in *The Old Ones* as a family ritual, but it's a dialectic of hope and despair which makes their relationship *work*. Manny lives out his senility in a confused darkness of anguished insomnia, spending his days in a Jobian search for the meaning of life through an interminable exchange of quotable quotes with Boomy, who is as convinced there is no meaning to life as Manny is hopeful there must be one (else he would not be searching). Boomy is the prophet of doom crying out passages from Ecclesiastes and Carlyle; it is Ecclesiastes who is traditionally read in the synagogue on *Sukot* (the festival of Tabernacles), the Festival of Joy. To Ecclesiastes Manny counters with one of Buber's sayings about the great Khasidic mystic Nakhman of Bratslav, that if one doesn't reach out to teach the multitude one will descend from one's rung on the spiritual ladder. Manny lives in expectation of the world converting to justice to-morrow, but his tailor's dummy, like Harry's in *Chicken Soup With Barley*, reminds him he has done nothing with his life. He nevertheless records himself singing a well-known tune full of warmth and love to verses by the Yiddish poet Itzik Manger on a tape of the Jewish partizans' defiant song of hope "*Zog nit keyn mol . . .*" ("Never say this is your last road"). The two brothers have been quarrelling all their lives, ever since Manny renounced the capitalist profits of his father's East End jewelry business by dropping the brothers' inheritance into the river. Boomy has always been bitter and he can quote, in retort to Manny's citation of Voltaire's rational optimism, Voltaire's cynical awareness that denial of evil only adds to the continual misery and suffering in the world. To Manny's first original thoughts attributable to himself which deny the existence of evil Boomy retorts with lines from Ecclesiastes which deny the purposefulness of new truths and deny the possibility of political action. To the making of books—and thoughts—there is no end.

The younger generation, on the other hand, must negotiate this ideological and existential impasse in their own lives. When Boomy's son Martin gets in trouble with the police after a political demonstration (the background is presumably the L.S.E. student riots of the early 1970s), the prodigal Jewish son comes back to ask his recalcitrant father for 100 pounds to be bailed out and to never be heard from again. Boomy can't take his son's cause seriously, and voices his hope that a spell in prison will make a *mentsh* of his son. But he has hardly been a positive model. All he can do in his old age is to fiddle about with old television sets trying to make sense of scientific reason (like Manfred in *The Friends*). Rudi, Sarah's nephew (son of a dead sister), is no more settled, hopping from one occupation to another. His present craze is painting—one of his primitivist works hangs in Hackney Public Library, others in an Israeli restaurant in Stamford Hill. Rosa, too, is an example of how her mother Sarah's ideals and those of Uncle Manny have rebounded on their children. Rosa is a careers advisor (she couldn't decide on a career so she advises others, as Sarah quips) and she tries to put Sarah's message of caring through to tough sixteen-year-olds about to leave school. She quickly earns their derision and only holds their attention when she sabotages her job by telling them they are powerless and haven't a hope of doing what they want in life or living where they want. All that can save them is books, culture. Sarah, however, still believes in the working classes, for, after all, what would one do without them to deliver letters, man electricity power stations and connect telephones? Yet three louts from that same working class cruelly mimic Sarah's sister-in-law, the crippled Gerda.[30]

It's important that Rosa is the one who reads out the instructions for building the *sukah* seen in various stages of construction in Sarah's council flat. She is representative of the next generation who must revive the old rituals through language, a particularly interesting variation of Wesker's earlier thesis that the intellectual can change others through "redeeming" language. Rosa quotes *Rabbenu* Bahya ben Asher that "'traditions which have their roots in the past must not be dismissed as obsolete but must be revived by the language and minds of new generations.' That's me! *I'm* supposed to tell you what to do?"[31] The consciously Chekhovian pause which follows speaks of the old idealists' failure to implant sufficiently strong roots to enable their children to make the ideals *work*. Ironically, the roots here are also spiritual and ethnic, since the old generation doesn't understand the meaning of the traditions they're rediscovering in their senility as a response to bitterness and self-doubt. Manny would like to extract from the festival of *Sukot* its universal content, Judaism's call for a brotherly union of all nations (he shares the messianic ambition of Louis Golding's Mr. Emmanuel). However, the only non-Jewish participant in the *Sukot* celebrations and the only non-Jew in the play is Jack, a cockney Stan Mann, a self-proclaimed dirty old man, who esteems the little old Jewish ladies because they're as hard as steel pellets.

The Jewish social message, secular as well as religious, recognizes the human condition as despairing but looks for the humor in the situation and in full awareness of the irony demands that man fulfill his appointed task. Ecclesiastes, as read in the synagogue on *Sukot*, ends (though these are not the last lines of the text) with an admonition to keep the divine commandments because this is the "whole of man" *(ki zeh kol ha-adam)*, that is to say it's his duty, or perhaps that's all he can do, he has no choice, as Manny says, claiming the thought for himself at the close of the play, when he reaffirms life in neo-Khasidic joy. "The chef, the architect, the man of reason, do what they must because men must apply what is in them to apply."[32] The end of man is dust, the possibility of action to change the world seems slight, but that does not justify cessation of action.

To write meaningfully out of this joy-in-despair is the task Wesker sets himself in his plays and particularly in his dramatic efforts to come to an understanding of how man becomes alienated from his work, from the managerial process of industry, how language itself becomes devalued, as does the jargon of brotherhood in *Their Very Own and Golden City*. It is in the process of *making*, in Hegelian *praxis*, that the worker must try to reclaim his humanity from the machinery of capitalist society. The kitchen is depicted impressionistically, not symbolically, to suggest this as a real experience in *The Kitchen*. So too in *The Journalists* (1974) the individual is confronted with faceless petty officials in dealing with Authority, yet those who would ideally awake the public to their manipulation, the journalists, are compromized when their enthusiastic *making* of news achieves something that threatens their self-respect.

The Journalists is the result of Wesker's controversial study of the workings of the prestigious British weekly, *The Sunday Times*, and speaks of the corrupting need to undermine the achievement and fame of others. At the same time it says something about the mediocrity of the newspaper industry, illustrating Karl Kraus's aphoristic definition of a journalist as someone with "no ideas and the ability to express them." The presses roll in the background, just as the ovens are always there, humming away, in *The Kitchen*, and there is a similar orchestration of rhythm in which the routine of each separate fragmented activity competes to meet the demands of the machine. But the characters don't come across as the *personalities* of the earlier plays, though there is a more refined sense of dramatic technique, of coordination of time and movement on the stage. On the other hand, the play makes a familiar statement about caring, this time the dire necessity to care about the way the mass media distort reality and obscure vital social issues (responsibility for collapsing bridges, teenage abortions) or exploit horror stories of human cruelty (the events in Bangladesh, Biafra). This ties up with the poverty of popular culture: it's assumed that the masses can't think for themselves; television and newspapers do their thinking for them. The play becomes almost overloaded with the attack on cliché and nearly every one of Wesker's favorite hobby-horses is dragged from the stables to be put through its paces or simply flogged: the sincerity of socialists, workers' control in industry, the conflict of state and science (*that* goes back to C. P. Snow and the two culture controversy), the betrayals of love and the betrayals of the revolution.

The Jewish element is less strong in *The Journalists*, despite the presence of the hardworking financial reporter Morty Cohen and his equally vivacious colleague on the sports page, Ronnie Shapiro. There's a "fink" with inside information on the World Jewish Conspiracy who happens not to be addressing the editors of *Der Stürmer*, though manipulation of public opinion was to be an issue raised more seriously over the coverage of Israel's 1982 invasion of Lebanon,[33] and in this case Wesker's warning is relevant to modern anti-Semitism. There's also a neurotic East European failed idealist, Tamara Drazin, on the brink of a breakdown. But these are mere aspects of a larger concern which for once doesn't depend on autobiographical experience and doesn't revolve around a Jewish moral thermometer. Also missing is the *kunts* of Wesker's earlier work, that magical act of lunacy, like Peter's arch in *The Kitchen*, Daniel learning to live life, Ronnie Kahn lighting a campfire, or *strudel* making in *The Four Seasons*. Yet there is a difficulty similar to that in *Chips with Everything*, of deciding between the intellectual's cynical slumming and a frustrated idealism. These are, after all, lilliputians who struggle to bring down giants by day and retire to safely conventional North London suburbs at night.

That the illusion of bourgeois comfort in the prospering suburbs of North-West London conceals vacuity of mind and spirit is the underlying premise of Wesker's short stories written between 1966 and 1977 and the theme of Anglo-Jewish novels which chart the abandonment of East End radicalism with the step up to suburban respectability (see the discussion below of Brian Glanville's *The Bankrupts*). In "Six Sundays in January" (1966) the ideals of the first generation of East End immigrants confront the aspirations fulfilled through their children—now adults rearing their own children—in an uncompromizing dichotomy. Marcia Needham has married out, to a non-Jew and into North London suburban comfort. She and her mother, however, can't forget the knowledge of sadness, that bittersweet Jewish melancholy unfathomable by gentiles, which brings Marcia back one bored Sunday morning to familiar East End haunts (like Zangwill's children of the ghetto who also go back time and again to East End origins). Katerina Levinson is drawn back to roots for the same reason. Crispin Peterson, an English architect, questions the honesty of the two women's search for identity, for they seem to assume a Jewishness they do not practice; moreover, they make wide generalizations about humanity all because one bus driver spitefully steps on the gas just as a man runs to the bus-stop. But that's just the point that Wesker, like Litvinoff, is making to the non-Jewish visitor to the East End. The East End taught caring, you couldn't be complacent, but, as Wesker says time and again, you have to learn to live with your mistakes. Katerina Levinson finds *that* harder to do. In despair she commits suicide, knowing this also to be a mistake. Nor can Marcia be on easy terms with domestic bliss. She breaks from the family weekend to run in the cold and damp of Hampstead Heath, in wild pursuit not of her runaway hat but of the right to act madly. The material security of motherhood and matrimony proves only too frail under the scrutiny of intro-spection.

Unsuccessful marriage and coming to terms with aging and death pervade Wesker's later work with a retrospective sadness that almost purges his earlier anger. "Love Letters on Blue Paper" (1973) looks at the irreversible effect of a symbolically incurable disease on a leading trade union leader, forcing him to rethink his life-long con-victions and the possibility of an afterlife. Wesker commands the Yorkshire ethnicity of Victor and his wife Sonia as naturally as he handles the dialogue of the Jewish East Enders in the *Trilogy*. None-theless the Jewish intellectual remains central in the person of a university lecturer motivated by artistic and political ideals, yet cynically aware of his own failings and lack of faith. Sonia sends her husband anonymous letters through the mail, touching on her love and her memories, and a picture is built up of their changing relationship and attitudes to success. She ends with a belief in a "blinding light" of truth which will come with death, a painful light when the false will fall away from the true. Another example of coping with disillusion is Sheridan Brewster, in "The Man Who Became Afraid" (1972), who like Harry in the *Trilogy* retreats childishly into the womb. He is tempted by his friends into collecting pictures, books, wines, anything to preserve the delusion of material prosperity. He, too, has made the mistake of the wrong marriage and his wife turns unresponsively aside when he tries to find new meaning to his successful but disillusioned life. His endless tumbling eventually brings about a metamorphosis into a man who really is afraid of everything.

These stories provide a kind of commentary to *The Friends* and *The Old Ones* and like the plays take a look at what happened to the idealists after they despaired of fulfilling their ideals. The question "what more is there?", which Sarah asks in the *Trilogy* and which is asked again at the end of *The Kitchen*, finds a somewhat sceptical and ironic reply, though not without a touch of loving sentimentality, in the coming to grips with living life, in the effort to deautomatize perception and values that have become estranged through being tarnished and scuffed by contact with bourgeois apathy, when privileged luxury has become routine. It's rather like the candlestick in "The Visit" (1977) which must be rubbed and polished until its original or ideal sheen is restored, just as it's with wild physical exertion that Marcia Needham has to throw off the cobwebs and remember who she is. In "The Visit" two couples, one Danish and ill-married, the other English, spend a five-day holiday in a country retreat. Out of the tranquil affluence of the Cambridgeshire countryside emerge real problems: personal, emotional and ideological. Raphael, the assimilated Jewish intellectual, embodies a biblical concept of brotherly love as opposed to the cruelties of the ideologies of our time. He tirelessly offers *khola* to the gentiles (an ecumenical bread-and-salt) and generally busies himself with the role of alienated Jewish intellectual/catalyst. Wesker shows that people can't face the brutality and catastrophe of reality and prefer the deceptive protection of a less confusing vision. Raphael draws parallels between Isaiah and Fidel Castro, but he's also responsible for the tape of Isaac

Deutscher, the biographer of Trotsky and Stalin, lecturing on Marx: ideology becomes inhuman when it stops forecasting and says what *must* happen. Raphael returns to a sense of Jewish identity out of a *kvelling* at his family rather than out of an image of the Jew as a "barometer by which to measure other people's inhumanity," though the Daniel Deronda type of ecumenical Jew must also affect the modern Jew's role-playing. The Jew benefits from the vantage point of an ancient people which knows that history is cyclical, that even in a socialist society there are going to be contradictions. Maddeau's energetic household chore provides the final truth. That easy gadget the spray can makes the candlestick immediately dully mediocre; only hard work with one's heart and soul in it can kindle the "blinding light": "The answer shone obviously. There was no alternative. It would have to be cleaned again and again, by hand. A family heirloom, to be kept constantly burnished, aglow. No other way. The sparkling surface had to be exposed. There was no protection. Heartbreaking! to have to take all that battering from the elements and then—all that work again. And again. But there it was: no relenting, the old cycle."[34]

PRAISE FIVE BOB A POUND, THANKS TEN A TANNER

We go back to that dusty family heirloom, the Jewish condition, in Wesker's best play for some years, *The Merchant* (1976). This is a rewriting of Shakespeare's *Merchant of Venice*, but it's also more than that. There have been adaptations of Shakespeare's masterpiece before, from Lansdowne's eighteenth-century *Jew of Venice* through modern interpretations such as Charles Marowitz's. Among the most famous previous attempts to reinvest Shylock with the sort of humanity which Shakespeare's ambiguity allows (in contrast to Barabas's transparently deceitful virtue) and which his tragedy demands is Kean's performance in the last century which did away with the traditional stage-Jew and his red-haired, grotesque-nosed Judas/Devil guise. Wesker, however, indicts Shakespeare's world famous humanity as being inhumane. Shylock's defense before Salerio ("Hath not a Jew eyes? Hath not a Jew hands, organs, dimensions, senses, affections, passions? . . ." Act III, 1) passes, in Wesker's version, to Lorenzo, who uses it to deflate charges of anti-Semitism and inflate the enormity of the Jew's crime in the trial scene. Wesker's Shylock will have none of it:

Lorenzo: If you prick him does he not bleed?
Shylock: No, no, NO! I will not have it. *[Outraged but controlled]*
I do not want apologies for my humanity. Plead for me no
special pleas. I will not have my humanity mocked and apol-
ogized for. If I am unexceptionally like any man then I need
no exceptional portraiture. I merit no special pleas, no special
cautions, no special gratitudes. My humanity is my right, not
your bestowed and gracious privilege.[35]

The Jew is sick and tired of being society's eternal scapegoat, forever
alien, the enemy within, portrayed as arrogant, insolent, obstinate
in his perfidy. Why should he make any special claim to be accepted
as human when humanity is already his? Shylock's silence and
obduracy in his insistence on the bond becomes a proud self-sacrifice
to defend the interests of the Jewish community. The bond must be
honored to maintain the credibility of the Ghetto, not the Venetian
legal system. Shakespeare's rhetoric over usury, the pros and cons
of "excess," and his concern for equity, are used to point an accusing
finger at modern society which transfers guilt for social evil to the
Jew. It is not that the Jew, like Dickens' Mr. Riah, is tragically forced
to play a distasteful role that creates misunderstanding about his
true character, but it is the system which washes its hands of poverty
and blames the Jew for extorting high interest rates from the poor,
a practice not confined to Jews and without which the economy
could not turn. The Jews are made the mythical bogey-man, on the
one hand, and fleeced by the State, on the other, so that if they are
to make a living and pay exorbitant discriminatory taxes they cannot
escape the socioeconomic function which they served in England
under Edward I, a function that is present in the image of the
mythical Jew in Shakespeare's *Merchant of Venice,* as it is in Chaucer's
Prioress's Tale:

Sustened by a lord of that Contree
For foule usure and lucre of vilanye,
Hateful to Crist and to his companye.

Moreover, Portia is allowed to drop the logically awkward disguise of stand-in public prosecutor/judge and speak as a woman in
her own right. She despises the leaders of Venice for their mediocrity,
for their unimaginative inflexibility in not realizing that the law must
change with changing reality. The final scene replaces Shakespeare's
last Act with the self-congratulating dull-witted young patricians, the

future rulers, to whom Shylock offers his knife to sharpen their wits. Instead of happy matchmaking and love-pairing Wesker ends with an accusation not against Venice but against capitalism and against Western concepts of justice, with its ambiguous symbol of sword and scales.

Shylock Kolner is an exuberant self-taught German Jewish immigrant, and if Wesker has read up on the historical details of sixteenth-century Venetian Jewry, then this doesn't diminish the feeling that we're back in the East End, just as Shakespeare touches on much that is relevant to contemporary England, even though *he* didn't have to stir abroad to read up on Venice.[36] True, this is 1563 and among the Marranos fleeing the Inquisition on the Iberian peninsula are Rebecca da Mendes, daughter of a Portuguese banker, and Solomon Usque, a playwright. But the benevolence with which Shylock receives them and his eagerness to arrange shelter for the refugees en route to Salonika speak for the caring attitude of East End Jewry as well as the charitable precepts of Judaism. This is a warm, bustling household dominated by an exuberant East End Jew who can't restrain his enthusiasm for knowledge, for moral philosophy, for personally supervizing plans for a new synagogue (once again an architect walks on stage), for living life. Like Mankowitz's antiques salesman, he knows you have to specialize to survive, to appreciate the beauty of things. He breathes the Ghetto, he *is* the Ghetto, whose sights he proudly shows to visitors. He is as Venetian as the East Ender was "real English." The Ghetto may be confining, it may be oppressive, but it's bursting with life, with culture. Like Manny in *The Old Ones*, Shylock feeds on the world's wisdom (not Christian flesh!) and he has got it all worked out, a grand scheme of things. Every little scholastic detail fits, but so carried away is Shylock over the historical development of the Renaissance (in Act I, 7) that he seems to forget it's not *his* Renaissance. As the bells ring Antonio reminds Shylock it's time to return to the Ghetto, to don his yellow hat that identifies him as an alien and a misbeliever. The plight of Shylock is the tragedy that history locks him in: however much he'd like to believe in the enlightened tolerance of the Renaissance, modern society makes him play the eternal role of usurer. His also is the inevitable, existential tragedy that his fate has already been written by Shakespeare (and by *his* sources), just as Stoppard's Rosencrantz and Guildenstern can't escape from *Hamlet*. They are as doomed as Annouilh's *Antigone*.

Shylock Kolner is a destereotyped, unstereotypable, loving, lovable human being, and a Jew whose Jewishness is not defined in the religious sense of leading a Torah-oriented life but in the more universalistic meaning of the Jew as a "light to the nations," bringing monotheism and brotherly love to the world (which hates him because that moral burden is so hard to bear), and suffering the lot of a cursed people running from one massacre to another, safe neither in France nor England (witness the martyrdom at York in 1190 of an earlier Anglo-Jewish poet and scholar, Rabbi Yom-Tov of Joigny). The Jews are chosen "to bear witness to what is beautiful in creation, and just,"[37] a task which requires them to be better than any other nation and which makes them unbearable to live with. "What can I do?" reasons Shylock the radical iconoclast, "I'm chosen. I *must* be religious."[38] Being religious is synonymous with being Jewish:

> Religious! It's the condition of being Jewish, like pimples with adolesence, who can help it? Even those of us who don't believe in God have dark suspicions that he believes in us.[39]

Shylock extends the Torah's commandment *ve-ahavta le-ra'akha kamokha* ("and you shall love your fellow as yourself") to embrace all mankind. He loves Antonio, the non-Jewish merchant, because that's part of being Jewish, and he wants his heart because that's the part of his friend which pleases him most! (Compare Shakespeare's original, Act I, 3: "I would be friends with you and have your love . . . This is kind I offer.") Antonio insists on drawing up a bond because the laws of Venice must be respected, yet Shylock would lend the money freely, out of friendship, so the friends mock the law with a nonsense bond not dreaming of the tragic consequences when Antonio's ships are attacked and he is ruined. Shylock has indeed "poisoned" the Christian, but with intellect. The Jew is the catalyst who opens Antonio's eyes to the real state of corruption and injustice in Venice, making him restless in his old age and sick, as he tells the Doge in the trial scene, of the intrigues and boredom (the ultimate enemy for Wesker!) that go with administration. Let us not forget that the merchant of Wesker's title, as of Shakespeare's title, is Antonio. His is the central tragedy because his eyes have been opened too late and brotherly love is thwarted. This makes the play a human, not just a Jewish tragedy.

Shylock is punished by forfeiting to the state his most treasured possession, his books, which have only recently been brought out of hiding, but he has also lost a daughter. Jessica, like Ronnie Kahn in the *Trilogy*, cannot bear her parent's grand scheme of things, the nagging to care, the presumptious wish to embrace the whole world. She resents Shylock's secret ambition to live his ideals through her, which prevents her becoming individual and apart, and she commits suicide as a daughter and as a Jew by eloping with Lorenzo. Only later, when she sees Shylock's admiration for Portia, the feminist aware of what goes on around her and the idealist ready to manage her estate herself, the woman Shylock would have liked to have for a daughter, does Jessica realize she has lost her father. But it's too late. She has rejected her father's idealism as too repressive, too impractical, and has opted for Lorenzo and his poetry of despair. Yet it's with horror she discovers Lorenzo will take her only if she turns Christian. The oedipal wheel turns full circle. Jessica is cut off from her Jewish home and unaccepted by the gentile world, a world which negates the Jew's money-making as playing with a dead sterile thing and won't see it as making things live through working with them by hand. Work redeems consciousness of one's surroundings, as Wesker has been saying all along, work redeems the word.

Deprived of his books ("you take his life when you take his books," says Antonio),[40] Shylock despairs of life, of men, even of books; as Boomy knew from Ecclesiastes, they don't help in the long run except to add to distress and confusion. To the background of a valedictory Ladino song *Adio querida*, the scene shifts to Belmont and Shylock prepares for a final pilgrimage to Jerusalem. But it's not the ideal Jerusalem of Dave Simmonds. Shylock has lost his appetite for life, worse, he has lost heart. He has failed to win Antonio's heart, he has failed his ideals and, despite all the warnings from his more pragmatic sister Rivka, he has been blind to his daughter's needs and differences, in the end failing her too. Shylock must learn the same thing as the Jewish entrepreneur in *The Wedding Feast* (1974), freely adapted by Wesker from Dostoevsky's short story *A Disgraceful Affair*, about the difficulty of living up to ideals: he has the lesson beaten into him (literally) that he is deluding himself in thinking that ideals are realities. And yet for once a Wesker character avoids making a mistake, a mistaken marriage and a mistaken life: Jessica refuses her non-Jewish lover Lorenzo, though her position is left unclear. Hers is the ambiguous situation of the new generation, who, for all their parents' caring, have no roots to hand on to their children. Jessica is left marginal to Jewish and Gentile society, yet she carries within her that seed of sadness which Marcia Needham wants to impart to her children and the bitter knowledge of failure.

Intermarriage and assimilation don't solve the problem of being Jewish, and for the relevance of this to modern society note the de-Hebraicization of the young people's names. Jewishness is after all too precious a gift to waste; it's a privilege, in fact, that the Jew can't get out of because it's part and parcel of his existential identity. Vanity of vanities, all is vanity, but in the end one must be a Jew and act Jewish, *ki zeh kol ha-adam*, because that is what it is to be a human being. The dream of Jerusalem lives on, even if time has made the author wiser, and it is not to be bartered for the loose change of stallholders or businessmen; the dreamers and idealists deserve praise because they have had the vision to see through petty bourgeois aspirations and everyday estrangement and they have had the courage, not to mention the madness, to believe the dream could be made reality. Dostoevsky dropped utopian socialism when he saw the dangers to which idealism led and Wesker knows the frustrations of putting ideals into practice. Yet *The Merchant* shows he hasn't given up the day-to-day values of living socialism (as he would call his secular brand of Judaism), he hasn't sold out, as a playwright at any rate, to the comfortable illusions of North London, where he lives with his family. No doubt he knows something of the grievance of Dave Simmonds in *I'm Talking About Jerusalem*, that his ideas and his plays haven't always received the kind of widespread support and praise Wesker might have hoped for.[41]

> *Dave:* Yes, praise! It would hurt, any of you? There isn't enough generosity to spare a little pat on the back? You think we're cranks—recluses? Well, I'll surprise you, look—no long hair, no sandals. Just flesh and blood. Of course we need a little praise. *[Dips in his pocket for coins.]* Or maybe you want me to buy it from you! Like in the market! Here, two half-crowns for a half-minute of praise. I'll buy it! You can't afford to give it away? I'll pay for it! Five bob for a few kind words, saying we're not mad. Here y'are—take it! Take it![42]

To which Aunt Esther retorts,

> You want to build Jerusalem? Build it! Only maybe we wanted to share it with you.[43]

Dave Simmonds' failure becomes for Shylock Kolner an existential irony.

EAST END WRITERS: CONCLUSION

Anglo-Jewish writing in the postwar period was dominated by the first works of East End writers Arnold Wesker, Bernard Kops, Wolf Mankowitz and Emanuel Litvinoff. They drew on their personal memories of the Jewish East End in the poverty-stricken, fascist 1930s, they rode on the wave of kitchen sink drama and looked back in anger at what had become of the closeknit Jewish community in the East End of London together with its ideals. Mosley and Hitler had thrown menacing shadows over the secure togetherness of the Jewish East Enders, while those who made it out of the East End into the more wealthy districts of North-West London betrayed the radical ideas of socialism and anarchism in which they had grown up.[44]

We recall that for Wesker in *I'm Talking About Jerusalem,* the final play in the Wesker Trilogy, the ideals remained true, only the idealists had failed. However, the suppression of the 1956 Hungarian uprising, the 1968 invasion of Czechoslovakia, the Soviet treatment of Jews and dissidents, not to mention countless other injustices around the world in the name of socialism, seriously undermined the Jewish intellectual's continued subscription to the Cause. No doubt by 1980 Wesker was beyond embitterment at the lack of labor movement support for his ambitious project for a cultural center for the masses. His new play, *Caritas* (1980), features a fourteenth-century Anchoress who has herself immured in a cell for life in order to achieve union with God. After three years she changes her mind, but it is too late: the vows cannot be broken. This question, what to do when one is imprisoned by what one once thought was an ideal, is the one which concludes Wesker's open letter to Soviet dissident Viktor Nekipelov of July 1980.[45]

The barbarity of Hitler's persecution of the Jews and the exposure of Stalin as perpetrator of brutal purges (among which the 1948 anticosmopolitan campaign and the 1952 execution of Yiddish writers were directed specifically against Jews) made inevitable a crisis in the radicals' faith in the ends which supposedly justified the means and which had seemingly solved problems of allegiance.

The post-Holocaust, post-Stalinist perspective may partly explain why the East End writers put forward the Jewish immigrant experience as a subject for general interest and concern, for the first time on the British stage if one excludes American imports such as Montague

Glass's *Potash and Perlmutter* (1914) or Clifford Odets' *Awake and Sing!* (1935). One reason for their success is the new acceptance of the working-class writer, another the altered social position of the British Jew, increasingly middle-class and influential; crucial is the relevance of the Jewish experience to fears of a nuclear holocaust. Instead of the medieval stock-type (resurgent precisely in the twentieth century) or the music-hall comedian, a Jew comes on stage to make the message of Jewish history and the Hebrew prophets relevant in the widest possible way. Clifford Odets' line from Isaiah, "Awake and sing," is, by contrast, a call to break with the Jewish immigrant experience, rather than to learn from it.

Wolf Mankowitz's *The Samson Riddle* (1972), for example, probes the riddle of man as much as the riddle of the Jews and Jewish history in the wake of Israel's victory in the Six Day War. This is an attack on both Philistines and Philistinism, a complaint of having a Yiddishe Mama and the woes of marrying a *shiksa*, as well as a parable of the male menopause and a satire on women. Bernard Kops draws on the theme of social decay in Shakespeare's *Hamlet* to draw a topical parallel in his Jewish East End Hamlet; Kops' punning definition of diaspora as a post-Holocaust despair in his collection of verse *Erica I Want to Read You Something* (1967) regrets a general loss of family and religion. Arnold Wesker goes back to the lost ideals of the Jewish East End in the thirties, to the ideals of Spain and Communism, to call a primarily non-working-class, non-Jewish audience to "respond"; similarly, Ada's feeling that she has murdered her father in *I'm Talking About Jerusalem* is indicative of the generation gap which accompanies the ideological crisis.

Wesker has been compared with G. B. Shaw and Arthur Miller; his acting as action has at the same time linked him to the theater of revolt. However, Wesker and Kops are not simply Jewish versions of the Angry Young Man, although neither they nor Pinter could have put on their plays before 1956, and their distinct Jewishness marks them out from the run-of-the-mill Outsiders who were all too often trying to be Insiders and were too sceptical of any belief to commit themselves to an ideal. V. S. Pritchett, John Holloway and Stephen Spender castigated the Angry Young Men as new barbarians, wrecking culture and avenging themselves for frustrated opportunities. This may be unkind, but the shock-tactics of protest on the stage after 1956 assured John Osborne and others a place in the upper tax-brackets, as well as in bourgeois pseudo-intellectual fashion. To a certain extent these were provincials seeking arrival, like the heroes of novelists Amis, Wain and Murdoch whom George Scott characterizes in *Time and Place* (1956) as "forever running away from some largely imaginary mess, seeking escape in the *graffiti* of their private thoughts" and being saved by a millionaire *deus ex machina.*[46]

Possibly poverty may always be an incentive to poetry as Charles Williams has it (bringing us back to Shylock), when he spots Shakespeare at an Underground station, *The Merchant* in his pocket, "But his chief thought was to be earning more money."[47] However, Wolf Mankowitz apart, the East End Jewish writers could never be at ease with the middle-class comforts awarded by success because, while they do not refuse these comforts, they oppose moral stagnation. Culture for them was to be worshipped, not attacked. Wesker went so far as to call the beatniks "pretty little fascists"[48] and we have seen in *Roots* Wesker's resistance to pop culture. The impulse of Jimmy Porter's generation is, after all, to despise idealistic caring attitudes as old-fashioned liberal humanism; even if Jimmy does care for a sick working-class woman and does try to enthuse a response, his offensive and hurtful vehemence makes his stance almost noncommital. Dixon in Amis' *Lucky Jim* satirizes the academic jargon of "integration of social consciousness" or "identification of work with craft"; socialism for him is as phony as Toryism. Wesker's socialism is at odds both with this complacency and with the violent nihilism of the next wave of playwrights, Brenton, Hampton and Bond.

Wesker fails and knows he fails because no one is listening, for he advocates culture for the masses when the masses are sold to the cheap mass-produced culture of the jukebox, as in Wesker's sketch of an expresso bar in North-East London ("The Hill," 1958), or the mass entertainment described in Richard Hoggart's *The Uses of Literacy* (1957). *Roots* is not a slice of naturalist drama, it is a battle of socialism with inertia, where socialism cannot be equated with the working-class ethos. John Mander, comparing the commitment of Wesker and Osborne, distinguishes here between dialect and dialectic;[49] Ronnie Kahn's dialectic presents a full-blown theory of culture and the irony, as Dave Simmonds learns to his cost, is that you cannot convince the workers that the dialectic is right by putting on the right dialect. *Roots* is misunderstood because the political content of commitment is generally deemed to weaken artistic merit. "What Wesker is trying to do is to *wake us up*"[50] and this is no consciousness-raising session with the local guru, but something which lies at the core of the Jewish writer's existence.

The warmth and vigor of Wesker makes all the difference between *The Old Ones* and Beckett's *Endgame;* the assurance that tomorrow can be made different is the knowledge of Mankowitz's
tailors and salesmen, of Litvinoff's East End adolescent and it even
penetrates Kops' devout pessimism. This is no doubt what the Shakespearean scholar G. Wilson Knight has in mind when he gives Wesker
and Kops as illustrations of the potential of kitchen sink drama to
make us think about live issues and to recognize that its low-born
heroes are nearer to life.[51] There is a common energetic anger in
Chips with Everything, The Long and the Short and the Tall and *Sergeant
Musgrave's Dance,* and there is a tragic, Shakespearean dimension to
the existential problem of the modern Hamlet, but their Jewish East
End origins mean that the "to be or not to be" of Kops and Wesker
is also a primary question of their identity as playwrights.

East—North-East

Chapter Five
Hackney and Other Provinces: Harold Pinter and Peter Shaffer

UNHACKNEYED HACKNEY

There is so much to say and for all that has been written we have only begun talking about Pinter. What Pinter has said about himself and his plays has created even more confusion among the critics. Take that famous early exchange on the radio which sent scholars frantically ferreting out innuendoes:

> "But what would you say your plays were *about*, Mr. Pinter?"
> "The weasel under the cocktail cabinet."[1]

There may be some hidden significance here, but basically the weasel is as elusive as a red herring. It does, perhaps, say something about hidden skeletons lurking in cupboards in certain social settings, a subconscious absurd presence in the most mundane dialogues of Pinter characters. But, like many of Pinter's other public statements, it is about as relevant and meaningful as any weasel would be under a cocktail cabinet.

There seems little point, therefore, in interpreting the words of the text as anything more or less than what they say, but there is some point in analyzing the sociological and linguistic context of the words, which are spoken, after all, by someone and somewhere, even if that information frustrates attempts to pin the author down to one meaning.

We have already seen how Wolf Mankowitz and Bernard Kops universalize their Jewish settings and how Wesker preaches universal messages from specific Jewish situations. Pinter is most successful when he writes the Jewish content out of his plays, leaving a writing that has everything and nothing to identify it as Jewish. As examples I want to take the more obvious plays with "Jewish" references, *The Birthday Party* (1957) and *The Homecoming* (1964), although what I have to say will be relevant to other plays and will show thematic concerns common to the East End Jewish playwrights, among others who came into British theater after 1956. At first glance there's little to connect them and certainly Pinter's approach to the stage and to being a playwright couldn't be more different. He is not committed as a writer, and distrusts "definitive labels."[2] He denies political or religious affiliations and he doesn't see the writer's role as putting across a message.

I certainly don't write from any kind of abstract idea. And I wouldn't know a symbol if I saw one.[3]

Writing is, on the other hand, a very personal act of creativity for Pinter and he does write about people in particular situations, very often working-class or lowlife characters, something which should not, however, make us hasten to lump Pinter together with Brecht and Beckett (who certainly have influenced him) or the kitchen sink dramatists—though a kitchen sink is shifted about on stage in *The Caretaker*, a play which shares the theme of a tramp's existential peregrinations with one scene in Wesker's *The Kitchen.*

In fact, the kind of debt Pinter acknowledges to personal experiences obliges us to examine his use of origins and ethnicity, though his taping of the local vernacular comes across more poetically and with a wider appeal than the East End speech recorded by Kops and Wesker.[4]

Hackney, a five-minute busride out of the economic insecurities of the East End, had an estimated Jewish population of 50,000 in 1938[5] and a reputation for a lower-middle-class respectability. It was a step up the social ladder from the East End toward the eventual destination of the prestigious commuter-belt of Golders Green and Edgware. But after the Second World War those who passed through had passed through and those who found themselves stranded on the steppingstone watched the area dilapidate, "go to the dogs," as one local resident put it.[6] Economic forces held them captive, making them despair of ever moving to a more densely Jewish and more "respectable" neighborhood. The Hackney community lacked the cohesion of the East End and there was more intermingling with the local English population, even if the relatively widespread independent occupations of taxi driving and tailoring reflect the pretensions of Jews working their way up; both groups looked down on the new black immigrants, though most Jews would have denied racial prejudice. Roland Camberton (pseudonym of Henry Cohen) wrote about the frustrations of young Hackney Jews in *Rain on the Pavements* (1951), a novel which gives a very real sense of the childish fears of the unfamiliar world outside East London and conveys the stigma of being a Jew on a scholarship at a private school. The make-believe play-acting (including an attempt at intimidation like Goldberg's in *The Birthday Party*) and the typically adolescent drifing into poetry and into Soho's Bohemian life (scarcely different from Bernard Kops' *The World is a Wedding*) end with the schoolboy heroes, or most of them, achieving success in the professions, with fast cars and suburban houses; only the central character, David, remains uncertain and adrift.

Hackney isn't poor enough or wretched enough to qualify for an Orwellian *Down and Out* or Lawrentian *Sons and Lovers* treatment, nor could it inspire the folksy lyricism for a local *Under Milkwood*, but the novelist Alexander Baron has successfully portrayed the almost sinister undercurrent in the banal monotony of Hackney in *The Lowlife* (1963). The narrator is Harryboy Boas, a drifter, a *shlemiel*, who gambles away any penny that comes his way and then runs to his sister and brother-in-law in their comfortable house in the smartest part of North-West London for a handout. If he is a pain to them, he despises their philistine mentality. A gambler addicted with Dostoevskian compulsion, Harryboy makes a philosophy of not settling down with "a nice Yiddishe girl"; he will go on gambling without release, he will give himself no peace until he has annihilated himself. Yet his fantastic dreams of success sometimes get the better of him. An English couple move in downstairs, the Deaners, and change his life without his willing it. To the humble clerk Mr. Deaner Harryboy's stories of the big time are true—he needs them to be true for relief from the pointless mediocrity of Hackney—and the poor man catches the betting fever. Harryboy, the *mentsh* at heart, tries to help him out and gets involved in the family's domestic squabbles. Mrs. Deaner, it turns out, fancies Harryboy for his manliness, for being everything her husband fails to be, but her snooty dreams of moving out of the "temporary arrangement" of a rented apartment in Hackney to an "own home" in Ilford (then quietly respectable) don't have much more substance than Harryboy's daydreams of a millionaire's paradise in the Canary Islands. When Harryboy runs into trouble with some Soho gangsters who come to collect a debt which he has gambled away, unassuming, prosaic, dilapidated Hackney lends the scenario for a spine-thrilling chase through back streets and railway yards. The way domestic scenes turn nasty—on the street and in the Deaner household—reminds us very much we are on Pinter territory, and there is also that ominous memory from the past which returns to irk the present. Before the war Harryboy lived with a woman in Paris whom he abandoned carrying a child. The Holocaust cut off that past he would rather not think about, but casual coincidences and daily pressures remind his conscience of the son he may have lost in the Nazi genocide. Guilt preys on his mind and he works out his confused identity through the Deaners and their little boy, for whom he is spiritual and physical father figure and Malamudian universal Jew.

HAROLD PINTER'S BIRTHDAY

It was Pinter, naturally, who made that most unlikely of all places, Hackney, into a most unhackneyed locus of universal concerns of betrayal, distrust and frustration. Harold Pinter was born in October 1930 and lived, until evacuated in 1939, on the Clapton side of Hackney Downs. Pinter's father worked extremely hard as a ladies' tailor but eventually he had to give up the independence of his own business and work for someone else. The melancholy, drab ugliness and futility of Hackney's industrial wasteland are striking in Pinter's childhood memories:

> I lived in a brick house on Thistlewaite Road, near Clapton Pond, which had a few ducks on it. It was a working-class area—some big, run-down Victorian houses, and a soap factory with a terrible smell, and a lot of railway yards. And shops. It had a lot of shops. But down the road a bit from the house there was a river, the Lea River, which is a tributary of the Thames, and if you go up the river two miles you find yourself in a marsh. And near a filthy canal as well. There is a terrible factory of some kind, with an enormous dirty chimney, that shoves things down to this canal.[7]

Baker and Tabachnick have shown the importance of Pinter's Hackney Jewish background for understanding his plays[8] and Pinter's schoolmate Barry Supple, in his review of *The Homecoming*, has drawn attention to the way Pinter effaces clear references to Jewishness in order to endow his plays with universal meaning, though the local idiom and characters are recognizable to anyone who knows Pinter and knows Hackney.[9] There may well be, as Alexander Baron suggested, talking in 1963 about the identity of the Jewish writer, something of the painful wound to which Edmund Wilson pointed in *The Wound and the Bow*, which drives the artist to write out of autobiographical circumstances and to write those circumstances out of him. Pinter once composed a school essay on Shakespeare which saw a similar kind of wound, a "peopled" wound, in the Elizabethan playwright.[10]

The specter of the past haunts Pinter's characters in surprising and disturbing ways and Pinter seems obsessed by his own. Rediscovering the past unlocks hidden, sometimes unwelcome, problems of identity and sexuality, as L. P. Hartley put it in the opening of his novel *The Go-Between* (1953), which Pinter adapted for the cinema: "The past is a foreign country: they do things differently there."

The autobiographical basis of much of Pinter's writing is vouched for by an unpublished novel *The Dwarfs* (ca. 1950–56), on which the play of the same name was based and which draws on Pinter's boyhood milieu of Hackney and Bethnal Green. The ambiguity of Jewish identity in Hackney[11] merges in the novel into the general problem of *verification*, though more information is given than in the play about the main characters, two of whom, Leo Weinstein and Mark Gilbert, are Jewish. They are part of the intense intellectual life among the Jewish population of East London, a closed world in which there was a self-conscious awareness of language.[12]

Violence was never far away in East London, from Jack the Ripper in the last century to the dreaded Kray Twins in modern times. The Mosleyite marches of the 1930s through the streets of East London stirred Kops and Wesker, looking back on what they could barely remember as children, to passionate indignation; Pinter was too young to run into Mosley's boys before the war, but during the mild fascist revival of 1946–47 he had a number of encounters, "some of them very nasty."[13] In the *Paris Review* "Writers at Work" interview Pinter recalled how dangerous it was to walk the streets if you looked at all Jewish. Pinter sees violence as an inescapable part of the modern world, though his own experiences of violence was as a Jew. Pinter frequented a Jewish club and on the way to the club would be confronted by a gang with broken milk-bottles. Note how language becomes a response to violence in which physical threats are just below the surface structure of everyday banalities:

> There were one or two ways of getting out of it—one was a purely physical way, of course, but you couldn't do anything about the milk bottles—*we* didn't have any milk bottles. The best way was to talk to them, you know, sort of "Are you all right?" "Yes, I'm all right." "Well, that's all right then, isn't it?" And all the time keep walking toward the lights of the main road.[14]

Attacks on intellectual-type Jews, who were commonly taken for Communists, were directed at the ontological existence of the Jew:

> they'd interpret your very being, especially if you had books under your arms, as evidence of being a Communist. There was a good deal of violence in those days.[15]

Destruction had threatened at home, too, as gas attacks were expected at any moment during the "Phoney War" and in 1944 the first flying bombs darkened local skies. Pinter remembers seeing his family's garden in flames.[16] The evacuation of children during the first stages of the war inevitably caused personal dislocation; for Jewish children it was often the first encounter with both the countryside (as in Wesker's case) and with an unfamiliar, uncomprehending, non-Jewish milieu that suddenly strained family relations and questioned traditional religious values (a crisis affectionately conveyed in Jack Rosenthal's award-winning television play *The Evacuees*, 1975, set in the North of England). The castle in Cornwall Pinter was sent to was hardly idyllic and during the days there before returning to London he was lonely and disoriented.[17] The possibility of aerial bombardment makes the tranquility of English life seem surreal; Baker and Tabachnick have noted that Pinter's presentation of such English pursuits as cricket at once suggests the continuity of the English people and belies the threat to that continuity, a threat that was actually carried out against the Jews.[18]

Social displacement is another factor that explains the uneasiness we feel in the ambiguities of Pinter's language and it characterizes the speech of many proletarian intellectuals (non-Jews as well as Jews) who found themselves moving in the upper circles of the Establishment after the Second World War. There is a lot left unsaid between Pinter's own displaced persons and those gaps are an entire continent which must be explored. Pinter's silences, so refreshing and uncanny after the forceful rhetoric of Jimmy Porter and Dave Simmonds, are not indications of failure of communication, "that tired, grimy phrase" which Pinter resents;[19] there is all too much nakedness in the blanks between words usually covered by clichés and catchy definitions. The smoke screen of language masks the frightening fact that there is no common ground, no shared reality. Speech is a continual evasion of this realization and a means of protecting the privacy of one's own vacuity: "To disclose to others the poverty within us is too fearsome a possibility."[20]

Pinter didn't make it to university but after leaving school at sixteen he got an LCC award to study at RADA (the Royal Academy of Dramatic Art). RADA didn't do much for him, in fact he spent a lot of time in and out of love and tramping the streets while continuing to draw his grant. At one point he faked a nervous breakdown. After answering an advert he toured Ireland with Anew McMaster. One senses the identification of a Hackney Jew with what Pinter called the "terrible loss, desolation, silence" at the center of the Irishman's performance of *Lear*.[21]

Shakespeare's greatest tragedies prefigure the postapocalyptic mourning and world-weariness of the modern age and there is in Pinter a schoolboyish love of the *fun* of Shakespeare,[22] of that wildly poetic vocabulary mixed in with adolescent play-acting and pseudo-Joycean ingroup slang.[23] For provincial acting Pinter adopted the stage-name David Baron and played opposite the actress Vivien Merchant, whom he married in 1956. The poisonous atmosphere of infantility, frustration, obscenity and filth in digs in Eastbourne gave birth to the situation of the *Birthday Party*,[24] while the sordidness of a raucous, brawling public house comes across in a poem called "New Year in the Midlands," which

> reveals a Jew's powerful vision of the failure of Christianity to control and heal the suffering that man inflicts on himself.[25]

Some of Pinter's early poems were published in small magazines under a pseudonym, Harold Pinta, which may be meant to indicate a Sephardic origin, though Pinter thinks his father's family came from Hungary.[26] Whatever the case, evasion from or concealment of identity reflects the anxiety of the Jew on alien territory, cut off from roots but uncertain where he does belong. Notice the confused nationality of Len and of the things in his room in *The Dwarfs*; in

Pinter's first play, *The Room* (1957) old Mr. Kidd can't remember if his mother was Jewish, but then his memory is suspiciously faulty, and the play ends with a vicious attack on a blind Negro who challenges the identity, status and at-homeness of an English house-wife, Rose, though that might not be her real name.

Pinter's language probes realities we'd sooner not face. Everyday conversations house inescapable dangers which stand the characters face to face with what words mean, instead of what they appear to say as phatic labels; there's a parallel here with Wesker's redemption of the word, though his characters have to work hard and rather obviously to free the signifier from overfamiliarity. Pinter's is the particularly Jewish knowledge that security is an illusion, you are not safe anywhere, not least in your own home, from the most surprising, irrational intrusion, Pinter takes an absurd everyday scene of a couple of people in a room and shows how they defend their territory from the intruder.

> The germ of my plays? I'll be as accurate as I can about that. I went into a room and saw one person standing up and one person sitting down, and a few weeks later I wrote *The Room*. I went into another room and saw two people sitting down, and a few years later I wrote *The Birthday Party*. I looked through a door into a third room, and saw two people standing up and I wrote *The Caretaker*.[27]

The terror of the midnight knock at the door which permeates *The Birthday Party* is something very recent in European countries that were under Nazi occupation but it's also something that has been going on for the last two to three hundred years.[28] It only needs an intrusion from outside to catalyze an unloading of hidden wishes, exacerbate frustrations and elicit confession of fears; the unexpected intrusion undermines basic assumptions and delusions. Pinter writes about people "at the extreme edge of their living, where they are living pretty much alone, at their hearth, their home hearth."[29] Before one can even think of involvement with sexual relations or the vital issues of politics there has to be an existential adjustment.

It follows from this that Pinter's lack of commitment as a play-wright does not mean that he holds no political views. Pinter refused National Service at the age of eighteen as a conscientious objector and was fined. His statement on Britain's proposed entry into the European Economic Community has often been quoted, "I have no interest in the matter and do not care what happens,"[30] though we know of Pinter's opposition in a school debate to a motion that a United States of Europe would be the only means to prevent another war.[31] Then again Pinter is openly pro-Israel and he opposed American involvement in Vietnam.[32]

Harold Hobson, in a defense of *The Birthday Party*, has hit the nail on the head when it comes to the day-to-day relevance of Pinter's plays:

> Mr. Pinter has got hold of a primary fact of existence. We live on the verge of disaster. One sunny afternoon, whilst Peter May is making a century at Lords against Middlesex, and the shadows are creeping along the grass, and the old men are dozing in the Long Room, a hydrogen bomb may explode. That's one sort of threat. But Mr. Pinter's is of a subtler sort. It breathes in the air. It cannot be seen, but it enters the room every time the door is opened. There is something in your past—it does not matter what—which will catch up with you.[33]

Before one can ask about ethnic or political affiliation one has to ask basic questions about identity. Those who ask *who* the characters are in *The Birthday Party* may well ask who *they* are, where *they* come from and whether *they* are "normal," and that's exactly the question Pinter reportedly put to a woman who wrote in asking who the characters were in *The Birthday Party*. In the postwar nightmare of a nuclear attack in Pete's dream in the play *The Dwarfs* people's faces start peeling and blistering during a panic in a tube station, but then we suddenly realize our own faces may be rotting away, our own outer personality may be just as frightening.[34]

The Birthday Party comprises a complex poetic summation, as Esslin calls it, of the totality of existential anxiety. Goldberg and McCann are not only walking questions of identity, they exist also as subversive and disturbing presences in the minds of others.[35] They are the catalysts in all of us of doubt about ourselves and about the familiar world in which we live. From the outset the play breaks down assumptions about the social status and identity of the characters, about their relationship to the space in which they act and to each other. The vacillation between whoredom and respectability, as in the unpublished novel *The Dwarfs* and the play *The Room*, alters our perception of the characters on stage and surreptitiously blurs the usual borderlines of normalcy. The breakfast routine in the seaside boarding house suggests a doting senility in Meg that touches on imbecility.[36] Stanley tells her "they're coming in a van," playing on her fear of being taken away by two Mental Health Officers, but in fact he is transferring his own paranoia awakened by the arrival of Goldberg and McCann.

Goldberg and McCann turn up out of the blue, like some Jew-and-Irishman comedy team who work their music-hall routine of wisecracks into an ominous catechism of Stanley's conscience that parodies the talk of rough boys in a Hitchcock movie. Lulu has already challenged Stanley to look at his face in a mirror and has called him a "washout": now Goldberg and McCann give him a working over, accusing him of heresy, lechery, incest and dirty habits. "You verminate the sheet of your birth"[37] reminds us of the way the army broke down raw conscripts by degrading their humanity. Echoing the protest in Arnold Wesker's *Chips with Everything* and Willis Hall's *The Long and the Short and the Tall* against the way Authority bullied the raw recruit into acquiescence, a broken Petey at the end of the play advises Stan not to "let them tell you what to do!"[38] as he is taken away.

Stan is on the run from something in his past and he invents an alibi for a lifestory set in respectable stockbroker-belt towns like Maidenhead and Basingstoke. His aspirations for respectability and social standing are telling in his insistence that he lived well away from the main road. Similarly, his delusions of becoming a concert pianist, an artist, fool nobody except Meg who misinterprets the tip he got as financial rather than the threatening kind. All through the play language covers evasions from what is better unsaid. If Stan ever played the piano it was not in a "concert" but in a show on the pier (the kind of show a Goldberg-McCann comedy act would fit into quite nicely) and it's in mockery of Stan's pretensions that Meg (wittingly or witlessly) gives him a toy drum as a birthday present. Stan is not only not an assimilated Jewish artist, as has more than once been claimed,[39] but he is also not trying to break out of an oedipal relationship with a Yiddishe Mama. There *is* something obscurely sexual in the sixty-year-old landlady's mothering of her pet lodger; she *is* afraid he will leave her and he *is* dependent upon her. But he is running away from himself. He has nowhere to run to (as we learn from what he says to Lulu) and no home to go back to. His is the rootlessness of a nonentity in a yes-man's land. If the drum is a sexual symbol (like the bongo drum in *The Lover*) and if it does trigger off Stan's secret desires, to strangle Meg and rape Lulu, these are the fantasies which everyone needs and which awaken universal sexual longings. Stan is a "Jew" only in the sense that Leopold Bloom is everyman in the *Circe* episode of *Ulysses* when he is being accused of every crime against humanity and womanhood and to the extent that Goldberg plays the role of Yiddishe Mama, pouring out all the anxieties, pain, incriminations and frustrated hopes of Mrs. Portnoy on the castrated son.

Goldberg is the Jew of the play in more ways than one. It is he and McCann, both aliens, who gate-crash domestic tranquility to realize the worst fears of ordinary people about the unclean demonic spirits embodied in social outcasts. As a mythical stereotype, Goldberg is the Devil-Jew-Judas, the calculating, fiendish Shylock with all the ambiguity Shakespeare built into the archvillain of the Elizabethan stage, and no less terrible than Graham Greene's Colleoni; quite possibly we are in Brighton again, this is hell, nor are we out of it (to paraphrase Marlowe's Mephistopheles), and comparison of Sartre's *Huis Clos*, 1944, known in the U.S. as *No Exit*, is all that is needed to give the theme an existentialist context. Making the analogy with Shylock, Ellen Schiff speaks of the stereotyped image of the Jew which corporealizes "the primitive dread which is the real destroyer in *The Birthday Party*."[40] That dread could be quite actual if we recall the McCarthy witchhunt (McCann accuses Stan of betraying "the organization," which, whether political or criminal, is definitely clandestine).

Yet to take Goldberg solely as a bogey is to miss half the fun of the play and it *is* fun, even if it irritated critics trying to make sense of it in conventional terms. There is another, more positive side to the legend of the Wandering Jew, for since George Eliot he also comes to teach and to moralize. Goldberg and McCann take Stan away to Monty ("only the best") and that's no more sinister or reassuring (whichever way you want to look at it) than the end Dostoevsky arranges for *his* Doppelgänger, Mr. Golyadkin, in *The Double*. Goldberg the Jew enters an English household that thinks no further than the morning bowl of cornflakes and he preaches values of love and caring. He toasts the reluctant birthday boy (Stan denies it is his birthday) with a speech traditionally given at a *bar-mitsvah*, though curiously mixed up with a funeral oration ("may we only meet at Simchahs!") and wishes for the Jewish New Year ("well over the fast"). Stan's inability to face maturity may suggest this is a ritual of confirmation, with Goldberg in the role of rabbi and McCann as father-confessor, except that their theological-philosophical jargon is nonsensical and they are the ones who crack Stan until he is a stammering lunatic. On the other hand, Goldberg has come to make Stan see the light, to look at what he really is: the metaphors of seeing and not seeing are repetitive, as they are in other plays by Pinter, and the game of Blind Man's Buff, as well as the breaking of Stan's glasses, make obvious the play on seeing reality.

However, none of this will wash as a solution to what has been called an "infuriating crossword puzzle." Goldberg preaches the ethical system of *mentshlikhkeyt*, respect for others, honoring one's father and mother (though there's also honor among thieves if one thinks of Al Capone and Babel's Odessa Jewish gangsters), but when it comes down to it he can't name the belief to which he owes allegiance and his East London Jewish patter is as much an evasion as anyone else's meaningless talk. Goldberg and McCann ostensibly challenge the preconceptions of the hosts whose home they are visiting, but they, too, have to face the questions "who are they" and "where do they come from." Goldberg's attempt to sum up childhood innocence and family security are no less suspiciously contradictory than Stanley's "memories" and he even aspires to an identical English Gentile middle-class respectability: "a little Austin, tea in Fullers, a library book from Boots."[41] His is the suave gift of the gab of the door-to-door salesman and perhaps he has come down in the world from being "in the business" (the *shmata* business, or garment industry, that is), but he is essentially a conman (just like Kops' Solly Gold) whose identity is as questionable as that of the average householder whom he challenges.

Goldberg's evocation of his mother and the cosy homeliness *(heymishkeyt)* of his Hackney childhood are phoney. The sun falling behind the stadium and the idyllic lovers' walk along the canal are all part of the wishful thinking in which Goldberg sees himself helping poor little strays (who happen to be dogs) and walking briskly to the safe confines of his mother's/wife's home where gefilte fish or rollmop herring are getting cold (though neither dish is often served hot!). Moreover, in Goldberg's nostalgic trip down memory lane his name changes from Nat to Benny and Simey. Simey is a name he's very touchy about. Goldberg's memories focus on a specifically Jewish family experience and it's remarkable how he picks on "after lunch on Shabbuss" or "Friday of an afternoon" in order to reconstruct roots in a Judaism he may never have known. His ties with the past are tenuous to say the least, but, like the characters in Wesker's *The Old Ones* and Norman in Kops' *The Lemmings* or David in *The Hamlet of Stepney Green*, he is not sure what Judaism is or why he is a Jew. The old rituals are acted out but it's not the same. But then McCann has rosy pictures of Ireland and Stan lets himself "confess" he previously lived under a different name. Most of the characters, in fact, show symptoms of schizophrenia. Lulu identifies Goldberg as her first pure love and later tries to present in a different light her nighttime antics with Goldberg; Goldberg thinks of her as his supposedly dead wife. Meg has delusions that hers is a respectable guest house "on the list" and she is the belle of any ball, a "tulip," as she ridiculously styles herself. Even Petey is displaced, to judge by the misunderstanding between him and Meg about what kind of show he means. Whether or not he is really a deck-chair attendant, he represents the man in the street who finds a way of accommodating the most untoward events and covering them up.

There is another, perhaps final sense in which Goldberg is the deracinated Jewish everyman. I refer to the whole ambiguity of the relationship between tormentor and victim. After the Holocaust the Jew can no longer look upon himself as a victim with the same clearcut moral criteria as before because the Nazi murder machine made the Jew into his own executioner and into an accomplice in the process of dehumanizing cruelty. Just as the Nazis needed a scapegoat for the purposes of guilt transference so does every society; feelings of guilt pent up in Jewish intellectual survivors of the Holocaust are let loose on a scapegoat from among their own number in C. P. Taylor's comedy of menace *Happy Days Are Here Again* (1965). This play, like C. P. Taylor's study of the mentality of an S.S. officer, *Good*, deserves more discussion than there is space for here, but it's noteworthy that it shows the common need to expiate guilt, to find a candidate for crucifixion, and it probes moral contradictions relevant both to the postwar Jewish condition and to the existential condition of man. Similarly, Goldberg takes away Stan, the Judas scapegoat, in a big car without too much opposition from the other people in the house, who will return no doubt to their daily complacency; the fact that Goldberg himself has something to hide only increases the irony that everyone is guilty of trying to escape the past. Whom Goldberg is working for, what his "assignment" really is and what the "subject" has done (if anything) are mysteries as deep as who is giving the orders in *The Dumb Waiter*. We can only wait for Godot and in the meantime imagine horrifying possibilities behind the most ordinary and innocent situations. These possibilities, however, must make us ask what is really behind what we do not see and do not usually think about.

COMING HOME

The Homecoming (1964) goes one step further in presenting an unthinkable situation in a domestic setting and making us rethink the ambiguities of identity. In C. P. Taylor's *Happy Days Are Here Again* Liphitz bullies his niece's suitors, only to place the guilt for her whoredom on all of them, just as he makes them all guilty of murder; C. P. Taylor's Ruth is never seen, she is an invisible ambiguous presence with whom each of them furtively try to communicate, whom we do not know to be living or dead. In Pinter's *The Homecoming* the Jewish references are more elusive, yet it's the same sacred cow of the Jewish family being dragged through the mud until we believe the most incredible relationships are possible.

The play is set in "an old house in North London" and the vagueness of this location itself suggests the ambiguity of the social position of Hackney Jews; there is also a similar disparity between actual and aspired social occupation (Sam is a glorified taxi driver who dresses in a chauffeur's uniform while Lenny fantasizes a career in aeronautics for Sam's American passenger).

Yet the shocking crudity of the language of father and sons disabuses any notion that they live up to the ideal of Jewish family virtue. Max is as rough and vulgar as Mendel Krik in Babel's *Sunset*, though we should be wary of taking for granted his self-image as terror of the West End, a scar-faced gangster knocking about with MacGregor, known as Mac, who might well be any "Mac the Knife" in a gangster movie (compare McCann in *The Birthday Party*). On the other hand, the disrespectability of this family of lowlifes is relatively questionable. For all their open violence, mutual insults and obscene insinuations they have their own cupboard of silent skeletons which is unlocked by two strangers who arrive in the middle of the night. Teddy is the prodigal son, the specter from the past, who has made good—now he is a professor in the United States—and his breaking with the social and psychological prison of the Jewish family closely follows the traditional paradigm. His family wouldn't understand the vision in his work, while his departure from home is clouded in obscurity: we can only guess that the reason

Teddy went away without telling his family he was married is because Ruth is not Jewish.[42] Max lets us surmise as much:

> I mean, you don't think I disapprove of marriage, do you? . . . Anyway, what's the difference, you did it, you made a wonderful choice, you've got a wonderful family, a marvellous career . . . so why don't we let bygones by bygones?[43]

However, the assimilation and intermarriage pattern fits too well to be true and it ignores the ambiguity in the situation (for example Max denies disapproval of marriage, not "the marriage"). There is quite likely a play on the Book of Ruth, as well as Shakespeare's *Troilus and Cressida*,[44] and, like the Moabite, Ruth is brought back from a foreign land to her husband's family. Yet even if Teddy at the end is in some symbolic fashion dead there is no hint of Ruth's conversion. On the contrary, there is a reversal of the disrespectable union that is made holy, for Ruth returns to disrespectability. She was born "quite near here" and has fantasies just like Lenny's about the past she would have liked to have (she wishes she'd been a nurse in the Italian campaign!). Her "memories" of pin-up modelling, whether true or not, bear out her self-identification as a whore and for once her behavior realizes as fact the initial sexual slur placed on her character by Max. Looking at it another way she is schizophrenic, "not well," as Teddy says, and quite liable to expose the story of family happiness and academic success in America as a sham, an eventuality of which Teddy is wary and which he tries to avert by protecting his identity with platitudes. This, if anything, is a universalization of the tensions inherent in the Jewish family,[45] showing the breakdown of individual and group personality. As in *The Birthday Party*, we watch people who are thrown together torment each other in the struggle for domination of space and of the clan; it only needs one word for unspoken realities to boil to the surface and disabuse us of much that we take for granted about kith and kin, for secret apprehensions to come into the open about one's nearest and dearest.

Oddly enough, Teddy is the outside intruder who has come to make them see reality and rethink their habitual preoccupations, but the philosopher can't cope with simple empirical questions from Lenny about whether the cheese is in the cupboard. It isn't there because Teddy has taken it in a deliberate act as irritating and seemingly pointless as McCann's shredding of a newspaper in *The Birthday Party*. He is the one who doesn't belong, not Ruth—she belongs only too well!—and it is he who goes away, alone and dejected, at the end of the play, while Ruth begs him not to become a "stranger." The search for identity, as was pointed out above, must be preceded by existential verification and it's mainly Lenny who does the verifying. Talking to Ruth about the clock which Teddy suggests has been keeping him awake, Lenny says that it might "easily prove something of a false hypothesis," like anything in life:

> All sorts of objects, which, in the day, you wouldn't call anything else but commonplace. They give you no trouble. But in the night any given one of a number of them is liable to start letting out a bit of a tick. Whereas you look at these objects in the day and they're just commonplace.[46]

Lenny's fantasies feature quite a few details which suggest displacement of one sort or another: his language aspires to intellectual vocabulary, but its content is brutal; he goes out snow-clearing for the borough council but has "independent means"; he agrees to help an old lady move an iron wrangle, which is an anachronistic object in the wrong room. To his surprise Ruth responds to both the attempted seduction and the expression of physical and mental derangement. Later she answers Lenny's challenge to Teddy to define a table, to revolve the enigma of being, by drawing attention to the ambiguities in everyday commonplace things, and not least in the dots between her words, which excite in the imagination the unsaid and the unsayable, for example a simple action like moving her leg.

> Perhaps you misinterpret. The action is simple. It's a leg . . . moving. My lips move. Why don't you restrict . . . your observations to that? Perhaps the fact that they move is more significant . . . than the words which come through them. You must bear that . . . possibility . . . in mind.[47]

The silent pauses and the lack of reaction to the most incredible acts from those who should be most affected highlight the unwillingness of the average person to "bear in mind" such possibilities. The kind of business administration jargon which Goldberg uses gives an impression of moral indifference, but it is also a tool with which to verify the necessity of reality, as Goldberg would say, "The possibility can only be assumed after the proof of necessity."[48] Only when it is accepted that Ruth *is* acting the "Belle-de-jour" and Lenny *is* a pimp, can one grant the larger possibilities for which this situation could be a metaphor: the modern breakdown of family and marital relations, derangement from environment and self, the groping for some kind of past in order to keep a grip on the present, the reversion to childishness as an escape from maturity and ageing.

TAKING CARE: BREAKDOWN IN PINTER AND SHAFFER

Pinter often gives the impression he considers the psychotic state to be the usual human condition. In *The Caretaker* (1959) we feel even less on safe ground, although the idiom is recognizable as belonging to Hackney, as is the language of *The Dwarfs* (1960). Man is seen as cut off from everything that could tell him where he belongs and who he is. The homeless tramp has lost track of time and his past. He claims that the papers which prove who he is are in Sidcup. We don't know to whom the room belongs in *The Caretaker*, but Mick has plans for getting rid of the filth and turning it into a dream home. His brother Aston attributes his depersonalization and restlessness to electric shock treatment in hospital, which may possibly, but not *necessarily*, be true.[49] What kept him going was laying out the possessions which *belonged* to him, this gave him a sense of selfhood, though the things in the room, including a Buddha, are as vaguely multinational and ill-assorted as those in Len's room in *The Dwarfs*. Aston spends most of the time playing around futilely with an electric plug and only the illusion that things can be repaired or sorted out enables him to go on living.

To *take care* of surrounding objects, or surrounding space, is the sole means to any illusion of belonging to a time and place. Aston, Mick and Davies are vague when speaking in the past tense, and each hopes they can fix things "for the time being"; Davies is lost without a clock because "if you can't tell what time you're at you don't know where you are." Adrift from time and place, Pinter's characters must feel the difficulty of verifying the past or even the present:

> If one can speak of the difficulty of knowing what in fact took place yesterday, one can I think treat the present in the same way. . . . A moment is sucked away and distorted, often even at the time of its birth.[50]

The common ground we call a shared reality is in Pinter's view a quicksand of uncertainties. And the continuum of uncertainties called time is punctuated by threats from outside, the Scotsman "looking after" Davies, or Davies' fear of domination and fear of contamination by Blacks. Being on the road is hardly the beatific experience it might be for Jack Kerouac. Nobody owes Davies respect and his pretension of a higher social standing only emphasizes his non-rootedness in time and place, his displacement and his paranoia. Davies' false name on his social security card puts him in dread of the Authorities, and Mick plays on that dread in his own attempt to establish an identity. Mick's bluffing engages a pseudoofficial tone similar to Goldberg's and is just as funny when he offers Davies a lease with

> No strings attached, open and above board, untarnished record; twenty per cent interest, fifty per cent deposit; down payments, back payments, family allowances, bonus schemes, remission of term for good behaviour, six month lease, yearly examination of the relevant archives, tea laid on, disposal of shares, benefit extension, compensation on cessation, comprehensive indemnity against Riot, Civil Commotion, Labour Disturbances, Storm, Tempest, Thunderbolt, Larceny or Cattle all subject to a daily check and double check.[51]

The alternation of intimidation and caring hides the uneasy feeling that none of the characters belong and, while Davies is seemingly the interloper, there is finally no being sure about relations between them or whether they are telling the truth. As Mick tells Davies, "I can take nothing you say at face value."[52]

Despite his claim to sanity, Davies admits to having had a glimpse into a psychiatric hospital, a suffocating place, he complains, always too hot. In *The Hothouse* the suffocation of an overheated institution assumes metaphoric proportions, though surely, as Beckett once wrote, no symbols where none intended. Pinter wrote *The Hothouse* in winter 1958, but waited twenty-one years before deciding it should be staged. Like *The Caretaker*, it has the familiar ingredient of a newcomer, Lamb, who is victimized, while the process of victimization helps to point out the fears and inadequacies of the victimizers. Yet it is more obviously a logical puzzle, along the lines of Stoppard's *After Magritte*, and because more obvious perhaps less satisfactory. The patients never appear on the stage, only the staff; these are ministerial underlings, low-grade civil servants, who feel nevertheless a cut above the proletariat, the understaff of kitchen and cleaning personnel, and as they busy themselves officiously with filing reports, they affect an official jargon which maintains that illusion of superiority. Actually, the power structure is a chain of agressive, even murderous intentions. The society that is the hothouse is bestial and intimidating. Colonel Roote, in charge of the so-called caring institution, has stopped visiting the patients and is becoming distracted from his official functions by drink and sex; he, too, becomes intimidated and begins to think something funny is going on. He is right, just as Elias Canetti tells us that after Auschwitz a man who thinks that someone is trying to gas him is right; yet, whatever credibility this may give to Davies' fear of being gassed, the paranoia in *The Hothouse* is induced as much by personal griev-ances and private conspiracies as by the stifling repression of Au-thority. Roote's own authority is insiduously challenged during the Christmas levity and he is murdered during the patients' insurrection. Gibb survives to take his master's place, while Lamb is left as if in a catatonic trance following his electric-shock therapy, a particularly sexual form of victimization worked out elsewhere in the revue sketch *Applicant* (first performed 1964), and his mad chuckle reminds us very much of Stanley in *The Birthday Party*. The primal, irrational forces latent in the human condition are released, but the ambiguity of the situation is remarkable, complicating the social parallels of the play's metaphors and questioning who are the victims, who the assassins.

Pinter broaches insanity again in *The Dwarfs*, where Len's lunacy is intimated mainly by his friends' insinuations. Conspiracies and hallucinations increase Len's awareness of what is really going on in the world as well as of the impossibility of verifying an unstable reality.

> Occasionally I believe I perceive a little of what you are but that's pure accident. Pure accident on both our parts, the per-ceived and the perceiver. It's nothing like an accident, it's de-liberate, it's a joint pretence. We depend on these accidents, on these contrived accidents, to continue. It's not important then that it's conspiracy or hallucination.[53]

Len's world is degenerate; he watches the dwarfs acting their strange rituals of contamination and purification, he watches nature eating its own death, dripping with pus and excrement, yet the vision at the end, of the clean lawn and the flower, makes it possible to go even in knowledge of delusion. The obsession with cleansing arises from guilt and the desire to wipe it out by purification, central to the Jewish idea of atonement which is an at-one-ment both with

community and God. The interaction of solicitation and ugly insin-
uation drives the three friends on; to be destroyed they need only
be left alone and not change, while the interaction of a trio in a
room, far more discomforting than the inertia and lie of stability, is
the very stuff of the drama of plays like *The Caretaker* and *The
Dwarfs.*

Mental breakdown may even bring about a heightened awareness
of reality, like Mick's "clear vision," of things as they really are,
piercing the veil of moral hypocrisy in daily behavioral conformity
and the paper-thin security of home comforts. It stresses the dis-
harmony of reality and the disconcerting contradictions of aspirations
(enforced and personal) with that exitless reality. For derangement
as a metaphor of confused identity it's useful to compare Bernard
Kops' *The World is a Wedding* and *The Hamlet of Stepney Green*, and
it's a theme also of a novel set in the East End that won the
prestigious 1970 Booker Prize, Bernice Rubens' *The Elected Member*
(1969), published in the United States as *Chosen People.*

Bernice Rubens' presentation of the East End is at best sketchy
and she apparently knows little about Rabbis. Indeed, her novel
would be better placed in one of the London suburbs for it has
much in common with the protest against bourgeois philistinism
found in novels and plays such as Michael Hastings' dramatic fable
of schizophrenia, *Yes, and After* (1957), set in Stockwell. The South
London playwright Hastings presents a loveless world after the Big
Scream in which communication between parent and child has failed.
The teenage girl is possessed by a *dybbuk*, a former lodger with
whom she has formed an illicit liason. Both the possession by a
deranged imagination and the pain of betrayal are indictments of
the real world not easily exorcized by modern psychiatry. Neither
Hastings' *Yes, and After* nor Peter Shaffer's celebrated *Equus* (1973)
betray specific Jewish referents, though Hastings used Ansky's play
The Dybbuk, while in *Equus* the magistrate Hesther Salomon is presumably named for a paragon of Hebraic justice and exhibits a moral
as well as ethnic otherness that she can share only with another of
her kind. She tells the child psychiatrist Martin Dysart that his
colleagues will be as revolted and "immovably English" over the
case as her bench was. To which comes the reply:

Dysart: Well, what am I? Polynesian?
Hesther: You know exactly what I mean! . . .[54]

Peter Shaffer (born 1926) comes from a traditional Jewish home in Liverpool, but like Pinter he needs to camouflage any Jewish content in his play if it is to convey the all-embracing agony of the Jew as a healer and moral standard of a society whose education and language prevent us seeing how it kills the capacity for spirituality, passion and pain. For most modern Jewish writers that frustrated agony has been lived in what Shaffer once called the "neighborhood solidarity circle"[55] of Anglo-Jewry, but its applicability is much wider, to much of English society.

In concluding the discussion of modern Jewish drama in Britain, Peter Shaffer's *Five Finger Exercise* (1958) may serve as an excellent example of how the breakdown of the Jewish family is translated onto the stage as a typically *English* situation. This is not the conventional drawing-room drama in the Noël Coward tradition it would appear to be and it deserves attention for the themes it shares with the plays of Wesker and Pinter, as well as for the comparisons with Michael Hastings' *Yes, and After*, whose suburban English milieu contrasts with the specifically Jewish setting of *Don't Destroy Me*, which brought Hastings to public attention in 1956 as one of the "Angry Young Men."

Five Finger Exercise is set in the Harringtons' weekend cottage in the Suffolk countryside, fitted out with all too much Taste and too much Town. These are *parvenus* egged on by Louise, the French-born mother, to keep up with the Joneses. The father grew up in the tough school of life and built up his own furniture company; now the social distance from his wife irks him and he fails to understand why his son Clive craves education and poetry instead of the things he lived for, money and material comforts. In fact the country retreat is no retreat from the family squabbles half-smothered by the veneer of respectability. The fantasy play-acting of Clive and his teenage sister Pamela gives expression to the repression of identity and in particular of sexual deprivation, while the mimicry of U-speech makes evident that social maladjustment felt in the idioms uttered as idiocies in Pinter's plays (which have been analyzed from a socio-linguistic standpoint by A. K. Kennedy, *Six Dramatists in Search of a Language*, 1975).

In each scene Shaffer gives a twist to the situation until we perceive the most incredible relationships worthy of *The Homecoming*. The five finger exercise of the title originates in a piano exercise of five inter-related elements that are variously weakened or strengthened by interaction. As in *Amadeus* and other plays by Peter Shaffer, music strikes a keynote, and not just the chord of Wesker's real culture. The exercise in the play is an exercise in self-awareness and in awareness of the brutality inherent in family harmony. The mother's unwillingness to let go of her son suggests the oedipal conflict of East End writers Bernard Kops or Emanuel Litvinoff, but it also releases a violence akin to Albert's in Pinter's *A Night Out* (written 1959, produced 1960). Clive, too, comes to know he can strike a cruel blow.

The interloper is not a Jew, nor even a Pinteresque nonentity, but a young German called Walter who is brought in as Pamela's private tutor. Walter expects an idyllic English family but Clive warns him he is entering a "tribe of wild cannibals" out for each other's blood. Walter falls victim to the family's vengeful frustration and soon discovers they are far from the stereotyped ideal which he imagined. Walter becomes the final catalyst of family breakdown, seduced by each member in turn to hurt the others. Awful truths seep out and these illustrate Pinter's own defense of enigmatic characters:

> A character on the stage who can present no convincing argument or information as to his past experience, his present behaviour or his aspirations, nor give a comprehensive analysis of his motives is as legitimate and as worthy of attention as one, who alarmingly, can do all these things. The more acute the experience the less articulate its expression.[56]

Walter himself, the diffident, intelligent twenty-two-year-old tutor, is not what he seems. He hides a secret past. He invents a biography to kill his father, an Auschwitz concentration camp guard, who beat into his son the slogans against the Jews, the Catholics and the Liberals. Germany has orphaned Walter. Thrown out as a waiter in Berlin he has turned his back on what he sums up as the Devil's hearth; he has sought to adopt a new homeland, only to find that he can be no more at home with the Harringtons than in Germany. Walter, who would have introduced culture and sensitivity to the household, tries to gas himself in his room. Symbolically, as the gas fills the room, the needle sticks on the Third Movement of Mahler's Fourth Symphony.

Apparently devoid of Jewish content, Shaffer's play nevertheless looks at family strife from a post-Holocaust angle. Walter's socioethnic and moral rebellion finds its parallels in Clive's generational revolt. Walter tells Clive he must get out of the family prison and it is

Walter, the alien steeped in moral guilt, who sparks off the English undergraduate's articulation of commitment, his need, in Wesker's sense, to care:

> *Clive* [intimately]: I think I want . . . to achieve something that only I could do. I want to fall in love with just one person. To know what it is to bless and be blessed. And to serve a great cause with devotion. [Appealing.] I want to be *involved.*[57]

Commitment alone points the way out of emotional and moral imprisonment, it alone makes sense when words no longer connect. The play does not allow as much optimism as might be suggested here, but it does call for pity and courage where Ronnie Kahn knows despair.

Shaffer's throwing together characters in a room and letting them talk achieves a dramatic conflict different to Pinter's but no less powerful. From this standpoint *Equus* is total theater. Watch how the horses are never allowed to become crude symbols, however tempting may be apocalyptic parallels, how the games people play (to borrow Eric Berne's phrase) make impressive and violent ritual. In both *Five Finger Exercise* and *Equus* moral argument is orchestrated into dramatic action so as to give little impression of the didacticism which obtrudes into Wesker's plays. An early example of this is a television play *The Salt Land* (1955) in which two immigrant brothers clash in Israel. The philosophical dilemma of prophetic idealism versus urban cynicism is worked out in the violent struggle between the two brothers on a kibbutz. Metaphysics becomes drama in the manner of Greek tragedy.

The background of Peter Shaffer and his twin brother Anthony, also a playwright, is comfortable middle class, provincial Liverpool, public school and Cambridge scholarship. Like other assimilated Jewish writers, Peter Shaffer has negated the official Jewish community. However, uninformed of the real tenets of Judaism, he mistakes its ethical imperatives for a hypocritical mouthing of liberal humanitarian platitudes over the gefilte fish,[58] as crass and objectionable as Mr. Harrington's bigoted patronizing. This leaves Shaffer, no less than Dysart in *Equus*, spiritually in the dark, and not even, as Dysart says, a dark "ordained of God." Far from being the work of an atheist, Shaffer believes "both *The Salt Land* and *Five Finger Exercise* to be religious plays";[59] similarly at the heart of *The Royal Hunt of the Sun* (1964) "is the search for God—the search for a definition of the idea of God."[60]

Shaffer knows that social maladjustment can result in a gifted, if schizophrenic sight, but he also knows, as do Harold Pinter, Bernard Kops and Arnold Wesker, that delinquency is essentially destructive. In fact, Walter in *Five Finger Exercise* warns of the affinity of the English Teddy Boys with the fiends of Nazi Germany. The adolescent in *Equus* disturbs Dysart and awakens him to the aridity of his marriage and his academic interests, but while the root of radicalism in the schizophrenia and oedipal complex of the Jewish home remains debatable, the Jewish playwrights recognize that the breakdown of family is a destructive force that must be checked.

The transition of the Shaffer family to London in 1942 parallels the suburbanization of London Jews in the North-West postal districts and no doubt Shaffer's intimate knowledge of how social change affects the family situation contributed to vital concerns which his plays share with the novels to be discussed in the following chapter.

North-West

Chapter Six
The Golders Green Novel: Glanville, Charles, Rubens, Raphael

Sarah Kahn wouldn't move to Hendon and "forget who I am" and in *I'm Talking About Jerusalem* the former idealists who move out of the East End lose sight of their beliefs and their identity, a theme of the later work of both Arnold Wesker and Bernard Kops who themselves live in London's northern suburbs. Making it to suburbia was the goal of the second generation immigrants who worked themselves up from nothing, all the time aspiring to bourgeois security and comfort. Instead of pushing their children on in the world, as their parents had done with so much self-sacrifice, they wanted to see them preserve the same English bourgeois values they had assimilated to, yet their fear of anti-Semitism and their fossilized clinging to ethnic exclusivity required of their children conformity to an ill-defined, half-forgotten Jewishness, institutionalized into a hypocritical weekly or yearly synagogue attendance; they demanded that the children marry within the faith and into respectable, preferably moneyed connections. The revolt by what became known as Anglo-Jewry's angry young men against the uncultured superficiality of the centrally-heated, wall-to-wall carpeted "Judaism" was the subject of the "Golders Green novel." Chaim Bermant has included under this heading Brian Glanville's *The Bankrupts* (1958), Gerda Charles' *The Crossing Point* (1960), Frederic Raphael's *The Limits of Love* (1960) and Bermant's own *Jericho Sleep Alone* (1964), *Berl Make Tea* (1965) and *Ben Preserve Us* (1965).[1] It's a term, I suppose, that's as useful as any other, and Bernice Rubens' novels as well as some of Dannie Abse's poetry might be included (Abse will be discussed in the following chapter), despite the fact that Bermant came from Glasgow, Abse from Cardiff and Charles from Liverpool before settling in North-West London.

However, the "Golders Green novel" never became a vibrant genre of Jewish writing in the same way as the novels and plays of the East End and some of the Jewish community's reactions to Glanville's *The Bankrupts* may suggest why. *The Bankrupts* tells the story of Rosemary Frieman, the twenty-year-old daughter of a wealthy Jewish businessman, who refuses to be married off to money and respectability. The warmth of this Jewish household somewhere between Hampstead and Hendon is artificial and typical of the stifling materialism of Jewish society in North-West London. The Friemans have come far from the East End of their parents and they want to see their children succeed in marriage and the professions in order to enhance their respectability in the community and to perpetuate the same way of life. At the ritual bridge parties, in the golf clubs and in the plush Bournemouth hotels where boy meets girl under strict parental supervision, money is god. They aspire to Englishness but are overdressed, overloud, and foreign; only Rosemary could pass for an Englishwoman and she wounds her parents deeply by refusing to be moulded in their self-image. She rejects the mawkish compromise of Reform Judaism because it represents what her parents stand for, yet she is the only one to heed the rabbi's words when he puts the blame on the parents for not handing down the real values of Judaism. Actually, neither Rosemary nor her brother David, who has been given a last chance to pass his law exams, know what they want out of life; Rosemary only knows she does not want her parents' way.

Rosemary's revolt is fostered by a Jewish research student, Bernard Carter, in whom she finds ideals which the Jewish race and religion should stand for. To the Friemans' way of thinking Bernard is a worse match than a non-Jew because his pursuit of literature, like Rosemary's interest in further education and artiness, doesn't make business sense to them and his social standing is so much lower than theirs. Bernard has fought his way out of the Jewish parents' domination syndrome and he helps Rosemary get out, although at heart she is quite attached to the luxuries of home life. It's almost impossible to get out intact, in fact, for the moral bankruptcy of the parents cripples the children's emotional maturity as well as their capability for moral awareness. They don't come out of the experience well-adjusted. There is a parallel with the protest in contemporary English fiction against the vacuity of the suburban middle-classes, though Bernard Carter is more sympathetic to Rosemary's parents than Jimmy Porter is to his wife's family. There's also a difference in the relative vigor and keenness of Anglo-Jewry, although at the same time Glanville sees it as barren and stifling any dynamism or creativity in the younger generation.[2] For Glanville there is little point in perpetuating Anglo-Jewry in the impotent, assimilating form he portrays and therefore little point in trying to identify with the community he negates, while the storm of outrage that greeted his novel made it clear the hostility was mutual.

Glanville responded to the attacks with a critique of what he calls "defense mechanisms."[3] The community, like the Friemans, couldn't face the reality of their hypocritical stand or the bankruptcy of the values they indoctrinated in their children. They preferred to believe the novel wasn't true, by which they meant it didn't give a rosy, flattering picture of how the community would like to think of itself. Most distasteful was the peep behind the curtains in N.W. 11, especially at David's sordid relations with the Irish maid, although tales of extra-marital love and adultery were probably the spicy gossip Jewish readers wanted to read in a popular novel (just like the readers gathered at Mrs. Goldsmith's in *Children of the Ghetto*). What would the Gentiles think? The assumption that such things didn't happen and, even if they did, that they should be swept under the carpet, denied the Jewish intellectual any right to criticize the community. The novel was even described as "disloyal." Glanville has concurred with Philip Roth in a public statement that the Jewish writer must not give in to the argument that the ignorant and bigoted might misunderstand his criticisms because that would be to submit to their censorship[4] and I think this sums up much of the dilemma of the Anglo-Jewish writer. If he is to write on Jewish themes he must disguise them and address a non-Jewish audience, as Pinter and Shaffer have done, but he is more likely to write one "Jewish" book and leave the community, since to remain would mean self-denial as an artist.[5] The lack of allegiance to the community on the part of leading Jewish writers with whom Glanville conducted interviews for the *Jewish Chronicle* in December 1958–January 1959 caused a protest which accused the Jewish writer of self-hatred, when in fact it was the failure to impart knowledge of Jewish history, together with the middle-of-the-road compromise devoid of belief in Torah Judaism, which left the secular Jew confused and distrustful of Jewish identity.

The Bankrupts is written with a heavy-handedness and a tendency to generalize which sometimes spoils the sincere anguish of the author, but it was the first of a few novels which attained success and a high literary level (the two not always being compatible) beyond the autobiographical attempts to deal with identity and renascent anti-Semitism in postwar Britain by Dannie Abse (*Ash on a Young Man's Sleeve*, 1954) or Alexander Baron (*With Hope Farewell*, 1952). Very often it's outside the community, in public schools or in the army, that the Jew has to confront his Jewishness, but this confrontation provides the basis for a work of art usually only when the writer first grapples with fundamental, existential questions of being and identity, as I've argued Pinter does. The alienation of the Jew from self and community has something in common with the alienation of the artist and while I don't think one can make a case for all writing being Jewish[6], the problems are interconnected for the Jewish writer. Glanville is at his best when he expresses displacement and marginality in his masterly command of language, particularly the speech of East London characters who find themselves out of their world and out of their depth (some of the stories in *A Bad Streak*, 1961; *The Olympian*, 1969; *The Comic*, 1974), and when his characters are identifiably Jewish they're often lowlifes and betting types (like the characters of Pinter and Baron), because these are also social outcasts with a wider relevance.

Perhaps these are some of the reasons why Gerda Charles' *The Crossing Point* is less successful. Charles is not as estranged from the Jewish community as some of her contemporaries and therefore does not have the same sort of conflicts with identity. Nevertheless, *The Crossing Point* deals with all the controversial aspects of Jewish life in Golders Green, including such hot potatoes as marrying-out and revolt against tradition. The tasteless extravagance, overexcitability and materialism of Golders Green is even more vacuous than it is ugly. Jewish mothers like Mrs. Goldenbird press their daughters on stale but promising bachelors, pursuing them in Bournemouth hotels at the same time as tyrannizing their own husbands. The family is falling apart: "Where there had been a family there were now broken ends."[7] Soon the familiar tirade of the Jewish father hurt by his daughters' betrayal and ingratitude is heard. He, the "scholar," has been repaid with "evil" for all their education and his sacrifice of love. Mr. Gabriel is dismayed that his daughters refuse to live in the image in which he moulded them but his fury, like Mr. Frieman's in *The Bankrupts* or Mr. March's in C. P. Snow's *The Conscience of the Rich*, is little more than a pitiful posturing that covers up his own impotence and failure.

Essie Gabriel lacks the appealing naivety of Essie Ansell in *Children of the Ghetto* but she also revolts against the one thousand prohibitions of the Sabbath and desecrates the Friday night so sacred even to Anglicized Jews. She has already made the typical muddle-headed compromise of exchanging a suspected crab sandwich for an equally unkosher jello. She cannot disapprove of intermarriage or consider it treasonable; when she elopes with a non-Jew she abandons the snobbery of socioethnic status even though that is exactly what her lover deceitfully acts out with a borrowed car, a false posh accent and a phoney past. They both have to overcome sociological barriers which are no more than delusions. They are both misfits up against what Essie calls "misplacement."

Meanwhile Essie's sister Sara glimpses the assimilated highlife of *parvenu* Kensington Jews with their unhappy marriages to non-Jews and their charity committees which compete with each other in wealth. Sir Oswald Gould, for example, is ashamed of his immigrant origins; like Mr. Frieman he uses Yiddish phrases when provoked but otherwise they are "non-U" except in burlesque.

The North-West London Jewish clergy is represented by Rabbi Leo Norberg who has a "modern" approach to Orthodoxy. He eats out and holds women's hands as well as boasting a healthy sexual appetite (at one point he jokes that he'd rather eat crab than marry one of those staid Golders Green Jewish princesses). His interest in medieval Jewish thought highlights the potential of Judaism as a "crossing point" but Leo can't carry through his ideas and he ends up marrying a second-rate third choice (in contrast to Leon Raphael in *Children of the Ghetto*). Rabbi Norberg overcomes idealistic and romantic impulses in order to emulate the pulpit-figurehead as Minister of a well-to-do congregation. At the same time he acknowledges that the ministry must move with the times and must play down the more "restrictive" demands of the Jewish religion; indeed, when he considers the number of people who drive to the synagogue on Saturdays and park round the corner he's not surprised by a colleague's switch to the Reform Movement.

Of course the narrow-minded Jews of Golders Green are no less dull than millions of others, but Charles' point is that the Jews are supposed to be better and it's their heritage to be better. They have the vitality and the intellect for it, but their venerated geniuses are prophets without honor in their own country. Instead they honor chairmen of synagogue committees and are content with their role as entrepreneurs, the middlemen essential to the smooth running of society. Gerda Charles, a lonely spinster living with her mother in a Maida Vale flat, no longer hopes, but retains the conviction that the Jews have a moral obligation to behave well, that they are chosen for moral responsibility.[8] In her novels she explores the "region of everyday hurt,"[9] the petty hurts which people inflict on each other, the calculated torment which parents use to dominate their children. Her characters must learn to see through the superficiality of their environment, reaching a crisis when realities fail to match up to expectations. She exorts us to follow the unfashionable virtues of tact, delicacy and generosity and her seriousness may explain her unpopularity:

> In championing a sense of responsibility and sacrifice against the pull of thoughtless self-indulgence and what she calls 'easy come and go' she is clearly not striving to be either fashionable or ingratiating.[10]

Gerda Charles (pseudonym of Edna Lipson, born 1914) emerged from provincial poverty without much formal education to publish her first novel, *The True Voice*, in 1959. In 1963 she won the James Tait Black Memorial Prize for her novel *A Slanting Light*, and was awarded the Whitbread Literary Award for 1971, the year she published *Destiny Waltz*; both novels return us to the theme of frustrated artists who need to articulate their inner conflicts and grievances, but who have to contend with the discouraging animosity of the stifling Jewish family which doesn't appreciate their talent. Reviewing *Destiny Waltz*, C. P. Snow claimed Charles as one of the outstanding modern British novelists who had undeservedly been subject to "benevolent neglect."[11]

For Arnold Wesker *The Crossing Point* answered several personal problems of being a Jew in England and of being a Jewish writer. The "neurotic strength" of a retrospective Jewish melancholy is something the Jewish writer can contribute to English literature (he refers to Kenneth Tynan's regret that the British theater lacked the "Jewish vitality" of the American theater)[12] and it may be a blessing in disguise that Glanville and Charles are condemned to write their heightened neurotic sensitivities into their work. For neither assimilation nor immigration to Israel prove viable options, yet to be accepted by the Jewish community means to capitulate to the philistine mediocrity of hypocritical conformity; as serious artists they fear acceptance because it brings the risk of oblivion and moral compromise. It's easy to be seduced into that trap and turn into the kind of Golders Green Jewish mother as materialistic and uncultured as Mrs. Frieman whom her daughter has fought tooth and nail, as Bernice Rubens warns us in her short story "The Blood of the Lamb" (1973), in which the lambskin is both the inheritance of mind-deadening materialism and the child's own sacrificial blood. The young Jewish woman accepts the dead mother's lambskin, acquired at such emotional and moral expense, and becomes her mother, shutting out her former social and cultural life as she dons the mantle of North-West London respectability and conformity. The danger is not the Gentile outside world but the painful conflicts of emotional blackmail within the Jewish family which never lets go of its children's minds or stomachs and which wouldn't answer the door if the messiah came to N.W. 11.

Bernice Rubens was born in Cardiff in 1928 and grew up in a Jewish immigrant family in South Wales during the Depression and World War Two. An English graduate of the University of Wales, Rubens gave up her teaching and acting careers to make documentary films about the underprivileged and handicapped; the theme of emotional, psychological or social disability is important in her novels and it is a theme discussed earlier in connection with Pinter and Shaffer. Rubens explores the relationship between the family and the disabled and uses disablement to take a critical look at the Jewish family. Her first novel, *Set On Edge* (1960), centers on Gladys's childhood in the Sperber family and tells how the family members exploit each other, without actually breaking the family bond. The family alone grants Gladys a sense of belonging as a neglected child, the only child who does not get married until she is sixty. When a husband is found for her, he most unfortunately dies on the honeymoon. After her mother's death, Gladys is left alone in the house. The Jewishness of the family is the claustrophobia of that tight family circle itself whose stranglehold disables the child so that when the family circle dissolves, the grownup child is left a displaced person at sea in the larger, fluid and amorphous circle of society, ill-equipped to deal with the pressures of reality. A *Times Literary Supplement* reviewer called *Set on Edge* "Jewish writing at its best," and in her first three novels Rubens explores the destructiveness of marital and family relationships with a penetrating black humor that is Jewish without being stylized.[13]

In *The Elected Member* (1969) the burden of belonging again strains the family to breaking point. Norman, a gifted barrister and the pride of the family, becomes its shame and its guilt when he turns to narcotics to escape to a schizophrenic existence that opens his eyes to things unseen by others and to the sort of clearer vision claimed by the disaffected young men of Kops and Pinter. After Norman is taken away by two Mental Health officers in a big car, a nurse asks his father, Rabbi Zweck, whether he would not bless his son if he had seen the Burning Bush. Having lost the radical vision which fired the prophets, Jewish society fails to recognize the duality inherent in the average individual and by attempting to suppress that duality succeeds in displacing it. Norman's cure is to come to terms with the Jewish home and his own guilt in that relationship. His Jewishness wells up within him at the invitation to kneel in worship to Jesus, and there, among the mentally ill, he must discover his Jewish God and pray his way out of confusion.

The family attempt to suppress recollections of the past which in any way negate the delusion of a happy, united Jewish family. The facility shown by the Anglo-Jewish family in wiping out un-mentionable, painful stretches of the memory is threatened by facts, such as their daughter Esther's marriage to a non-Jew. Norman blames the suicide of his best friend David on Esther's elopement, but the way Esther remembers it, Norman persuaded her to elope by telling her his best friend David was a homosexual. Similarly, his sister Bella's ankle-socks accuse Norman of responsibility for her spin-sterhood, and piecing together the past we discover that the incest bred by the unhealthy closeness of the family has all the heady, stifling sexuality of Dr. Braun's memories of Tina in Bellow's "The Old System". These unpleasant and unspoken truths are avenged in the jealous cruelties which mother inflicts on son, which brother inflicts on sister and father; they are kept together by self-delusion, self-interest and mutual hatred. Here again is the scheme of *Five Finger Exercise* and the secret knowledge of cruelty latent in the Jewish family. Mrs. Zweck is the familiar Yiddishe Mama who con-tinues to exert her over-possessiveness after her death and leaves her bed as Norman's legacy, securing forever her hold over the child prodigy who is never allowed to grow out of being a child prodigy. Her greedy ambition claims in perpetuity the son's genius as a personal achievement of social aspirations, while her smothering

over-identification claims his body as an exclusively private possession, her own zealously guarded Peter Pan.

The psychology of disablement is probed further in Rubens'
following novels, which, though they do not deal exclusively with
Jewish themes, continue to explore breakdown of personality, as in
Sunday Best (1971), the journal of a transvestite, while *I Sent a Letter
to my Love* (1975) suggests a Welsh version of *Set On Edge*. *Spring
Sonata* (1979) returns to the emotional in-fighting of the Jewish family,
this time overheard, rather incredibly perhaps, by a child in the
womb. The child's refusal to be born is an accusation of moral
blindness and psychological imprisonment against the post-Holocaust
generation who exploit their young as scapegoats of sacrificial love
and submerged guilt and against the reproachful, disappointed, over-
expectant mother who passes on a crippling hereditary stranglehold.
The wonder progeny plays Beethoven's Spring Sonata *in utero*, a
passionate dialogue between the violin of the foetus and the piano
of the mother, but the thought of performing in public and being
used as a status-building symbol, devoured by possessive love and
ambition, makes the *wunderkind* despair of life after the womb. He
cuts the umbilical cord with his violin bow and literally breaks his
mother's heart. This vindictive pessimism is striking, given the author's refusal to apportion blame in *The Elected Member*, but it
similarly illustrates the transcendence into novel form of personal
displacement, as well as the anger at the bourgeois stratification of
the Jewish family.

Rubens' warm understanding of family crisis brings us to another
resident of North-West London who came from a provincial community, Chaim Bermant (born in Glasgow, 1929), whose novels match
the local interest and vitriol of his *Jewish Chronicle* column, but do
not generally have the makings of a great novel, although *Diary of
an Old Man* (1966) is an excellent evocation of the paranoia and
loneliness of an elderly widower. Among Bermant's satires of provincial and suburban Jewish communities or the Bournemouth Borsht
Circuit, *The Last Supper* (1973) records the dying moments of a Jewish
family with an incredibly guilty past, a general theme, apparently,
of recent Jewish writing, which suggests that the pain of guilt is
double-edged: the younger generation must share the guilt for the
damage it has done to the fabric of the Jewish home. *The Last Supper*
features one of those Holyday gatherings, the Passover *Seder* meal,
that are festivals of family disunion which celebrate the sacrificial
ritual of emotional blackmail; as in *Spring Sonata*, the by now oblig-

atory mourning rites for the Jewish family are solemnly performed, though Rubens and Bermant write within a referential framework of Jewish liturgy and ethics that does not rely totally on inaccurate Yiddishisms or on *shmaltz*. Jewish values, are, after all, amenable when middle-class English society is indifferent or hostile to Jews and Judaism, while the aridity and vulgarity of middle-class society are in no way preferable to the intense, if oppressive, passion of the Jewish family. It is a Jewish wisdom which Rubens quotes in *Spring Sonata*: "The fathers have eaten sour grapes, and the children's teeth are set on edge" (Ezekiel, 18, 2).

THE LINGUISTIC PHILOSOPHY OF FREDERIC RAPHAEL, OR
WITTGENSTEIN AND THE CYCLISTS

An author who observes the disintegration of the family with as careful attention to sociological data as Gerda Charles, but more cynically and entertainingly, is Frederic Raphael. Born in Chicago, Illinois, in 1931, Raphael had a public school education at Charterhouse before going up to Cambridge where he read classics, 1950–4. Born of a transatlantic union with roots everywhere, it's not surprising he belongs nowhere and is troubled by the philosophical-existential dimensions of ambiguous identity. His novels, stories and screenplays about Cambridge graduates tested by the ethics of fame, the moral dilemma of acceptance by community and society, resemble the popular family chronicles of G. B. Stern and Naomi Jacob, but differ in the display, at times rather irritating, of wit and knowing cleverness which owe much to his commercial sense as a successful film script-writer; the underlying serious search for identity through verification he owes to the ideas of Wittgenstein, who was at Cambridge until his death in 1951 and whose disciple, John Wisdom, left a lasting impression on Raphael.

As in Pinter's plays, the search for defining acts of being is a question of freedom and necessity, and in Raphael's novels these defining acts are determined by the linguistic facts of sociological data, for example status symbols such as makes of automobiles, prestige postal districts and telephone exchanges, even brands of cookies. Logical Positivism becomes both a philosophy and an aesthetics of writing, though it's doubtful in quite the way the philosophers intended! Fundamental to Raphael's understanding of critical reasoning is the radical indeterminacy of ordinary concepts, the realization that the boundary is blurred between ethics and aesthetics; aesthetic discourse is characterized by a logical plurality in which language cannot embody absolute truths.[14] The gaps between words are filled with self-doubt, and the criterion of validity of the speaker's arguments, while nominally linguistic verification, must ultimately be the acceptance of sophisticated verbal duels and wordplay because they convince.

In Raphael's novel *The Limits of Love* (1960) the challenge to the security of a North-West London Jewish family comes from a living specter of the past they'd rather not think about, the death of six million Jews in the Holocaust, in the person of Otto Kahane, who comes to *claim* his long-lost relatives, the Adlers. In the camp at Dachau he survived by assuming the identity of someone else, a doctor of the same name. In this way he has killed his own self and suppressed his memory, because it's impossible to live with memories of what was. His unexpected and unwilled freedom now comes as a burden:

> Freedom was too much for him. A prisoner, there had been cause to act; free there was none. In the camp he had belonged; to be on this street on this day, was a mere accident.[15]

His relatives have no wish to be claimed, as he knows ("no necessity bound him to them") and they'd rather not hear the grisly details of Jewish suffering at the hands of the Nazis.

Adler's Delicatessen is prospering in 1945, and once again it's suggested that there is some substance in the allegation that capitalist Jews made money during the war. The family can afford to move to the Finchley side of Golders Green. Mr. Adler would rather not have had the change, simply because he doesn't like change, whereas his daughter Julia had assumed moving out of the store would entail a break with Jewishness and with a family whose jokes and problems are incomprehensible. Having Otto visit them seems to her like "transplanting a weed to a new garden" and she retreats from memories of Jewish persecution behind the Livy she is studying at her fee-paying private school. The artificial fire, the pre-supper sherry, the over-new, over-comfortable furnishings contrast with the lone concentration camp survivor who hoards the warmth.

Another daughter, Susan, has betrayed her father's values and aspirations by marriage *downtown*—to a Jewish communist from the East End. She has broken with her home life and with the equally lecherous RAF men and self-hating assimilated Jewish heirs, but she doesn't feel quite at home among the Trotskyites and anarchists of Archway (halfway between Hackney and Hampstead). Her speech traits mark her out and her allegiance to the Party is little more than a bourgeois loyalty to her marriage. Ben joined the Communists after Mosley's attempt to march through the East End because they were the only ones to explain what was going on when the Board of Deputies advised Jews to keep away. Ben comes to commitment to social action out of the same conclusions as Dave Simmonds in Wesker's *Trilogy*, but he stays in the Party after de-Stalinization and Hungary, when his comrades have left. The situational dialogue of the radicals typifies the falsity of ideological positions, while as part of the dialectics between liberal humanism and socialism it remains unconvincing.

Mr. Adler's son Colin represents another trend, the conformity to the assimilatory pattern of Anglicized bourgeois suburbia. He doesn't take up the ambitious, imaginative projects of Marowitz, the *architect* of the postwar world, who wants him to test his limits and *care* for the people he builds for. Instead Colin opts for humdrum safe Wimbledon, a South London suburb where aesthetics don't go with the business of building standardized homes for standard young couples with standard nesteggs and building-society mortgages. Colin wishes to be accepted as a Briton and to lead a quiet life without thinking too much about being Jewish. He just hopes his father's fine for infringing the ration laws won't get into the newspapers and he deplores anything that might give the Jews a bad name. He's particularly uneasy at his neighbors' anti-Semitic responses to atrocities by Palestinian Jewish terrorists and at a stereotyped jibe overheard on a bus.

At the Southfields Golf Club, which doesn't have a bar against Jewish membership unlike the Royal, Colin meets the Riesmans who worship as Liberal Jews and vote as Conservatives. They detest North London Jews and are jolly pleased there aren't many Jews in Wimbledon. Their son Paul grows up into centrally-heated love and exortation to virtue, inheriting only a disdain for Jewishness and Judaism; he has no roots, nothing firm to believe and *be* in. The knowledge Paul receives from his parents of sexuality and divinity alike is cold and formal, useless.

At Benedict's, Paul's Public School, he works hard to ingratiate himself with his fellows and even shares their pleasure in persecuting Marion, the class "Jew," a label given to the ubiquitous alien and bedwetter. When his own Jewishness is rumbled he is ruthlessly victimized. His father wants him to be coached for his Confirmation, but has little sympathy for those who cannot bear pain, while the headmaster can only sigh over the trouble caused by the Jewish intrusion into his closed Anglican society. The priest can offer no consolation except that he must bear his cross, for all who suffer are Jews! Yet when Paul reads T. S. Eliot's *Gerontion* he must confront the world as a gray prison in which he is hated and vilified. Like Ben he suddenly realizes the full extent of the System and he determines to write a protest novel, except that his parents have given him no language and his expensive private education has taught him only the art of mimicry. The only tool with which to exhumate the "black, inner anguish" is an English sarcastic irony that allows of no originality. The "Jewy truth" within him stands in the way of his career and he exaggerates his monstrous and self-alienating image of himself until he becomes impotent. The only way is to write it out of himself, to kill it with satire, as the saying goes. Paul writes the Jewishness out of his hero, making him a "non-Jewish" Jew (as Pinter and Shaffer do in their plays), which is a form of literary suicide until Julia comes into his life to give him something to live for and to kill his death-wish. Yet he will not agree to be responsible for bringing another Jew into the world, which I suppose is a form of suicide by proxy.

At Cambridge Paul dives into moral philosophy and into Ayer's *Language, Truth and Logic* whose "icy articulation of language and the remorseless destructiveness of its arguments were alike agreeable to him. There was no outstanding problem which was not dealt with or eliminated. The world was the public world and all that was meaningful within it was patent and available to all; there were no secrets; save that there were no secrets." Paul is in sympathy with what he hears of Wittgenstein:

> The man who asks the question is in the best position to answer it . . . . The question which can be asked answers itself, the question which cannot be asked reveals its own absurdity. All problems which are real problems are capable of solution. Someone once said to Wittgenstein, "Professor Wittgenstein, I have a problem: I do not feel at home in the Universe." "That," replied Wittgenstein, "is not a problem, that is a difficulty!"[16]

Jewishness is not a problem, it is a difficulty, which Paul means to solve by dissolving it. Once he has detached himself from his own symptoms, he decides, there is no impediment to the extension of logical positivism to any problem in the universe. Until, that is, Paul comes to see that morality and marriage are more than expedients when given the chance to sleep with a different, non-Jewish Julia. Then he is a Jew and she is a Gentile who would prefer not to think about what the Nazis did to the Jews. To be his own self he is *forced* to be a Jew and Julia's, but to be *free* to write is to write one's self out, if one wishes to succeed.

The contradiction of being a writer and being Jewish is summed up in Paul's obviously unhealthy idea of Jewishness as a disease: "No one can cure you of being an artist. Or of being a Jew."[17] This ties in with what Bergman, a Swedish theologian Paul and Julia meet in France, says about Spinoza on freedom and necessity: to be free and necessary one must comply, one must be at one and in love with the world, with God and with nature. Hence the "absurdity of the Jew lies in his freedom, his unnecessary freedom."[18] In the end Paul agrees to a synagogue wedding, where he stamps on the traditional glass like "a man at a brothel." His is the self-consciousness of a solitary, unhappy Jew getting back at his enemies and his public school upbringing by earning success and fame. He belongs to the right clubs and subscribes on principle to liberal causes. However, success doesn't satisfy Paul and he thinks of Belsen. He speechifies that something must be done, yet there he is living with Julia in comfortable bourgeois suburbia writing about comic spies. They have neither courage nor convictions. Talking achieves nothing. In fact they are estranged from meaningful language: "words don't relate us to anything any more—all they do is make us think the unthinkable and drive us all rotten, with impossible ideas. In the end we aren't capable of anything except words, words, words."[19] This futility inclines Paul more toward wanting a child. A child would give meaning and, as Otto says, it is the only answer to Hitler. Marriage has altered Paul's freedom: to be really free the relationship between people must be necessary. Hence the "limits of love," which are tested by each character in turn. "Freedom's like contraception, it makes you think about what was never intended to be thought about."[20]

Paul discovers in the East End origins of Mrs. Adler's family a sense of community, which is meaningful and which he missed together with the "love-loving" and "life-living" Jewish tradition: "with all his heart Paul ached not that he was a Jew but that he wanted to be one."[21] However, the East End is dead and the young

Jews in the novel accept, albeit with the bitterest self-critical cynicism, the bourgeois aspirations of their parents, acquiring all the social markers of settled respectability they had earlier rejected.

Frederic Raphael would deny any affiliation with the Jewish community. For one thing, he does not subscribe to any doctrine of salvation, religious or otherwise. In any case his Jewishness is a disillusioned diaspora symbol of loneliness: "I feel myself alien from everyone. This is my kind of Jewishness."[22] Frederic Raphael illustrates the problem of the Jew born into marginality and assimilation who is confronted with the dilemma of relating to an identity enforced upon him from *outside*; as Sartre would say, "The Jew is one whom other men consider a Jew." Anti-Semitism brings the marginal, assimilated Jew to question his identity in the absence of any model of Jewishness, or at most in the light of a model contaminated by misconception and Christian symbolism. The complicity of the nations of the world—whether through action or inaction—in the Nazi genocide and the persistent prevalence of anti-Semitism, in conjunction with a rigid class structure, make it difficult for the Jew in England ever to think of complete acceptance by the Gentiles other than as a Jew. For nothing can be the same again after the Holocaust, although the petty mundane concerns of daily bourgeois living continue as if it could—a theme, incidentally, of the novel by a South African Jewish author living in England, Dan Jacobson's *The Beginners* (1966).

Such paradoxes are the stuff of which Raphael's novels and short stories are made. Moreover, identification with the six million victims of Nazism brings with it a guilt complex not only of having survived, but also of never having known the experience. One thinks here of George Steiner's self-definition as "a kind of survivor," wary of both nationalism (including the Zionist variety) and radicalism. Raphael himself comments:

> . . . the Final Solution—its vulgarity no less than its brutality, its greedy malice no less than its murderous factories—lies always at the back of my mind even if I myself, as a child growing up in England, suffered nothing more than its bad breath blowing in my face from across the Channel. It may be an indulgence for anyone who did not have closer experience to claim personal acquaintance with the holocaust; it is equally frivolous to ignore it.[23]

In his novel *The Glittering Prizes* (1976) Raphael has his Jewish hero Adam Morris carry around in his pocket the photograph of a little Jewish boy in a cloth cap with his hands up: "Me? I was eating bread and Marmite at the time—hated it—and learning amo, amas, amat."[24] Raphael had tackled the topic of identification with the Jewish victims of Hitler's Europe in *Lindmann* (1963) in which a British civil servant, a kind of Mr. Sammler figure, takes on the identity of a Jewish refugee, Lindmann, whose boat has sunk after being refused permission, with British connivance, to land in Turkey. This examination of moral guilt for one *Struma*-type incident in the destruction of European Jewry was described by its author as his "last word on the Jewish theme."[25] Yet *The Glittering Prizes* finds Raphael casting in the role of central character a Jewish writer who is sufficiently disturbed by the Holocaust to see it affecting his personal identity.

Adam—like Paul Riesman and his creator Raphael—went to a Public School in the best English tradition of private education. He gets his place at Cambridge, but leaves school with a grouse, a resentful grumble upon which he ruminates in the opening scenes. As usual, Jews must attend Chapel; the head advises, "They are not required to believe, but they are expected to attend."[26] Adam doesn't mind all that much conforming to English hypocrisy, but his blood does boil when the visiting preacher, no less than the Provost of Ipswich, makes an anti-Semitic remark in his sermon. Angered by the public endorsement from the pulpit of popular usage, Adam writes a rude letter to the school's guest speaker. Adam is soon called to the headmaster's study and given a dressing-down for accusing the preacher of "fascism"—after all, he had fought in the trenches in the First World War and was decorated for gallantry!

At Cambridge Adam has rooms with Donald whose aristocratic Catholic family are shown to be inherently anti-Semitic. Adam cannot restrain himself from bursting out that while millions were being sent to their deaths Roman Catholic priests all over Europe preached their anti-Jewish dogma and the same would have been repeated in England had Hitler crossed the Channel.

Raw youth in Cambridge in the early fifties encourages Adam to ask pertinent questions, but he is shown to be as naive and almost as ridiculous as those whom he mocks. Yet in Raphael's succinct dialogue with its seemingly facile wordplay deeply philosophical problems are being bandied about; the existence of God, Jewish identity, racial violence, the morality of commercial success and promiscuity are just some of the issues made the subject of badinage and verbal swordsmanship. Adam Morris eagerly imitates the professor who succeeded to the Chair once occupied by Wittgenstein and engages Sheila in philosophic discourse to prove the non-existence of God by showing that the existence of the deity is literally non-sense; the same test is immediately afterwards applied to the convention against premarital sex.[27] The fact that Adam wants to get Sheila into bed with him naturally cheapens his argument, but does not mitigate the agnosticism of a generation. Sheila is no intellectual match for Adam, but then few women are when he has designs on their bodies. The priest in Donald's family, too, comes to resemble something of a punch-ball; no serious intellectual opponents are stood against Adam's sweeping punches, but the ambiguities and contradictions in his position are no less clear for that.

Adam's family is a respectable middle-class Jewish household: propriety and candlesticks are prominent on the mantelpiece. The Judaism of the home is the magic ritual of candle-lighting on a Friday night, met so often in American and Anglo-Jewish fiction as the one symbol of religiosity. Of course, Adam's parents would like to see him meet a nice Jewish girl, but Adam has got better things to do on a Friday night, such as making love to Barbara who, unlike Sheila, is free of both Jewish and virginal anxieties. The usual conversation between Jewish son and Jewish parents may serve as an example of Raphael's use of dialogue for purposes of polemic; the father speaks first:

'There's a principle involved.'
'Your principle, not mine. Do we really have to pretend—?'
'Pretend what?'
'That God's in the heaven and all's right with the world. He isn't; it isn't.'
'That's your opinion.'
'That's my opinion. And I am, as they say, entitled to it.'
'You're turning your back on five thousand years.'
'I sometimes think that's the only sensible thing to do with five thousand years. Five thousand years of superstition, humbug and mumbojumbo.'
'That's what you think of your people.'[28]

This philosophical disagreement is typical of Raphael's treatment of problems of morality and identity, as Raphael puts it, "The question is, in a sense, of language."[29] Only through the dramatic conflict of words can emotional states and historical or philosophical situations be worked out in a clear form. And, one might add, in a popular form.

Adam's agnosticism (and his Jewishness) get the blame for weakening Donald's faith in Roman Catholicism. Adam's cynical disproval of all religious doctrines does encourage Donald's interest in sex, but this is an interest already awakened by the Kinsey Report which destroys for Donald the myth of the celibacy of the priesthood. Donald is dying from leukemia, but his family withholds this deadly revelation. Adam accuses the Church, embodied by Donald's uncle the priest, of purveying falsehoods while hiding truths, but Adam plays along with the ruse and lets himself be used to keep Donald in blissful ignorance. Adam the Jew is both catalyst and victim, unable to resolve the moral questions he raises. Adam reads of Donald's death when he is on holiday in Italy with Barbara and walks straight into a church with its sickening, false piety and leans on a pew as if praying.

Adam Morris is after all symbolic. He is firstly symbolic of a generation which reacted with indifference to the postwar era of austerity and gloom, to disillusion with the socialist Welfare State, to despair at the human capability for cruelty and destruction. Their response to vital issues is the zany humor of Cambridge Revues and the BBC radio series *The Goon Show*. When confronted, in the section entitled "An Academic Life," with the student activists of the next generation on the new red-brick university campuses, who march against American involvement in Vietnam, the Bomb and racial discrimination, their position is the general Cambridge "no position." Adam settles down to a happy bourgeois suburban marriage and a prosperous career as scriptwriter and novelist. Yet his is the "Double Life" of the title of his latest book and of the last section of Raphael's novel. He remains faithful to his conscience and to his non-Jewish wife although there are plenty of temptations not to. In fact he pays poor drunken Anna not to take off her clothes. He tells the ex-stripper Carol he feels guilty and it is not just something that comes with being successful. It is then that he pulls out the photo he always carries of the small Jewish boy in the Holocaust. He was only a schoolboy, learning (as quoted above) how the Romans declined "love":

> Nothing happened to me at all. I've had a charmed life, I really
> have. I don't really feel guilty about the money. I feel guilty

about being alive. At being so nice, so *agreeable.* I'm a lot nicer than I want to be, hard though that may be to believe.[30]

Indeed, he leads the life of Riley, he really wants to enjoy all the pleasures that wreck the lives of his fellows. His control over his duality is his key to survival, as the novel concludes:

> As long as he could keep just one chamber of his castle locked and its contents safe from scrutiny, Bluebeard was model husband, reliable father and responsible citizen.[31]

Adam is, if you like, an unwilling *mentsh,* the Jew despite himself. He marries a *shiksa,* but has his son circumcised. Adam does not want to be a Jew, he does not want to be a gentile, he does not know what he wants to be, yet the six million stir his emotions.[32] Marginality and assimilation are not satisfactory solutions for the Jew who has been brought up with an idea of Jewishness as an empty, meaningless symbolism, who has forsaken the Jewish home. Life continues regardless, but the very insistence on the theme suggests dissatisfaction, just as the irony of the writing presumes both mockery and disquiet.

After

Chapter Seven
Anglo-Jewish Poetry After the Holocaust: Dannie Abse and Jon Silkin

DANNIE ABSE: THE SURVIVING MISFIT

Of the many Jewish poets writing in Britain today two deserve special attention because the rootlessness of their identity is a prime force behind their being poets. However, one couldn't find two more dissimilar examples of postwar British poetry than Dannie Abse and Jon Silkin. Jon Silkin shares an instinctive distaste for Hampstead in *The Re-Ordering of the Stones* (1961) with Dannie Abse's satire of the tidy, mowed lawns of Golders Green (in "Here," *Funland*, 1973), but their approaches to the sociological actuality of Anglo-Jewry couldn't be further apart.

Dannie Abse was born in Cardiff, Wales, in 1923, and described his Welsh Jewish childhood in his novel *Ash on a Young Man's Sleeve* (1954). Here are all the usual complaints of an unbearable, interminable, fusty Jewish ritual; the mother with the endless reserve of tears; the father ambitious for his sons to be doctors and lawyers, educating them so that he can't understand what they say to him; the Rabbi mourning as dead a son who married a non-Jewess; the brother dedicated to Communism. Familiar, too, are the themes of exile and despair in Abse's depressing picture of his National Service in the Royal Air Force in another novel, *Some Corner of an English Field* (1956). Abse is one of many who took up the spirit of the times, angry at the betrayal of postwar hopes for politics, literature, education and the Welfare State. But as a Welsh-Jewish doctor-poet

Abse is the outsider among outsiders for whom England, to invert Rupert Brooke's line, will always be foreign. This double outsideness has the advantage of the ability to deftly switch personalities, the Jewish and the Celtic, as deftly as Leopold Bloom in Dublin, and it suggests a similar parallel between two threatened cultures and minorities.

In his introduction to the *Mavericks* anthology (1957), which he edited with Howard Sergeant in direct opposition to Robert Conquest's *New Lines* (1956), the programmatic anthology of the Movement, Abse defended the emotionally charged poetry of Dylan Thomas and, to explain why he was anti-Movement, equated "the romantic with the Dionysian and the Dionysian with that mysterious, permanent element in poetry that irradiates and moves us and endures."[1] From this standpoint Abse works out his alienation without identifying as a Jew, a Welshman or even a poet; in a 1963 interview on being a Jewish writer, he quotes Dylan Thomas saying that "art is an accident of craft" and goes on to say that "poetry is written in the brain but the brain is bathed in blood."[2] Poetry-making isn't a rational business and if Jewish themes creep into his work they do so, Abse claims, without conscious design, but he admits that he is a Jew aware of the situational predicament of the Jew in the twentieth century. This influences his selection of images, for instance the choice of a misfit of a tree struck by lightning rather than a tall, straight, beautiful elm, or a slow, slave-like shunter instead of an express train. In other words, far from allegorizing the Jewish condition, being a Jew conditions his poetic vision without his having to delete his self in the poem; in his poems the Jewishness is unobtrusively there and does not need to be written out to be made universal. That may be why Abse feels his more obviously Jewish subjects work less well as poems. In any case, the Holocaust has made Abse's poems more Jewish than they would otherwise have been, and, as with his contemporaries, his Jewishness is a different kind from what it would have been before Hitler: "Hitler has made me more of a Jew than Moses." The Freudian explanation of evil in society makes it inevitable and subconsciously present in our early Oedipus complex, unlike the more optimistic Marxist view of environmental determinants; as physician and father Abse must therefore see himself as a survivor and be wary of anti-Semitism even in liberal democratic England.[3] His drama *The Dogs of Pavlov* (1969) takes up the conclusions of Professor Stanley Milgram's experiments which showed how ordinary subjects could without hesitation perpetrate the worst pain on another being. As a Jew he is aware of the "night without end" afflicting the chronically sick, though he may not understand, and he questions the suffering of an "Auschwitz thin" terminal case ("In Llandough Hospital"). He is affected because being a Jew is inescapable and, even if he regards poetry as artistic fiction which doesn't necessarily reflect his own point of view, he would surely not be true to himself if it didn't deeply affect his writing and increasingly so, as can be seen in the explicit Jewish themes in *Poems, Golders Green* (1962), as well as in the rediscovery of Jewish sources (Midrash and medieval legends) in *Way Out in the Centre* (1981).

In "Surprise! Surprise!" *(Poems, Golders Green)*, Abse asks us to

Talk not of loneliness, but aloneness.
Everything is alien, everyone strange.[4]

We cannot call the familiar our own, and if we look at the world afresh, as if for the first time, one's neighbor and one's lover are revealed as unrecognizable, estranged objects. When Abse the physician looks at his patients and friends he must ask himself whether they could be beneath the familiar skin as capable of Nazism as their counterparts in Germany. Being alien one can see this and not take clichéd exteriors for granted. The sexual metaphors in "Shunters" evoke a post-Holocaust "despair beyond language" at the sight of these "numbered proletariat," "the colour of grief,"[5] for even everyday phenomena of the modern world, such as diesel engines, cannot escape the potential parallels with the Jews who were numbered and enslaved, made into things good for mechanical, repetitive, dehumanizing hard labor but not for thinking about as individual humans. That same familiarization of concepts persists in our society and calls for the alienated poet to speak his despair.

To refute the overfamiliar is to question the belonging to a hometown. In "Return to Cardiff" the poet goes back to Wales to try and catch on to "mislaid identities", while in "Red Balloon" the Jewish child's red balloon becomes a symbol of himself as a persecuted Jew. It is red with the "dear Lord's blood" in the eyes of Christian boys fed for centuries on the blood libel. Some of the boys get their knives out to circumcize it. They assault the balloon out of jealousy and longing, for, inflated and floating, its sexual function is suggestive. This Freudian version of the famous *Red Balloon* film becomes a self-searching for identity, a universalization of a personal victimization.

As writer and as Jew, or rather as writer because as Jew, Abse feels duty-bound to speak out on the release of Ezra Pound from imprisonment for collaboration with the Fascists ("After the Release of Ezra Pound"). The release of Ezra Pound is praiseworthy, but the sweater-and-jeans *intelligentsia* should not excuse

> the silences of an old man,
> saying there is so little time between
> the parquet floors of an institution
> and the boredom of the final box.[6]

If the brevity of life were to span no more than the circumference of a concentration camp, writes Abse, it would be sufficient to rouse Walt Whitman to eloquence and Thomas Jefferson to anger.

"Odd" contrasts loud, dirty but alive Soho with the conformity of Golders Green, while in "Even" (in *A Small Desperation*, 1968) Abse looks with repulsion at the hatted Jews carrying their prayerbooks to the synagogue. Afterwards his conscience frets with the "dodgy thought" that he could be an anti-Semitic, self-hating Jew, but he feels better when he reacts in the same way to a procession of Christians carrying their prayerbooks to church, because he can distinguish between his own identification with Jews and his dislike of the "pathology" of all religions, both Jewish and Christian "zealots of scrubbed excremental visions."[7] The word "dodgy" plays on risk and evasion and underscores the uncomfortable tensions between clinical diagnosis and personal involvement.

In "A Night Out" the poet takes his wife to the trendy Academy Cinema in London's West End. They watch a film about a concentration camp. Children no older than their own go "without fuss" into the gas chamber. After the film they return home, where their children have gone to bed, presumably also without much fuss, and are sleeping safely under the care of the German au-pair. The cloud-gray dreariness and futility of suburbia is clothed in a hypocritical fabric of virtue and patriotism, just as in other poems popular culture deadens awareness of violence in the real world and makes the cruelties committed in Vietnam seem untrue. The real world is absurd and insane. Only the insane and the eccentric can see that (the neurotic Jew is a bit of both). The conformists to bourgeois materialist comfort are dead to life and dead to death. The conformist goes on with daily familiar routine as if the Holocaust had never been. In "A Night Out" predictable, cautious Golders Green is juxtaposed with the personal meaning of the Holocaust and the paradox undermines the conventional marital relations in the last lines, but at the same time suggests that love is possible.

JON SILKIN IN RETROSPECT

Jon Silkin was born in 1930 of mixed Jewish and Christian parentage and attended the fee-paying Wycliffe College and Dulwich College. During the war he was evacuated to Wales where he experienced the kind of socioethnic alienation from self and community which affected Pinter, Raphael and Abse. Silkin has spoken of this in a recent poem "We Were Evacuated in the War,"[8] turning, like Wesker, to the popular image of the Jew as Shylock to express the split-personality of the Jew as writer and human being. The poet exploits the stereotype of the gold-lusting Jewish usurer, while the metaphors of mineral prospecting extract the mixed alloy of the Jew's identity and quarry the proud indignity suffered by the modern Shylock. The "dishevelled outsidedness" of the Jewish boy contrasts with the authentic gold he detects in his school-mates who enjoy an easy-natured brutishness and a belonging to clean surroundings, pastoral in comparison with the uncomfortable in-dwelling of the urban Jew. But it's with this self-knowledge that the poet comes to sexual maturity and to the rich seams and cross-shafts of language.

On completion of his military service, Silkin abandoned his comfortable Home Counties background and worked as a laborer in London. In 1952 he founded the magazine of committed writing *Stand,* which he still co-edits, and in 1958 he was appointed to a poetry fellowship at Leeds University. He has become one of the leading figures in British postwar poetry, a distinct, if at times a difficult and terse voice. To categorize him as a Jewish voice would, I am convinced, be a grevious misunderstanding of his work and his views. In his response to the Daiches-Roback-Rabin debate on Anglo-Jewish literature in the *Jewish Quarterly,* Silkin made it abundantly clear that he operates outside ethnic and national frameworks, which is not to say that he ignores the value of the writer's ethnic and national roots, but he must address the reader first as a fellow-human and only second as a Jew; the advantage of being Jewish is to be able to speak as part of a persecuted minority which, like other persecuted minorities, has something to say to the rest of humanity.[9] Elsewhere he has identified with Isaac Rosenberg as an extraterritorial writer (to borrow Steiner's phrase), a cosmopolitan poet of Judah preaching a universal moral. Silkin's Jewishness is a humanitarian universalism in which the Christian Jesus functions as a Jewish symbol of love of mankind.[10] Silkin is a committed writer in the sense that he feels we must *respond* to other cultures and realities as one way of coming to terms with post-Holocaust actuality. Since Auschwitz smoke and soap, even chairs and trees, have become frightening phenomena because of the murderous purposes they have been made to serve; language itself can never be innocent again.[11] In questioning, with Steiner, the purpose and integrity of post-Holocaust poetry, Silkin seeks to treat all human activity (which is to include *inhuman* activity) from the standpoint of the hunted fox who views nature and man as contiguous, a creature "that symbolizes much of the desperate fear and strength and cunning the hunted animal must show to the enemy":[12] "My country is a fox's country," as the poet writes in "No Land Like It" (*Peacable Kingdom*, 1954). Silkin has disdained the unequivocal identification of the fox with the poet as a Jew,[13] though Dannie Abse was not alone in reading the animals in *A Peacable Kingdom* as paradigms of the modern victim, with whom the poet, as a Jew, identifies.[14]

In his "Flower Poems" (in *Nature With Man*, 1965) the poet suggests correspondences with the human situation by substantiating the life process of each particular species of flower. Though his intelligence sets him apart, man is born of nature and one doesn't have to make nature anthropomorphic to show the contiguity of man's nature with nature. Man and plant inhabit the same existence: "I see the garden, in fact, as a kind of human bestiary."[15] The plants chosen by the poet are wild and undomesticated, but they're found in the domestic garden where they claim their own power and sensuality, their own being. "Dandelion" invites political parallels as a space-seizer, a hungerer after *Lebensraum* (compare the wind in a later poem "Brought Up With Grass"). "Bluebell" similarly explores the theme of nature's preying nature. Weeds and uncultivated plants demand observation for, like man, they are creatures which change with alarming tenacity and vicissitude.

"Milkmaids" differs from the other "flower poems" in the replacement of contiguity with direct confrontation between human and plant life. In absorbing the conditions of a prison camp the Milkmaids are themselves deeply changed:

They mount the incline breathless
Pale violet. Their eyes wide,
They halt at the wire. This is the camp.
In silent shock a multitude of violet faces
Their aghast petals stiff, at the putrescence
Of the crowd wired up. This halts them:
The showing bone; the ridges of famine,
Protusions, want, reduction.[16]

In "Nature with Man," man, unlike the ordered and and human existence of nature, is a "treacherous creature."

Monstrous and huge eye:
The entire process
of nature perverted
Into the search for him.[17]

"The Religious West," in the same collection, which draws upon Bialik, is similarly relevant to a barbaric kingdom below the Divine source of light; the sun illumines both the poem and a heap of shoes piled hgh in what is, though never identified as such, a concentration camp. Man ignores the uncomplimentary analogies with the insect and plant world and yet labors to destroy his humanity. If not actually godless, the universe has at least not endowed man with the sense of reciprocal moral care.

The Australian, Northumberland and Hebridean settings in *The Little Timekeeper* (1976) serve as a good example of how the poet localizes his experience while engaged in a search for the peaceable kingdom that never wanders far from Jewish landmarks. In "The Excellence of an Animal," a run-over cat triggers thoughts of "our dead," while the lush pleasures of connubial living jar with the brutality of the murder of six million; the plump fruit, maidenly flowers and the poet's words are rendered barren in comparison. "A Prayer Cup" is an *Akedah* poem for the "blood of six million," mixing the Jewish and Christological motifs of the sacrifice of Isaac in a communion cup. The irony is underscored that

I who write
a factious poem want the means
to bless a christian.[18]

Local roots do not confine the poet's existential fears to a single place: "The locale is an exploration of becoming; it is a means to habitation."[19] The poet's faith wavers between, on the one hand, existential fears before an immortal, everlasting eternity and, on the other hand, anxiety at a universe perceived through Clausius's formulation of entropy, which reversed a crucial assumption about the nature of cosmic energy.

> My background is a mixture of rationalist agnosticism and dilute orthodox Judaism; the bases of my spiritual clichés are identifiable in the familiar approximation of anthropomorphised eternity.[20]

If the universe is running down and cannot be wound up without some help from God, confirmation is found in the laws of nature for the poet's pessimistic vision. Theology and physics have been divorced. The poet's search for God is localized in his lament that there is no restoration of the former order, as when Jews return, after their readmission under Cromwell, to Newcastle, which had bought their expulsion, but trade has declined ("Centre of Absence"): the melancholy is irreparable.

The lament over the irreparable loss within nature itself is discernible, too, in the exilic quality of the Gaelic night in "In the Place of Absence," but nowhere more obviously than in the famous "Death of a Son" (in *The Peacable Kingdom*, 1954). The death of a son aged one in a mental hospital creates a poignant and questioning, almost accusing, absence.

> Something has ceased to come along with me.
> Something like a person: something very like one.
>   And there was no nobility in it
>   Or anything like that.[21]

The child is as a dumb stone watching his own silence within, he is as a house of mourning building the habitation of his breathing, inward silence. Despite his pathetic inability to reciprocate love, he cherishes a deeper meaning, now lost. He is not brick and stone, but flesh and blood, and worth the pity. Similarly in other poems in the same collection, such as "A Space in the Air," the noticing of absence gives rise to a realization of the fear of death of one loved, a realization of loss of what is close and meaningful. The contiguity with the animal kingdom in that poem questions man's relationship with animals and with man. In "Caring for Animals," as in the "flower poems," the creatures are domestic but not domesticated, and we are awakened by an unusual perspective on familiar objects to the need for humankindness and mercy. The mourner carries a responsibility for the suffering of the dead, who are in a way his victims, as in "A Death to Us," where contemplation of a dead fly gives meaning and purpose to the death of an insignificant frail being. George Steiner has said that genocide preempts the future by depriving it of part of its body and soul; what pains us is "absence from our present needs"[22] and much of Silkin's verse is an act of requiem for the absent dead, rather like the Jewish mourners' prayer, the *kaddish*. The mourning of the smallest, unnoticed deaths both occasions celebration and praise of life and determines the meaning of the gaps in our lives.

The martyrdom of York Jewry in 1190 in "The Coldness" (*Re-Ordering of the Stones*) creates an accusing absence which touches directly on the Holocaust, for indifference to the deaths of the city's Jews itself "deadens" York; André Schwarz-Bart chose the martyrdom at York as the starting-point of the long road to Auschwitz in *Le dernier des Justes*. Silkin writes

> All Europe is touched
> With some of frigid York
> As York is now by Europe.[23]

The irreparable absence of Jews (few returned to York) is a bodily wound, a physical lack, but it is also a corrosive on the conscience, turning the heart cold. Silkin's new poem on the York Jews, "Resting Place" (*The Psalms With Their Spoils*, 1980), looks to retribution more than indignation. The poet thinks of the irony of a municipal parking lot built on a medieval Jewish burial plot but accords his Jewish brethren—for he is also one of the dead—poetic justice. That corroded false god of Christendom, the automobile, leaks oil which drips through the clay to annoint the dead (note the play on "Judased" and "Judah'd with oil"); the oil also camphors the poet's consciousness in amnesia as he loses memory of his brethren. It is for the Church to pray the Angel of Death "made of desire and mercy" to shelter the poet's ancestors.

Fortressed in the local castle, the Jews of York chose the example of the mass suicide at Massada rather than accept forced baptism at the hands of the mob. "The Malabestia" (in *The Principle of Water*, 1976) tells the story of one of three women who left the castle, enticed by a promise of safe conduct. She recounts her conversion in spiritual and sexual terms. The arch-villain of the piece, Richard of Acaster Malbis, a baron in debt to the Jews, earns the nickname Malabestia by his merciless "charity" in according rape and death to the women who have deserted their Jewish God. Their bodies are tenanted by the god of the Church whose grace barely reaches, but the conflict of the soul betraying its God to a god betrayed, the inner conflict of the Jew in hostile Christendom, "my failed desertion, my gently abandoned roots," offers an excellent opportunity for the rootless poet to furtively enquire after rootedness.[24] The direction that enquiry may be leading can be guessed by increasing use of Jewish standpoints and Jewish sources (for instance, the Talmudic story in "It Says" of a rabbi who made his wife wait for his return and died when she shed tears.)

The collection *The Principle of Water* includes "The People," Silkin's most direct attempt to tackle the Holocaust. A concentration camp survivor, Stein, enters the life of a couple called Finn and Kye who have suffered the loss of a little boy in a mental hospital, a tragedy described in "Death of a Son," Stein brings his own record of death, a ritual of untold suffering told with sensitivity, yet which may still be untellable.

> There is no language, some say, that could speak
> of this. And some, no language that should speak.[25]

Language itself disturbs, unsettles, a hard, sometimes cruel taskmaster. It is with this knowledge that the poet melts into the grazed field in "Isaiah's Thread." He is unwilling to take up the prophet's cry, "flesh is grass," but when he sees men "automatic with rifles" defiling (in single file and defiling nature), he protests the tearing of human beasts by each other. The animal and human species are no longer merely analogous: man has usurped and perverted predatory instincts. It is to nature that the poet directs his hope for messianism:

> The fly will be appointed, the sweated ox;
> and a furred leopard, over the kids it has pastured.
>
> Lie together, grin, creep, pant, assemble;
> convene the kingdom.[26]

Biblical motifs function in a specifically post-Holocaust actuality in Silkin's poetry, but also in the context of the mutual influences of modern English and Israeli poetry (which Silkin has helped to translate, mostly Natan Zach). As for Yehuda Amichai, Amir Gilboa, T. Carmi and other modern Hebrew poets, David and Isaiah are contemporaries, albeit at times unwilled, of the linguistic crises of modernity. Silkin's acquaintance with Israel and the transmission of

Judaic images through a rural Northern English voice make the explicitly Jewish content of his universal moral no less problematic. A caged parrot in a pet-shop gives occasion to "A Word about Freedom and Identity in Tel-Aviv" (in *Amana Grass*, 1971). The parrot is also human, and being human also Jewish (like Malamud's *Jewbird*). Taught to repeat "Torah," the parrot utters its religious and Judaic plea with the harsh, hoarse devotion, which for the poet is characteristic of Torah Judaism. Its cry was placed

> by one Jew inside another. Not belonging though;
> an animal of no distinct race,
> its cry also human, slightly;[27]

The contiguity of species and race extends to the meaning of Jewishness: "suffering begets suffering." The poet, too, is a caged bird who, in the earlier "The Two Freedoms," violates the gilded freedom of two birds to satisfy man's avarice for power, although their pain makes him think of his own wings "cut and trimmed by my grey God."

If the Jew is the ultimate human being, the modern State of Israel is the ultimate place, yet not a homeland, possibly *the* land of the homeless or, as Natan Alterman has it, the most alien of all lands. Scavenging of waste products, in "Jaffa and Other Places" and "Reclaimed Area," suggests the site of an extermination camp, the Jew representing man as a refugee, but also occupier of the Arab. Nor is the Jew the unique victim—the "hunted skin" of the Negro is darker than his absence among the scorched corpses. "Divisions" uses the natural geography of the Middle East to universalize local conflicts in zoological and botanical terms. The bodies of the male dead are distinguished by their foreskins, but the female organ mourns the unique instrument it was, regardless of tribal differences. Sex anticipates absence of the dead and the intensity of that pain is one reason why the poet doubts the belief he'd partly wish for in life after death; another reason is that death delimits the act of love, qualifying its pleasure; a third that the light of a candle is defined by the limits of darkness, permanence already charred and extinct ("Conditions"). These three conditions on belief are no less terrifying than the oblivion the poet perceives in Judaism as glimpsed in a synagogue. But then he acknowledges the mystic meaning ascribed to the blanks between the words in the written Torah and it's in those spaces that the poet must seek the Divine presence.

What sustains is the love that grows from nature and the skill man puts into work before overcome by violent death (see *Killhope Wheel*, 1971), although in the opinion of Anthony Rudolf, "Silkin has *not* sought to merge poetically" the identity of Jews and English working-men but he is "a Jew true to the prophetic tradition of Judaism—which is the inspiration or origin of many radical social movements."[28] Love proves more permanent and transcendent than a flower or rock formation, or man himself; in "To My Friends" (in *The Re-Ordering of the Stones*) the agony of human life is bearable only because it must be to have meaning, whether or not overseen by a divine omnipresence; this applies even to those

> Grains of love that are burned
> In complex and primitive agonies
> In concentration camps.[29]

Silkin's Lawrentian conception of sex teaches that man matters and it matters how we treat each other, whether in intimate relationships or in international relations. In this way Silkin hedges the theological difficulty of God in Auschwitz, or the larger problem of squaring human suffering with faith in Divine Providence.

It is perhaps an historical paradox that Jews born in Christendom, after centuries of Christian psalmists, should write in the same uncircumcised tongue as they, yet with the timelessness of the Hebrew prophets. Like Dannie Abse, Ruth Fainlight, Elaine Feinstein and other Anglo-Jewish poets, Jon Silkin must, in the mediatorship of biblical imagery to contemporary social problems, contend with the Christian messiah. By the 1970s social protest in Britain had exploded into the senseless violence of the Angry Brigade, and for Silkin it is only in the prefiguration of messiahship that meaning can be returned to the earth. His Jerusalem is at once earthly and of the spirit, a theme running through the collection *The Psalms With Their Spoils* (1980):

> where flesh is, the spirit does good
> masonry; the two Jerusalems
> compact branches of stone and soul,
> a huge stark weft of praise.[30]

The cynical despair of Silkin's worldview is close to Rosenberg's picture of a cruel, ruthless Deity in *Moses*, and Rosenberg's "God Made Blind" is here relevant to Silkin's Jerusalem poems because he has jealous God kneeling to man who has fulfilled the "conditions" of being human. Jerusalem is praised for the heavenly beauty of its sensuality but also in acknowledgement of Jewish suffering in 70 C.E. at the hands of the Romans—in "Jerusalem" the phrase "Yiddisher flesh concaves" anticipates the Holocaust. The burning Temple is a Sabbath candle of white light and the white of Jerusalem stone merges into a "serene absence," the meaningfulness of overfilled space, as the poet stands by the remaining Western Wall (the *kotel*) of the temple. The poet's is to praise, for "praise is comely," as the title page quotes Psalm 147, but it's a praise which updates Shelley and Wordsworth because the modern predicament has exposed the heart of nature as man's fellow alien and beast, not consoling or sympathetic in the Romantic tradition. The Judaic desanctification of nature repudiates the Hellenistic deification of nature and brings man together with all fellow-creatures in a "fellowship of praise," as Abraham Joshua Heschel calls it.[31] Man is "in league with the stones of the field" (Job 5,23), but the community of praise in the Psalms denies anthropomorphic pantheism by speaking *to* the Creator. Silkin, as we have seen, is sceptical about sharing that object of praise, and the despair within the modern poet's blessing, addressed to a human, not Godly, reality, is that the loved one doesn't respond.

Silkin's syntax forces his poetry into sense. That sense is modified in a cryptic combination of semantic ellipsis and suggestive phonetics. As Silkin quotes Walter Benjamin on Brecht's poetry, "lapidary" describes the style developed for Roman inscriptions: brief because the chisel is heavy and brief because one speaks to posterity's many generations. "The *Lapidary Style*, brief as a cut/in stone, for it is hard to cut that."[32] "Lapidary words: for it is hard/to chisel stone; and to detain/the reader at the tomb."[33] Each poem sketches a highly visual image of a thought. As the artist draws, each line wantonly entices an interpretation and teases meanings out of signifiers unused to the strain. Silkin has been much impressed by the possibilities of language opened up by the Authorised Version of the Bible and by the Jew Osip Mandelstam (see "The Old Version"), though he has spoken also of the technical influence of Marianne Moore.[34] Silkin's concern for language, like Mandelstam's and Rosenberg's, is that of a Jew coming to his native language as to a foreign tongue, even though he is not rooted in any other language and is least fluent in Hebraic sources. This is something like the linguistic alienation attributed by George Steiner to Franz Kafka and by T. W. Adorno to Heinrich Heine: "Only he who is not truly at home inside a language uses it as an instrument."[35] Silkin's verse has been criticized as too weighty with abstraction and he has developed an even tighter style, even meaner with keys to meaning, but his invective against linguistic and moral imprisonment remains forceful. The written word *is* political and metaphysical statement, but when polemic rises above rhetoric it is usually called poetry.

Mundane concerns continue but daily joy can never be the same again after the Holocaust. However, nothing has been the same since the Roman destruction of the Temple or the medieval tragedy of York Jewry. In his recent poems collected in *The Psalms With Their Spoils* Silkin despairs at the violent cruelty of sexual passion and perhaps the despair is too great for the contractual ring of man and woman to be made whole ("Wife and Man"). In this barbarous kingdom, where Hell's Angels razor a little boy's penis ("I in Another Place"), the ploughshares are still swords, but the poet continues to celebrate that strange joy of which Isaac Rosenberg spoke in "Returning, We Hear the Larks" (1917):

> But hark! joy—joy—strange joy.
> Lo! heights of night ringing with unseen larks.
> Music showering our upturned list'ning faces.

Rosenberg's sensibility of rootlessness clearly attracts Silkin who seeks to teach wider, less Jewish lessons from Jewish suffering, but who comes back to more obviously Jewish themes in his inability to resolve the contradictions between the Jewish and Christian traditions in postwar Europe.

Chapter Eight
The Poetry of Survival

"All novels about Jewish suffering written in the post-Holocaust period must implicate the Holocaust, whether it is expressly named or not" (Alvin Rosenfeld)

". . the key concept for the Jewish creator is not marginality but relationship, not solipsism but the transmutation of tradition" (Arthur Hertzberg)

THE GUILTY SURVIVORS: RECENT TRENDS IN POST-HOLOCAUST LITERATURE IN BRITAIN

Recent developments in contemporary Jewish writing suggest a significant reappraisal of Jewish themes, primarily under the impetus of the Holocaust, or rather its delayed impact on public consciousness. Rober Alter has surveyed in the pages of *Commentary* aspects of the culture that has grown out of remembrance of the six million, and others have drawn attention to the effect of the European genocide on American fiction.[1] English poetry has been affected (see W. H. Auden's *Refugee Blues*, or Peter Porter's *Annotations of Auschwitz*), yet if for Gentile writers the fate of European Jewry teaches something about the nature of totalitarian society (as in Alan Bold's poem "June 1967 at Buchenwald") or bears witness to Freudian versions of a Christian apocalypse (as in *The White Hotel* by D. M. Thomas, 1981), then for those with Jewish blood it inevitably has personal meaning.[2]

My concluding hypothesis is that the former conflict between Jewish roots and assimilation has been succeeded by a reassessment of identity together with a reevaluation of morality under the impetus

of the Holocaust. Marginality has become no longer tenable. It was useful as a way of looking in from outside, of redeeming the word by recognizing experience as estranged, but the moral despair it entailed couldn't allow the most earnestly self-searching Jewish writers in Britain an easy identification with the culture to which they came in protest in the 1950s and which awarded them commercial success, even arrival.

The event which helped to start Anglo-Jewish writers thinking about their Jewish identities (after they had succeeded as writers who happened to be Jewish) was the 1961 Eichmann trial and especially Hannah Arendt's account of it (published in book form as *Eichmann in Jerusalem*, 1963, at the time of the premiere of Hochhuth's play *The Representative*). Arendt's own paraiah status is of course relevant, even if not entirely analogous. to the marginality of the Anglo-Jewish writer, and it served as a personal example of the first major postwar confrontation of Jew and German. What came out of the trial, or rather from Arendt's conclusions, was the utter banality of the man who was accused of sending so many human beings to their hideous deaths. He was primarily concerned all the time, Arendt insisted, with doing his job and doing his duty. His resentment at being outranked, his ambition for promotion and his elation at hobnobbing with his social superiors are all shown to be symptoms of his being absolutely ordinary. The obsession with certain memories of the past betrayed the petty vanity found in the man in the street, just as the dubious nostalgia of some of Pinter's characters shows up their frustrated mediocre aspirations. The employment of the "language rule" wraps up murderous intent in innocuous administrative procedure and immunizes personnel from confronting the human reality of their cold-blooded deeds. To penetrate euphemism language must be penetrated searchingly and to do so is a precondition of linguistic and moral survival. In *Lindmann* Frederic Raphael has inverted the "language rule" to play Wittgensteinian "language games" in order that his civil servant, faced with the awful responsibility of an order which sent hundreds of Jewish refugees to their deaths, may test the truth of language to the point when his assumed identity of Jew and survivor is shown to be a lie. When the Jewish community asks Lindmann for his mandatory contribution, he pulls out his member to show he is not one, drawing attention to the contradictions in modern man's pose as survivor and at the same time to the irony of the Jew's moral position as Holocaust victim and survivor.

The Eichmann trial was supposed to demonstrate Jewish humanity, but why should the Jews have the right to judge others? The trial, Arendt claimed, left out of account Jewish collaboration with the Nazis: she accuses them of being no less susceptible to the collapse of moral conscience. Wasn't discrimination also involved in deals with the S.S. (whether justified or not) and in the selection of eligibility for work-permits (that meant life) or in the selection for the transportation lists (that meant death) for which the Nazis calculatingly invested responsibility in Jewish bodies? And what was the meaning of judgment of a crime so unimaginably monstrous? For Arendt the trial was an attempt to publicly expiate guilt (didn't Eichmann offer to hang himself as an example to German youth?) and to find a scapegoat for all Nazi crimes against the Jews, instead of seeing Eichmann as part of a crime against humanity inflicted on the Jews. The community's need to expiate guilt through a scapegoat has been treated in C. P. Taylor's *Happy Days Are Here Again*, as well as in Bernice Rubens' *The Elected Member*. In *Good* (1981) C. P. Taylor explored the conscience of an S.S. officer attached to Eichmann's outfit who remains, to the end, a "good" person; in fact, his neuroses suggest everyman on the psychiatrist's couch, and we are reminded of our own complicity in the Auschwitz perpetrated against the peoples of the Third World, as well as our compliance with a future, final, nuclear holocaust. Halder hears bands playing at the time the Nazis come to power and this imagined music accompanies his own long march from alarm to compliance and complicity. At the gates of Auschwitz he still thinks he is hearing Schubert in his head, but this time it is real: the camp inmates are made to play while the gas chambers perpetrate the barbaric work of a music-loving nation.

George Steiner's novel, *The Portage to San Christobal of A. H.* (1981), published the same year as the first performance of *Good* and itself adapted for the stage by Christopher Hampton, goes a step further and gives Adolf Hitler, tracked down by Israeli secret agents in the South American jungle, the opportunity to justify himself. There is, of course, a danger in humanizing evil to the extent that it becomes all too understandable and even excusable. Hyam Maccoby, one of Steiner's more reasoned critics, has complained that in playing the Devil's advocate Steiner runs the risk of putting convincing arguments in Hitler's mouth which, apart from being quite untypical of his erratic racist demagoguery, might be misread as valid.[3] Indeed, A. H. repeats some of Steiner's own arguments that anti-Semitism was rooted in Gentile resentment at the impossibly demanding Jewish monotheism (see Steiner's adoption of Freudian theory in his *In Bluebeard's Castle*, 1971). According to this formula the Jews are guilty also as agents of Culture, for society would like to return to the "silence of the jungle." The Jewish writer who claims that the anti-Semitism which made the Holocaust possible is natural to the human condition, a condition of being human, does so not out of moral superiority but out of the recognition that all are susceptible to evil. Gerda Charles—who is about the last person who could be accused of self-hate—identifies anti-Semitism with universal, not national, characteristics, and fights within the Jewish community and everywhere the evil ordinary people do to each other:

> . . . from my earliest years I have seen low natures, meanness, cruelty, despicable acts committed against men's dignity and self-respect everywhere. I detested that part of my own society which bullied and despised the weak and the defenceless amongst them so much that I spent most of my early life trying to avoid it by a sort of willed sleep of my own sensibility.[4]

Only the concept of Divine Justice, "the thought that *somewhere*, somehow, the balance is being redressed,"[5] gives her faith to live on.

Arnold Wesker responded to the Eichmann trial by declaring his dream of universal disarmament, starting with Israel. The trial had failed because no judge or politician had yet summoned the imagination of a poet to see that their own thinking was conditioned by an unjust civilization bent on self-destruction.[6] Jewish commitment to nuclear disarmament was deepened by awareness of the Holocaust, as expressed in the Jewish protest group JONAH or in the plays of Bernard Kops. Yet it is surely paradoxical that on the one hand the Jewish writer claims to speak on suffering and the human predicament because he is more aware of the consequences of indifference and because he cannot deny the personal significance of Jewish history, while on the other hand he claims that to isolate specific theological, social or moral concerns in Jewish writers would be tantamount to the same kind of racism which the Jewish writer negates. One could do so, says Michael Hamburger (born 1924), speaking of German-Jewish writers (though this is equally applicable to his Anglo-Jewish colleagues), but not without running the danger of doing the same kind of violence to them in order to glorify them as the Nazis did in order to expunge them from German literature. The reason, quite simply, is that one's criteria would be reduced to racial ones . . .; and if racialism is wrong, as I believe, it is wrong for everyone.[7]

Michael Hamburger, Karen Gershon, Lotte Kramer and other refugee poets were born in Germany and came as children to England before the outbreak of war. Those who came as children often lost close relatives, sometimes all, and grew up in a lonely, strange, unchosen land, feeling guilty they had not been *there*, as Karen Gershon (born 1923) has written in "I Was Not There" (in *Selected Poems*, 1966):

The morning they set out from home
I was not there to comfort them
the dawn was innocent with snow
in mockery—it is not true
the dawn was neutral was immune
their shadows threaded it too soon
they were relieved that it had come
I was not there to comfort them . . .[8]

If she had been there, the poet would have been able to do nothing, except to, perhaps, comfort her parents, but being alive she has not even the knowledge of what she has been deprived: once her father was taken to prison "and now I have no means to know/ of what I was kept ignorant." She must atone because she is alive: "I could not have saved them from death/ the ground is neutral underneath." Unlike the camp inmates, whose lives are a memorial to what happened, whose writings, as Elie Wiesel testifies, are a remembering, the refugees do not even have the memory with which to commemorate. Their guilt at being alive (like Adam's in *Glittering Prizes*) makes their writing a *kapara* (penance) without remission.

They have been, moreover, doubly cut off from German culture, and they have had to learn all the cadences of English as a foreign language.[9] Their learned (and even learn*ed*) English opens up new possibilities, but the challenge is arduous, for they are not simply exiles: their native tongue has denied them. In 1966 Hamburger declared he was writing "for the horror-stricken. For those abandoned to butchery. For survivors. We learnt language from scratch, those people and I."[10]

Hamburger grew up in no less ignorance of Judaism than his contemporaries, Jon Silkin, Frederic Raphael or Brian Glanville, in England and with no less schooling than they in Christianity; their similar upper middle-class backgrounds bestowed upon them the privilege of Public School education. But it was Nazism which caused Hamburger to delve and explore the trauma which brought home his Jewishness. His poem on Eichmann, "In a Cold Season" (in *Weather and Season*, 1963), is one of several which record the delayed breakthrough. That poem failed, Hamburger says, because it was meant to do good, not just be good; it was meant to penetrate the complacency that mercy was somehow inferior to justice: the Jews to whom mercy was denied should have accorded it. "Retribution only buries the stench."[11] The men and women whom Eichmann had killed were to him no more than words on official papers.

Words cannot reach him in his prison of words:
Whose words killed men because those men were words.[12]

The poet could not bring himself to add one more death, Eichmann's, to the six million, because to silence the murderer of words does not flesh one word; therefore to pity Eichmann, who had no pity, for the sake of those who died for lack of pity, is to affirm the human in his victims by sparing the human in him: "Dare break one word and words may yet be whole."

In the light (or darkness) of T. W. Adorno's dictum that there can be no poetry after Auschwitz, Hamburger has called the making of language as an aesthetic object "a harmless but ludicrous and childish occupation."[13] But not only is poetry possible, it is necessary if we are not to live as if nothing had happened. In a world, as Sartre remarked in *What is Literature?*, that can do very well without literature and still better without man, poetry is the sole means to a human existence. In the case of Holocaust diarists Chaim Kaplan or Anne Frank, writing is their posthumous guarantee of at least some sort of existence, and if Celan's *Todesfuge* sounded to Adorno incongruously and even obscenely lyrical, it speaks nevertheless, or perhaps more so, because the lyricism disturbs.

Both the refugees and Jewish writers who didn't have the misfortune to have to escape Hitler must regard themselves as survivors who have to force some sense out of living *after*. They are guilty survivors who didn't have to face the prospect of being a personal victim, but they do have to face up to being victims of something much more universal and perhaps more menacing. Their proclaimed universalism is a Jewish response (the contradiction between universality and Judaism is an often-held fallacy) and Stephen Spender has suggested that survivors like Nelly Sachs may be able to deal with the Holocaust more readily than the Christian writer whose concept of tragedy is the Hellenistic idea of the personal hero.[14] The Jewish idea of national tragedy and tragedy of everyman is rooted in the Bible, it's there in Job and Jeremiah who are immediately accessible for this reason to poets as distant as Nelly Sachs and Jon Silkin.

> Your voice has gone dumb,
> having too often asked *why*.[15]

If the best expression of the Holocaust is silence, it's the silence that's inside poetry, a silence as brimful with meaning as the silences of God in the Bible, even perhaps the silence of God at Auschwitz.[16]

Hamburger's poem "Treblinka," in *Ownerless Earth* (1973), is prefaced with the words, "A Survivor Speaks," words that are charged with the anguish of one who was not there. The vividly imaged rainbow flare over the camp where the corpses are burned resembles the coat of many colors of Joseph, the chosen son and scapegoat-victim of his brothers' jealousy. The voice of the opera singer drives away cold and fear, gushing as blood from a wound with the cry of Jesus on the crucifix, "Eli, Eli . . .". That, too, is a question of the silence of God, but one which was used to justify two millenia of persecution of the Jews:

> Long we'd been dirt to be wiped off, dust to be dispersed—
> Older than he, old as the silence of God.
> In that light we knew it; and the complaint was praise,
> Was thankfulness for death, the lost and the promised land,
> The gathering up at last, all our hundred hues
> Fierce in one radiance gathered by greater darkness,
> The darkness that took our kings, David and Solomon
> Who living had burnt with the same fire;
> All our hundred languages gathered again in one silence.[17]

As for Silkin, praise for life is qualified by death, the sure knowledge of mortality and the final, determining silence. Hamburger's "At Staufen" (in *Real Estate*, 1977) looks to a contiguity with nature similar to Silkin's in the juxtaposition of mass destruction in the insect world with the man-made mass killing in the East. In Germany there remain not even gravestones to mark the poet's origins ("The

Search," in *Weather and Season,* 1963), and in the confrontation with the Christian culture in which he writes there is no return home, not even a home to return to as there was in Abse's poetic visit to Wales.

Hamburger has translated the Holocaust poets Nelly Sachs and Paul Celan, but he is also well-known for his translations of Hölderin and Rilke. What of that culture which symbolized liberal humanism, the premise of European civilization, and which was the culture of Nazi Germany? Steiner would say that when great literature or music is enjoyed down the road from the death camp (or even in the death camp) the only option is silence. But he also believes it to be the role of the critic after Auschwitz, in the age of bestiality, to preserve the values of humane liberalism by showing what to read and how to read it. The possibility of humaneness lies in the cathartic power of literature. Jon Silkin is far less optimistic about literature's civilizing role than Steiner, but he is more convinced that poetry isn't merely written out of a mimetic urge, it can change individuals, "for just as we cannot assume that the concentration camp officer wasn't reading Rilke 'well,' we may also question whether he was reading 'properly.' There is no way of knowing. There is only the parallel and endlessly disturbing coexistence of cruelty, which is worse than barbarism, with art."[18] Living *after* irrevocably alters our appreciation of the literary past. We must reread Keats, just as modern Jewish writers come to English literature with a peculiar rereading of Yeats, T. S. Eliot, Pound and the modernists, and just as Silkin would have us reread the First World War Poets, in particular Isaac Rosenberg and Wilfred Owen (Silkin's polemics in his introduction to the *Penguin Book of First World War Poetry* are highly instructive in this respect).

Owen spoke of the pity that was in the word and his poetry revealed a cruelty that preluded the Holocaust. But can poetry do justice to an unspeakable cruelty of the magnitude of Auschwitz? Certainly Silkin had to overcome apprehensions in writing "Death of a Son" that he might be desecrating the memory of the child's death,[19] but the fact that he and others have made poetry out of the deaths of six million speaks for itself. Auschwitz has rendered useless many basic moral and semantic values and the poet must find a language not debased, must fight the continuing devaluation of language and morality by the mass media which employ vulgarity and parascientific jargon, as did the Nazis and other totalitarian regimes, to obfuscate live issues. The violence of the Holocaust is a possibility to be guarded against and it requires incredible courage and gift to render imaginable the unimaginable, to make readable the unbearable (indeed what must not seem bearable!). The function of the writing act and the reading act has changed, although in the context of Jewish understanding of the literary text as the hammer breaking the rock (see Sanhedrin 34a on Jeremiah 23, 29) it has been restored.

The violence of the Holocaust overshadows the atrocity literature of the postwar years, the best of it ranging from Hiroshima scenarios (including William Golding's apocalypses) to what might best be termed the punk prose of Ian McEwan. Even the prelapsarian tranquility of Tolkein's *Lord of the Rings* is disturbed by black riders and in retrospect the century opened with an evil boding in L. P. Hartley's *The Go-Between*. The Holocaust has also been appropriated for commercial profit by William Goldman (*Marathon Man*, 1974) and Sol Stein (*The Resort*, 1980), both of which relate Hitler's attempt at genocide to sex and violence in modern America; it has even provided material for pornography (which just goes to show how much moral and semantic values have deteriorated).[20] Then there are non-Jews William Styron, in *Sophie's Choice*, and William Gass, in *The Tunnel*, who have attempted to reclaim the horrors of the Holocaust as legitimate literary material and to reclaim it from its place in Jewish history. They risk, no doubt with intent, reducing the Holocaust to another ex-taboo subject in the attack on public morality and in vindication of the sex ethic. Clive Sinclair is an example of a young Jewish short-story writer for whom the Holocaust is a literary obsession that haunts his pseudoautobiographical persona. Laughing over abortions or advertizing soap bars ("The Creature on my Back," 1978), may be good therapy for exorcizing the *dybbuk* of the Holocaust, but this makes living *after* obscene. In "Scriptophobia" (1983), set in North-West London, Sinclair exposes Hendonites as secret hedonists in a rehash of *Portnoy's Complaint* in the worst taste that explodes the Jewish community's taboo on Auschwitz in a sadomasochistic rite of expiation: the Jew sexually ravages the Daughter of Germany, relieving her of guilt while satisfying suppressed sex mania. Sinclair needs the Nazi as a sexual fantasy because the young Jew of the postwar generation bears the victim's mark of Abel, here an eternal reproach for having missed the train, for not being *there*, but also because post-Holocaust society demands desecration of both self and history, a public masturbation of both private and ethnic fantasies, as the price of admittance; and the pen is the phallic symbol *par excellence*. The sacredness of the Jew's history accuses the failure of the West in not preventing the Holocaust, while Jewish separatism is another kind of moral threat which is averted by equating it, in a perversion of logic, with fascism.

Extremist art may tend to trivialize when it breaks down the taboos on private and mass pain, but the border line between poetry and obscenity must lie somewhere within the control Alvarez accords Sylvia Plath, defending her in *Beyond All This Fiddle* (1968) from the charge of narcissism in making Dachau and Hiroshima relevant to private experience. Sylvia Plath is another sort of "guilty survivor" and perhaps it is only the poet who can approach the extremities of the unimaginable and create a way of handling despair which denies trivial responses.

However, modern Jewish writers, along with modern German writers (including Böll, Broch, Mann and Grass), have to face the effect of the Holocaust on the Western consciousness as a socioethnic, national and moral, as well as literary, dilemma. Auschwitz and Belsen may be beyond comprehension and beyond description but Frederic Raphael and others need to comprehend that it did happen and could still happen. Raphael "wouldn't try to write about Dachau,"[21] and it's not a subject directly tackled by Anglo-Jewish writers, but the very fact they were safe while their brethren were burned across the narrow stretch of the Channel threatens their tranquility and disturbs their conscience. Obsession with identity may be explained in terms of the need for expiation, while in coming to terms with the Holocaust, nearly two decades after the Final Solution, they had to come to terms with a Jewishness forgotten or unknown and negated by their inbred marginality and assumed status of assimilation in a society largely complacent about the fate of six million Jews.

Having learned from centuries of persecution and degradation, the Jew erroneously thought that abolishing tribal differences would end discrimination. Disillusion, resentment and cynicism have crept in. On the one hand, such barbarism might seem to reinforce the liberal humanist standpoint that Auschwitz and Hiroshima serve identical warnings on intolerant mankind. On the other had, more and more it is remembered that the horrors of the Holocaust exceeded anything in the realm of the human imagination and that it was the Jews who were systematically and impassionately singled out for extermination, albeit together with Gypsies and other "undesirables," in the heart of civilized Europe, while the world remained silent.

So What After Marginality? Instead of a Conclusion

The general popularity of ethnicity, exemplified by Alex Haley's *Roots*, and the particular rise of Jewish consciousness have spread, on a smaller scale, from the United States to Britain, while the international mass screening of the television series *Holocaust* has certainly done something to make the tragedy of the Holocaust widely accessible, if it has achieved nothing else. There does not exist a large Jewish readership in Britain and one cannot speak about Jewish writers in England of the stature of Bellow, Malamud or Roth. On the other hand, English has become the international language of Jewish culture and Jewish cultural mediatorship as previously German was for Heine and Zweig, Rosenzweig and Buber, Kafka and Herzl. Yet the Jew in English literature has a special and complex history, from *The Prioress's Tale* through the Shylocks and Fagins to both James Joyce and T. S. Eliot.

Anglo-Jewish writers who have recently dealt with Jewish themes are, by and large, removed from a Jewish background, may be highly assimilated and, in quite a few cases, have married out. They can speak of no direct experience of traditional Jewish life; there would seem little motivation for them to chronicle contemporary Jewish actualities and, indeed, they would not always agree to be labelled Jewish writers. Yet almost all of them have been moved by the Holocaust into re-examining Jewish identity. To take a couple of examples, Alexander Baron established himself as one of the first writers of Second World War fiction with his *From the City, From the Plough* (1948), yet a personal incident aroused his identification with the victims of the Holocaust; his interest in the survivor's guilt is expressed in his novel *The Lowlife* (1963), whose hero Harryboy Boas could only be a Jew.[22] Brian Glanville, another popular novelist of the 1960s, calls himself the first to write serious fiction about football and he often emigrates to Italy in his books; yet he has spoken of being obsessed and horrified by the Holocaust.[23]

One does not have to refer directly to Jewish themes for the influence of the Jewish experience to be felt, and several of the writers discussed in this book have translated it into universal terms or else written it out. Alexander Baron, for example, has spoken of unavoidable Holocaust associations in almost everything he thinks of, though he deletes such associations from his writing when they appear irrelevant: this is one therapeutic way of dealing with an unavoidable fact, or mental blockage, in the writer's creative self, though not as productive, I think, as the translation into metaphor, of which Harold Pinter and Dannie Abse are examples. In this they share an identity with the so-called refugee poets—those who came as children—who metaphorize the Holocaust into a poetry of survival, and this is one means by which they cope with their Jewishness, with their burden, or gift, of suffering. Karen Gershon, for example, has returned to biblical motifs in *Coming Back From Babylon* (1979) and has described the helplessness and guilt of one who must lose a son in "The Death of King David's Baby," a poem not nearly as powerful as Silkin's "Death of a Son" but which also sees bereavement as a fact of life's joys. Similarly, in Gershon's obviously allegorical tale of a woman condemned to die from chronic poliomyelitis, *Burn Helen* (1980), the prospect of sure mortality gives new meaning to moral responsibility and emotional relationships. Life as a struggle with death is akin to Elie Wiesel's appraisal of the protracted death of concentration camp inmates. And it should not be surprizing that traditional Jewish responses should be appropriate to the modern predicament of living *after*, even if the experience is no longer to be thought of as an exclusively Jewish burden.

The consciousness of exile, of being a victim, of bearing guilt not one's own is now

> the common heritage of a generation of survivors and displaced persons. Auschwitz has entered deeply into the soul of modern man: it functions as fundamental metaphor, as archetype. All mankind is waiting for Godot in a treeless wilderness in which fear, insult, barbarism, and outrage form the quotidian reality.[24]

Whether or not one recognizes the Jewishness of these central themes in modern literature, the sense of alienation and exile that is the Jew's do provide a key to the concerns of Saul Bellow, Bernard Malamud and Philip Roth, as well as Harold Pinter, Dannie Abse and other Jews writing in Britain.

> 'We are all Victims,' replied the old man. 'All of us. The Age of the Martyr is over; the Age of the Victim has begun.'[25]

Speaking of Bellow and American Jewish writing, David Daiches defined the Jew in modern literature as the archetypal victim, the thermometer of social injustice:

> The Jew is more vulnerable than others, more sensitive, more troubled by the relation between his true self and the society

in which he lives, more anxious to find out the truth about the problems which enmesh him.[26]

The universalization of the meaning of being Jewish appears with variations from Arthur Miller's novel *Focus* (1945), in which anti-Semitism teaches moral action, to Malamud's notion in *The Assistant* (1957) that being Jewish is to suffer, it is being human, only more so. In both these cases the role of Jew is usurped by a Gentile, as it is in Raphael's *Lindmann*. In Wesker's *Trilogy*, too, the lessons of the Jewish intellectual are directed at the Gentile working-class, in the case of the play *Roots* an uneducated Norfolk family. Whatever anti-Semitism the Jewish writer may have encountered during National Service and whatever the misgivings aroused by the sinking of the *Struma*, the Anglo-Jewish writer addresses an English audience and more often than not the poetic metaphors are set against English landscapes.

For none of the writers mentioned has Israel provided a real alternative of Jewish identity, not even the alternative tried and failed, as in Dan Jacobson's *The Beginners*. In Raphael's *The Limits of Love* Israel raises, briefly, the question of divided loyalties during the Suez Crisis. The availability of a Jewish homeland for the committed Jew in Glanville's *The Bankrupts* does little more than emphasize, as if further emphasis was needed, the vacuity of North-West London, whose armchair Zionists are mortally shocked if their children should think of settling there. When Bernard Carter is tragically killed by an Arab bullet, Rosemary horrifies her parents by deciding to have her illegitimate baby on a kibbutz—at once abandoning her parents' values and returning to the larger Jewish family. In Gerda Charles' *The Crossing Point* Israel is ideal as a fund-raising project and Zionism is heart-felt, but the reality of settling there is not so desirable. Disappointment with the experimental agricultural training scheme is felt here, as it is in Chaim Bermant's *Jericho Sleep Alone,* and there is an arrogant Israeli student who is criticized for his lack of English civility. The Zionist youth movement in East London attracted Bernard Kops and Arnold Wesker for a while, but even that small involvement was no doubt elicited by negative attitudes toward the British political scene, as well as a vague sense of guilt at not being more involved in the fact of Israel's existence after the Holocaust. Perhaps that is what Chaim Bermant had in mind when he wrote of his visits to Israel, "I keep returning like a criminal to the scene of his crime."[27] In 1967 Jewish writers rallied round when it seemed Israel faced annihilation, but enthusiasm faded together with fears of another Holocaust, though the prominence of Israel in the news was a reminder of threatened identity.[28] Indeed, the portrayal of the modern state of Israel, whether passionately for or against, with all its challenges of identity and survival, has attracted not Jewish but Gentile writers—Muriel Spark's *The Mandelbaum Gate* (1965) and Lynne Reid Banks' *An End to Running* (1962) and *Children at the Gate* (1968) spring to mind.

Apart from perrenial family sagas,[29] Jewish themes are dealt with mainly by serious writers with little affiliation and little affinity with the Jewish people. They are drawn to the problem of Jewish identity, and specifically to the problem of identity in relation to the Holocaust, to an extent incommensurate with their distance from the Jewish experience. Those writers who are committed to traditional Judaism (such as A. C. Jacobs) or who have plighted their troth to life in Israel (as Chaim Bermant finally did) clearly do not face the same conflict of identity, although their attitudes may be equally critical.

The documentation of Jewish life in England in the novels of Zangwill and Golding assumed the ability of Jews and Gentiles to live together; that assumption died at Auschwitz together with the humane ideal. The disillusion of the radical idealists and the disintegration of the Jewish East End in the novels and plays that came from the East End writers are themes which have run their course, although Bernard Kops and the South London playwright Michael Hastings have offered the lessons of the Jewish immigrant experience to the new generation of immigrants from Asia and Africa.[30] It seems, as Albert Memmi said in 1966, as though the Holocaust has "inaugurated a new era in the history of Jewish literature as . . . in that of the ex-colonized"[31]: it is the ex-victims' turn to speak and to write history. Now has come the turn of a new search for symbolic identity and moral responsibility in a demoralized post-Holocaust world. If the Jewish experience during the Second World War taught universal lessons, then universal themes have, in a sense, become Jewish themes, and Wesker, Raphael and Silkin serve as different examples of an increased awareness of this.

The obvious paradox in modern Jewish writing in English suggests that "one possible definition of a Jew is to say that he is a man who, when he speaks of his condition, will in some measure speak for all other Jews but in a great measure for none,"[32] or as

Nathaniel Tarn once saw himself before adopting his American identity, locked

> In the synagogue of my body,
> in the flesh that is all Jew,
> though that flesh has thoughts
> which are all men's and not bound
> by race or kinship, . . .[33]

Beyond marginality the Jew must accept the responsibility of ethnic community and yet be accepted as a member of the writer's community. In many ways the reappraisal of Jewishness has enabled that step beyond marginality, so that the Jewish view of things, not least the Jewish use of biblical themes, is gradually accepted as less parochial and also accepted less condescendingly than it was in Isaac Rosenberg's day. The Jewish voice claims as much place in British culture as the Roman Catholicism of Graham Greene or T. S. Eliot, as the Scots dialect of MacDiarmid, and as the reggae beat in music. Alvarez has suggested in *The New Poetry* that the Jewish contribution is the post-Holocaust European perspective; this "foreign" note may be welcome and legitimate in the regional and cultural devolution of British life, however unsure Britain's commitment to political devolution or to full integration into Europe may be. To resent the Jewishness of a poet such as Dannie Abse as "overdone" or "irritating" is to ignore the urgency of the Jewish message.[34]

Notes

NOTES TO INTRODUCTION

1. Whether the Jewish writer's attacks on the Jewish community are anti-Semitic has long been the subject of a debate in the United States that has ranged from Philip Roth's "Writing About Jews" and "Imagining Jews" (collected in *Reading Myself and Others*, 1975) to Robert Alter's "Defaming the Jews," *Commentary*, 55, 1 (1973), pp. 77–82. Alter's comment, that in the destructive satire of some Jewish writers "the tearing down is a moment of painful self-knowledge," hits upon a truth, I think, which illuminates the premise from which the post-Emancipation Jew writes: when acculturated and assimilated, the writer who secretly wishes to be a Jew at home and a non-Jew on the street must live within the reaches of schizophrenia.

2. Fein, "Contemporary Jewish-American Poetry,"*Judaism*, 14, 4 (1965), pp. 389–98.

3. Bloom, "A Speculation Upon American Jewish Culture," *Judaism*, 31, 3 (1982), pp. 266–73; Alter, "The Jew Who Didn't Get Away: On the Possibility of an American Jewish Culture," *Judaism*, 31, 3 (1982), pp. 274–86.

4. See Carole Gerson, "Some Patterns of Exile in Jewish Writing of the Commonwealth," *Ariel*, 13, 4 (1982), pp. 103–14.

5. For the problems of writing in English in Israel faced by poets Dennis Silk, Karen Alkalay, Edward Codish, Richard Flantz and Richard Sherwin, see Sherwin, "Writing Poetry in English in Israel," *Shdemot*, 16 (1981), pp. 54–61, and Jonathan Wilson, "English Poetry in Israel," *The Literary Review*, 26, 2 (1983), pp. 310–14.

6. George Woodcock and others have noted that for Jewish Canadian writers after the Second World War the angry youth at odds with family or

neighbors is merely the aspect they know best of the individual in revolt against society at large. Much of this is true for Anglo-Jewish authors as well.

7. Lucien Goldmann, "The Sociology of Literature: Status and Problem of Method," *International Journal of Sociology*, 19, 4 (1976). For a fuller discussion see Goldmann's *Pour une sociologie du roman* (Paris: Gallimard, 1964); Michel Zéraffa, in his *Roman et société* (Paris: Presses universitaires de France, 1971), argues eloquently for the integrity of sociology and aesthetics. J. L. Talmon declared in a public lecture of 1956 that only literature could define the intangible Jewishness of the Jewish experience: "Jewish impulses and reactions, attitudes and sensitiveness, Jewish modes of feeling and patterns of behaviour call for the intuition of the artist, and indeed can only be intimated by symbols, conjured up by poetic incantation, and communicated by the art of the novelist. In brief, the Jew is part of a collective destiny, even when he does not know it or is unwilling to share in it." (*The Unique and the Universal: Some Historical Reflections*, London: Secker and Warburg, 1965, p. 70). This is also cited by Harold Pollins in his argument for the historical value of Jewish writing, "Sociological Aspects of Anglo-Jewish Literature," *Jewish Journal of Sociology*, 2 (1960), 25–41.

8. Isaac Deutscher, *The Non-Jewish Jew* (New York: Oxford University Press, 1968).

9. The situation of the Anglo-Jewish writers who knew little or no Yiddish contrasts with the influences of Biblical and Yiddish styles on Bellow, Agnon, Borges and others which are explored in Murray Baumgarten, *City Scriptures: Modern Jewish Writing* (Cambridge: Harvard University Press, 1982). As will be seen below, the Yiddish tradition and Jewish values had to be rediscovered by Anglo-Jewish writers.

10. Josephine Zadovsky Knopp, *The Trial of Judaism in Contemporary Jewish Writing* (Urbana: University of Illinois Press, 1975).

11. On Nakhman as a model for Yiddish writers see Howard Schwarz, "Rabbi Nachman of Bratslav: Forerunner of Modern Jewish Literature," *Judaism*, 31, 2 (1982), pp. 211–24.

NOTES TO CHAPTER 1

1. A recent appraisal of Disraeli's literary output is T. Braun's *Disraeli the Novelist* (London: Allen & Unwin, 1981).

2. For the background of Anglo-Jewish history see Cecil Roth, *A History of the Jews in England*, 3rd ed. (Oxford: Oxford University Press, 1964).

3. See Harold Fisch, *The Dual Image* (London: World Jewish Congress, 1971).

4. Brian Glanville, "The Anglo-Jewish Writer," *Encounter*, 24 (1960), p. 63. The beginnings of the Jewish novel in England have been surveyed by L. Zatlin, *The Nineteenth-Century Anglo-Jewish Novel* (New York: Twayne's, 1982).

5. On Zangwill see Joseph Leftwich, *Israel Zangwill* (London: Clark, 1957); M. Wohlgelernter, *Israel Zangwill: A Study* (New York: Columbia University Press, 1964); E. B. Adams, *Israel Zangwill* (New York: Twayne's, 1971).

6. Harold Fisch, "Israel Zangwill: Prophet of the Ghetto," *Judaism*, 13, 4 (1964), pp. 407–21.

7. Ibid., p. 409.

8. Zangwill, *Children of the Ghetto: A Study of a Peculiar People* (London: Heinemann, 1893), p. 240.

9. Ibid.

10. Ibid., p. 241.

11. Zangwill quoted in V. D. Lipman, "Introduction," in Israel Zangwill, *Children of the Ghetto* (Leicester: Leicester University Press, 1977), p. 8.

12. *Children of the Ghetto* (London, 1893), p. 246.

13. Ibid., pp. 55–6.

14. Cf. Frank Montagu Modder, *The Jew in the Literature of England* (New York: Meridian, 1961), pp. 310–46; David Philipson, *The Jew in English Fiction*, 5th ed. (New York: Bloch, 1927), pp. 161–207.

15. Dan Jacobson, "Jewish Writing in England," *Commentary*, 37, 5 (1964), p. 50.

16. Jon Silkin, *Out of Battle: The Poetry of the Great War* (London: Oxford University Press, 1972), pp. 272–3.

17. Dennis Silk, "Isaac Rosenberg, 1890–1910," *Judaism*, 14, 4 (1965), pp. 462–74. For full-length studies of Rosenberg see Joseph Cohen, *Journey to the Trenches: The Life of Isaac Rosenberg, 1890–1918* (London: Robson Books, 1975); Jean Liddard, *Isaac Rosenberg: The Half-Used Life* (London: Gollancz, 1975); Jean Moorcraft Wilson, *Isaac Rosenberg: A Biography* (London: Cecil Woolf, 1975).

18. See also Alexander Baron's obituary for Louis Golding, *Jewish Quarterly*, 6, 1 (1959), p. 3.

NOTES TO CHAPTER 2

1. Walter Allen, *Tradition and Dream* (Harmondsworth: Penguin Books, 1965), p. 299. The impossibility of making *a priori* statements about England in the fifties and sixties, of knowing the direction anything was taking, is reflected in Arthur Koestler's entertaining collection of *Encounter* essays, *Suicide of a Nation?* (New York: Macmillan, 1964). Equally instructive are V. Bogdanor and R. Skidelsky, eds., *The Age of Affluence, 1951–1964* (London:

Macmillan, 1970); Anthony Sampson, *Anatomy of Britain Today* (London: Hodder and Stoughton, 1965).

2. Allen, p. 310.

3. Postwar British novelists who reach back to former pre-modernist, almost Victorian, modes and who are nostalgic of the past order (Anthony Powell, Evelyn Waugh, C. P. Snow) are often said to manifest a typically English ideology that still accepts the liberal humanitarian ethos as viable, that sees no crisis when everything seems to be in crisis; though Malcolm Bradbury denies the accuracy of this cliché in a culture as essentially eclectic and pluralist as postwar Britain (*Possibilities: Essays on the State of the Novel*, New York: Oxford University Press, 1973, pp. 172–3). However, there is no doubt something in it which emphasises a further reason for the modern Jewish writer's alienation from mainstream English writing and attraction to the fringe, to experimental writing, to symbolic fantasy or to the social realism of the angry school. The term "angry young man" was in fact a political label originally applied to the angry youth in left-wing politics in the 1930s by Leslie Paul in his *Angry Young Man* (1951); its misapplication to the youth of the fifties spread in the mass media to all kinds of areas which did not necessarily have anything to do with that generation of young men who burst onto the cultural scene and who expressed their distaste for both the establishment and the social caste system which had denied them admittance but now accorded them success.

4. See V. D. Lipman, *Social History of the Jews in England, 1850–1950* (London: Watts, 1954); Lipman, "Trends in Anglo-Jewish Occupations," *Journal of Jewish Sociology*, 2 (1960), 201–18. Stephen Aris has suggested that Jewish businessmen intuitively knew what the market needed (*The Jews in Business*, London: Cape, 1970) and Wolf Mankowitz has made the knack of caring about what the public wanted an integral part of his characters' Jewishness.

5. Many non-naturalized Jewish refugees were lumped together with resident German Nazis as enemy aliens and subjected to professional and personal restrictions, an experience described by Maurice Levinson, *The Trouble With Yesterday* (London: Peter Davies, 1946); Leo Kahn, *Obliging Fellow* (London: Nicolson & Watson, 1946). The alien's view which saw the funny side of the British is exploited by Hungarian-born George Mikes, *How to be an Alien* (London: Deutsch, 1946) and Victor Ross, *Basic British* (1956).

6. See J. Sonntag, "Editorial," *Jewish Quarterly*, 1, 1 (1953), pp. 5–8. Lionel Kochan gave voice to a common plea for a sort of gourmet Jewishness that would be demanding and versatile, modern and secular, but neither assimilated nor Orthodox ("Judaism for the Intellectual" (1967), reprinted in Jacob Sonntag, ed., *Jewish Perspectives: 25 Years of Modern Jewish Writing (A Jewish Quarterly Anthology)* (London: Secker and Warburg, 1980), pp. 51–63; henceforth *Jewish Perspectives*).

7. David Daiches, "The Possibilities of an Anglo-Jewish Culture," *Jewish Quarterly*, 3, 1 (1955), p. 39.

8. Chaim Bermant, *Troubled Eden: An Anatomy of British Jewry* (New York: Basic Books, 1970), pp. 163–4. Nominally it was a question of the Chief Rabbi's authority to approve appointment of ministers (local synagogue rabbis), but there was also the issue of Jacobs' unacceptable views on divine revelation expressed in his book *We Have Reason to Believe* (1957), which led to the blocking of his promotion to head of Jews' College, the theological seminary associated with London University, and then to the blocking of his reappointment as rabbi of the New West End Synagogue. The national press took up the affair and Jacobs led a small splinter group away from the United Synagogue (see the *Jewish Chronicle*, 29 December 1961 and 13 March 1964). But more than anything the Jacobs affair indicated that the United Synagogue was, at least in the eyes of the media, out of touch with its rank and file members, or, to look at it differently, had failed to meet the challenge because it lacked a new young dynamic leadership which might bring people back to Torah Judaism.

9. Lynne Reid-Banks, "Why Must They Indulge in Self-Flagellation?" *Jewish Observer*, 17 February 1977. See chapter 6 below.

10. See Stephen Sharot's comparative study of secularization and religious affiliation *Judaism: A Sociology* (Newton Abbot: David and Charles, 1976). In a British National Opinion Poll conducted in 1971, 68% of United Synagogue members said they drove on the Sabbath, compared with 84% of members of Liberal or Reform synagogues (Sharot, p. 162). 85% of Jews questioned by Krausz in 1963 in the North-West London suburb of Edgware lit sabbath candles, but only 31% refrained from eating non-kosher food outside the home and 11% did not ride on the Sabbath (ibid., p. 218). The overall statistical picture suggests that observance of domestic rituals (candle lighting, Passover meal, kosher kitchen) is higher in preference to observance of public rituals (Sabbath observance or the prohibition of eating out) which might mark Jews from their neighbors. Further, motivation for synagogue affiliation is frequently explained by a wish for the children to grow up as Jews, the synagogue functioning as a social meeting place and marriage market to deter exogamy. United Synagogue membership held its own in the years 1930–1970, and, as the synagogue does not have the sort of acculturating role which it has in the United States, one cannot resist the sad conclusion that private hypocrisy has been institutionalized.

11. Quoted in Bermant, *Troubled Eden*, p. 4.

12. See, for just one example, a poem by Frederic Raphael, one of the recruits to the 1967 Writers for Israel Committee, written during the Lebanese Civil War, "Ode to a Syrian Armoured Division," *Jewish Quarterly*, 24, 4 (1976), p. 48. Raphael has published his 1977 remarks on Jewish identity and Zionism as "Leaves from a Notebook," *Jewish Quarterly*, 29, 2–3 (1981), pp. 9–12.

13. T. R. Fyvel, "The Jewish New Wave," *Jewish Chronicle*, 13 September 1963, New Year Section, pp. 37, 44.

14. See Dan Jacobson, "Jewish Writing in England," *Commentary*, 28 (1964), pp. 46–50.

15. Pearl Kazin, "Jews in Cardiff," *Commentary*, 19 (1955), p. 403.

16. Brian Glanville, "The Anglo-Jewish Writer," *Encounter*, 24 (1960), p. 62. See chapter 6 below.

17. Ibid., pp. 62–4.

18. Philip Hobsbaum, "A Peep into the Mirror: Problems of the Anglo-Jewish Writer," *Jewish Chronicle*, Literary Supplement, 8 December 1967, pp. vii–viii.

19. Irving Howe, "The Lost Young Intellectual: A Marginal Man, Twice Alienated," *Commentary* (October 1946), p. 361.

20. Howe, *A Margin of Hope: An Intellectual Autobiography*, (London: Secker and Warburg, 1983), p. 137.

21. The influence of the demographic change has been previously noted in S. E. Tabachnick and W. Baker, "Reflections on Ethnicity in Anglo-Jewish Writing," *Jewish Quarterly*, 21, 1–2 (1973), pp. 94–7.

NOTES TO CHAPTER 3

1. V. D. Lipman, *Social History of the Jews in England, 1850–1950*, pp. 94–101.

2. Moses Angel, for over fifty years headmaster of the Jews' Free School, complained in 1870 that his pupils "were ignorant even of the elements of sound; until they had Anglicized or humanized . . . they knew neither English nor any intelligible language"—Yiddish supposedly being unintelligible and uncivilized (cited in L. P. Gartner, *The Jewish Immigrant in England, 1870–1914* (London: Allen and Unwin), p. 223). On the other hand, by 1911 Reverend S. Levy could report to a conference of Anglo-Jewish ministers that so few East End children spoke Yiddish that sixty percent would have to be taught it if they were to gain any benefit from the traditional evening Hebrew Bible classes at the Talmud Torah, which were conducted in that language (Lipman, *Social History*, pp. 148–9).

3. William Goldman, *East End My Cradle*, (1940; revised edition, London: Art and Educational Publishers, 1947), p. 204.

4. Emanuel Litvinoff, "Author's Note," *Journey Through a Small Planet* (Harmondsworth, 1976), p. 9.

5. Ibid.

6. Dannie Abse, "Portrait of a Jewish Poet," *Jewish Quarterly*, 1, 4 (1954), pp. 16–22.

7. "Struma", *The Untried Soldier* (London, 1942), p. 24.

8. Litvinoff, *Notes for a Survivor* (Newcastle, 1973), p. 9. For an account of the public reading of the poem see Dannie Abse, *A Poet in the Family* (London, 1974), pp. 130–3.

9. *Notes for a Survivor*, p. 9.

10. James Vinson, ed., *Contemporary Novelists*, revised edition, (New York: St Martin's Press, 1976), pp. 828–9.

11. "Author's Note," *Journey Through a Small Planet*, p. 10.

12. *Journey Through a Small Planet*, pp. 79–80.

13. *The Penguin Wolf Mankowitz*, Harmondsworth, 1967, p. 264.

14. "Writing for Discovery," *Jewish Quarterly*, 13, 1 (1965), pp. 13–14.

15. Jacob Sonntag, ed., *Jewish Perspectives*, p. 83.

16. Ibid., p. 82.

17. *The World is a Wedding* (London, 1963), p. 15.

18. Ibid., p. 114.

19. Ibid., p. 190.

20. Ibid., p. 219.

21. Ibid., p. 252.

22. "Children of Two Inheritances: How It Worked Itself Out," *Commentary*, 15, 3 (1953), pp. 272–9.

23. See David Aberbach, "Freud's Jewish Problem," *Commentary*, 69, 6 (1980), pp. 35–9.

24. Cf. Zena Smith Blau, "In Defense of the Jewish Mother," in Peter I. Rose, ed., *The Ghetto and Beyond: Essays on Jewish Life in America* (New York: Random House, 1969), pp. 57–68. Professor Fisch has suggested that the Yiddishe Mama is not originally a Jewish archetype at all, but is first found in the person of Mrs. Morel in D. H. Lawrence's *Sons and Lovers* ("Fathers, Mothers, Sons and Lovers: Jewish Patterns in Literature," *Midstream*, 18, 3 (1972), pp. 37–45), though the Biblical Matriarch Sarah seems a more obvious model. The Yiddishe Mama also appears briefly in the Circe episode of James Joyce's *Ulysses* when Bloom's father is blessing his son, prefigured as Isaac, *agnus dei*, with feeble vulture-like talons, while admonishing him for leaving the Jewish God and home, for running after *goyishe nakhos* (or *"goim nachez"* as Joyce has it): "nice spectacles for your poor mother!" Aubrey imagines his mother metamorphosized into a gigantic Kafkaesque spider that stalks the East End and prevents his escape; this fits the paradigm in modern Jewish writing of the weak father being devoured by the ravenous Yiddishe Mama, a mother creature of prey nagging about food. Aubrey feels just as guilty as does Bloom toward his father and as anxious about sexual attainment, though more virile (potentially) than Alex Portnoy turns out to be when he comes to roost, briefly, in the womb of modern Israel. The Yiddishe Mama breeds a disabling Oedipus complex (or mock complex), and a profane *akeda* (sacrifice of Isaac) symbolizes that castrating wound.

25. See Milton M. Gordon, "Marginality and the Jewish Intellectual," in Peter I. Rose, ed., *The Ghetto and Beyond*, pp. 477–91.

26. Kops, *Four Plays* (London, 1964), p. 21.

27. Ibid., p. 29.

28. Ibid., p. 86.

29. Ibid., p. 9.

30. Fisch, *The Dual Image*, pp. 127–30.

31. Ibid., p. 129.

32. Traschen, "*Hamlet's* Modernity," *Southern Review*, 18, 3 (1982), 522.

33. Kops, "The Young Writer and the Theatre," *Jewish Quarterly*, 8, 3 (1961), pp. 19–20, 22.

34. Kops, "This Time," *European Judaism*, 4 (1982), p. 46.

NOTES TO CHAPTER 4

1. "Some Aspects of Anglo-American Jewish Fiction," in *Jewish Perspectives*, pp. 103–11.

2. *Tradition and Dream* (Harmondsworth, 1965), pp. 342–52.

3. John Allin and Arnold Wesker, *Say Goodbye—You May Never See Them Again: Scenes from Two East End Backgrounds* (London, 1974), p. 2.

4. Wesker in *Encore* (1959), cited in Charles E. Spencer, "Arnold Wesker as a Playwright," *Jewish Quarterly*, 7, 1 (1959), p. 40.

5. See Jerry White, *Rothschild Buildings: Life in an East End Tenement Block, 1887–1920* (London, 1980).

6. Wesker cited in Spencer, "Wesker as a Playwright," p. 40.

7. *I'm Talking About Jerusalem* in *The Wesker Trilogy* (Harmondsworth, 1964), p. 206.

8. Allin and Wesker, *Say Goodbye*, p. 27. The nostalgia, not for the buildings themselves, which were scarcely appealing, but for the people in them, is an East London attitude that is not exclusively Jewish, as can be judged from a typical statement by one resident of Bethnal Green: "I suppose the buildings in Bethnal Green aren't all that good, but we don't look on this as a pile of stones. It isn't the buildings that matter. We like the people here" (Michael Young and Peter Willmott, *Family and Kinship in East London* (Harmondsworth: Penguin Books, 1962), p. 44). It was common for parents and close family to live a few doors away from each other and to be closely involved in each others' lives, a proximity which paradoxically was liable to cause friction.

9. See the September 1959 interview with Wesker in L. Kitchin, *Mid-Century Drama* (London, 1960), p. 135.

10. Ronald Hayman, *Arnold Wesker* (London, 1970), p. 4.

11. As can be seen from Robert Benewick's account in *The Fascist Movement in Britain* (London, 1972), pp. 225–32, Wesker has placed Dave and Prince in the forefront of the Battle of Cable Street, in contrast to other childhood memoirs where the narrator is more often than not a juvenile bystander.

12. *The Wesker Trilogy* (Harmondsworth, 1964), p. 41.

13. Ibid., p. 62.

14. Ibid., p. 63.

15. Ibid., pp. 72–3.

16. Ibid., pp. 73–4.

17. Note the way Ronnie symbolically replaces Harry on the stage and appears to Sarah as in a dream.

18. *The Wesker Trilogy*, p. 70.

19. Cited in Kitchin, *Mid-Century Drama*, p. 195.

20. Wesker cited in Hayman, *Arnold Wesker*, p. 4. Wesker gives an example of the boys in Edward Bond's *Saved* (1965), who stone a baby to death, and a recent illustration of what he means is Steven Berkhoff's *East* (1977) or the reactionary pig-headedness of Alf Garnett (the original Archie Bunker) in Johnny Speight's television series *Till Death Do Us Part*.

21. *The Wesker Trilogy*, p. 145.

22. Ibid.

23. Kops, *Four Plays*, pp. 253–4.

24. *Wesker Trilogy*, p. 163.

25. For a discussion of the connection between Marxist alienation, Brechtian *Verfremdung* and Shklovsky's estrangement, see the debate between Stanley Mitchell and Ben Brewster in *Screen*, 15, 2 (1974), pp. 74–102, and cf. Bertolt Brecht, "Binocular Vision in the Theatre: The Alienation Effect," *The Messinghauf Dialogues* (London: Methuen, 1965), pp. 76–83. Richard Schacht has tried to clear the mist over use and abuse of "alienation" in *Alienation* (New York: Doubleday, 1970). Clifford Leech has related these examples of estrangement in Wesker's plays to Coleridge's words in *Biographia Literaria* on "awakening the mind's attention from the lethargy of custom, and directing it to the loveliness and the wonders of the world before us; an inexhaustible treasure, but for which, in consequence of the film of familiarity and selfish solicitude, we have eyes, yet see not, ears that hear not, and hearts that neither feel nor understand" ("Two Romantics: Arnold Wesker and Harold Pinter," *Stratford-Upon-Avon Studies*, 4 (1968), pp. 10–31).

26. Compare Jimmy Porter's "There aren't any good, brave causes left."

27. *The Wesker Trilogy*, p. 218.

28. Ibid., p. 7.

29. Hayman, *Arnold Wesker*, p. 5.

30. The mimicry of the uncouth louts can be traced to a scene in *The Menace* (1963), a television play about lonely, looney people in bed-sitter lodgings, which drew political and moral parallels in the menace situation of the Berlin Blockade as well as the menace situation of inner-city poverty.

31. *Wesker—Plays*, volume 3 (Harmondsworth, 1980), pp. 181–2.

32. Ibid., p. 193.

33. See Norman Podhoretz, "J'Accuse," *Commentary*, 74, 3 (1982), pp. 21–31; Edward Alexander, "The Journalists' War against Israel: Techniques of Distortion, Disorientation and Disinformation," *Encounter*, 59, 3–4 (1982), pp. 87–97.

34. *Love Letters on Blue Paper and Other Stories* (Harmondsworth, 1980), pp. 207–8.

35. *Wesker—Plays*, volume 4 (Harmondsworth, 1980), p. 259. There is an earlier attempt to present the Jewish side of the story in the trial scene in Michael Dines' one-act play *Shylock in Justice, Jewish Quarterly*, 7, 2 (1960), pp. 9–14. Interpretations of Shylock's role have been discussed from a modern viewpoint by Charles Marowitz, "Giving Them Hell," *Plays and Players*, 24, 10 (1977), pp. 15–17, and C. Itzin, "The Trouble with Shylock," *Plays and Players*, 24, 10 (1977), p. 17.

36. See the excellent introduction by W. Moelwyn Merchant to *The Merchant of Venice* (Harmondsworth: Penguin Books, 1967), pp. 7–60.

37. *Wesker—Plays*, volume 4, p. 199.

38. Ibid.

39. Ibid., p. 198.

40. Ibid., p. 261.

41. Wesker expressed something of the frustration he experienced in a diary he kept during the New York rehearsals of *The Merchant* (July–November 1977). He does not succumb to paranoia (perhaps he has achieved too much success for that), but he does almost feel that his plays are jinxed: his father died on the first night of *The Kitchen*; the Broadway run of *Chips with Everything* coincided with the assassination of John F. Kennedy; his mother died on *The Merchant's* first night in Stockholm; and Zero Mostel, cast for the role of Shylock, passed away during the U.S. tour, robbing the play of its warm, effusive Jewish star (Wesker, "A Zero's Death," *Jewish Quarterly*, 26, 3–4 (1978), pp. 89–94). *The Merchant* flopped after eight previews and four public performances, at a cost of $736,131. A longer, revised version opened at Birmingham, England, in 1978, but closed after 3½ months.

42. *The Wesker Trilogy*, p. 207.

43. Ibid.

44. Wesker writes that his family story begins where the story of the East End radicals ends ("A Zero's Death," *Jewish Quarterly*, 26, 3–4 (1978), 92), and the *Trilogy* is a kind of postscript on the disillusion of that radicalism.

45. Wesker, "Not Tea and Sympathy, Just Words of Courage," *The Times*, 9 July 1980, p. 18.

46. Quoted in G. Feldman and M. Gartenburg, eds., *The Beat Generation and the Angry Young Man* (New York: Citadel Press, 1958), p. 297. Also see John Holloway, "'Tank in the Stalls,'" reprinted in the same collection, and

compare Stephen Spender, *The Thirties and After* (London: Macmillan, 1978) or Kenneth Allsop, *The Angry Decade* (London: Peter Owen, 1964).

47. Charles Williams, *Image of the City* (London: Oxford University Press, 1958), p. xi.

48. Theodore Roszak, *The Making of a Counter-Culture* (New York: Anchor Books, 1969), p. 73.

49. Mander, *The Writer and Commitment* (London: Secker and Warburg, 1961), pp. 194–211.

50. Gerda Charles, "Trends in Anglo-Jewish Writing," *Jewish Quarterly*, 10, 1 (1963), p. 11. Charles' italics.

51. "The Kitchen Sink," *Encounter*, 21, 6 (1963), pp. 48–54.

NOTES TO CHAPTER 5

1. Cited in John Russell Taylor, *Anger and After*, 2nd revised edition (London, 1969), p. 323.

2. Harold Pinter, "Writing for Myself" (1961), *Plays* (London, 1979), volume 2, p. 12. Further references will be to this edition of Pinter's plays and essays.

3. Ibid., p. 10.

4. One rather unsympathetic American critic has accused Wesker of having "as much feeling for language as a suet pudding" (G. E. Wellwarth. *The Theater of Protest and Paradox: Developments in the Avant-Garde Drama* (New York, 1971), p. 282).

5. Including Dalston, Canonbury and Highbury: see Lipman, *Social History*, pp. 169–70.

6. Cited in J. W. Carrier, "A Jewish Proletariat," in M. Mindlin and C. Bermant, eds., *Explorations* (London, 1967), p. 128.

7. Interview in the *New Yorker*, 25 February 1967, quoted in Martin Esslin, *Pinter: A Study of His Plays* (London, 1973), pp. 11–12. Pinter later claimed that he had exaggerated the decay and poverty in this description (ibid., p. 12).

8. W. Baker and S. E. Tabachnick, *Harold Pinter* (Edinburgh, 1973).

9. B. Supple, "Pinter's Homecoming," *Jewish Chronicle*, 25 June 1965, pp. 7, 31. In the same way Peter Shaffer's *Five Finger Exercise* (1958) is widely recognized as a camouflaged Jewish family situation.

10. "A Note on Shakespeare," in Esslin, pp. 54–55.

11. Alexander Baron, cited in Baker and Tabachnick, *Harold Pinter*, p. 7, speaks of a kind of "osmosis" which he recognizes in Pinter's plays.

12. Pinter's novel is discussed in Esslin, p. 120 ff.

13. Letter to W. Baker, 31 January 1973, cited in Baker and Tabachnick, *Harold Pinter*, p. 12. Compare the anti-Semitic violence directly encountered

in those years by the frustrated narrator of Alexander Baron's fictionalized memoir of growing up Jewish in Hackney, *With Hope Farewell* (1952). Baron's invalid air-pilot, who had thought to get away from the Jewish problem by joining Fighter Command, comes back from the war to the disappointment of latent hostility and is forced to reconsider his lack of sympathy with his fellow Jews. The threat to their existence is at times couched in such everyday language that it is not always easy to tell friend from foe. Living with that threat can result in extreme forms of behavior.

14. G. Plimpton, ed., *Writers at Work: The Paris Review Interviews*, 3rd series (New York, 1967), p. 363.

15. Ibid.

16. *New Yorker* interview, cited in Baker and Tabachnick, *Harold Pinter*, p. 11.

17. Ibid.

18. Baker and Tabachnick, *Harold Pinter*, p. 20.

19. 1962 speech, *Plays*, volume 1, p. 15.

20. Ibid.

21. Pinter, "Mac," *Plays*, volume 3, p. 16.

22. Pinter's tribute to McMaster quotes (ibid.) Yeats' *Lapis Lazuli*, a poem which conveys the knowledge of the "gaiety transfiguring all that dread" in *Hamlet* and *Lear*.

23. For Pinter's poetic, dramatic and sporting achievements at Hackney Downs Grammar School, as well as a most revealing early interest in the French avant-garde cinema, see the appendix in Baker and Tabachnick, *Harold Pinter*, pp. 149–50. For the relevance of Shakespeare to the condition of Jewishness, compare Bernard Kops' use of *Hamlet* and Arnold Wesker's *The Merchant*, discussed above.

24. G. Plimpton, ed., *Writers at Work*, p. 352.

25. Baker and Tabachnick, *Harold Pinter*, pp. 19–20.

26. Esslin, p. 11.

27. Pinter, *Plays*, volume 2, p. 10.

28. See Pinter's March 1960 radio interview cited in Esslin, p. 36.

29. October 1960 BBC interview, cited by Esslin, p. 34.

30. "'Going into Europe': A Symposium," *Encounter*, 19, 6 (December 1962), p. 59.

31. See Pinter's school record in Baker and Tabachnick, *Harold Pinter*, pp. 149–50.

32. Esslin, p. 32.

33. *Sunday Times*, 25 May 1958.

34. There is a similar scene in an underground railway station in Kops' *Home Sweet Honeycomb;* during the war, night-time shelter in East London underground stations posed the constant danger of being crushed to death or electrocuted, as well as the possibility of flooding and direct bombing, and added to a shared experience of homelessness and depersonalization.

The eerie sleepers on the platforms waiting to go nowhere also embody the helplessness of the individual in the crowd: in both Pinter and Kops no one heeds the young man's desperate call to move away from danger, just as the call to stop the Bomb fell on deaf ears after the war.

35. In a poem "A View of the Party," dated 1958, the year of the first performance of *The Birthday Party* (which was originally entitled *The Party*), Goldberg and McCann are forces in the *thoughts* of each of the characters (Esslin, pp. 81–2).

36. Pinter suspected a "deficient order in the upper fretwork" in his own landlady in Eastbourne (G. Plimpton, ed., *Writers at Work*, p. 352).

37. Pinter, *Plays*, volume 1, p. 61.

38. Ibid., p. 96.

39. See Baker and Tabachnick, *Harold Pinter*, p. 65.

40. Schiff, *From Stereotype to Metaphor: The Jew in Contemporary Drama* (Albany, 1982), p. 76.

41. Pinter, *Plays*, volume 1, p. 66.

42. The first to publish this conclusion was Barry Supple ("Pinter's Homecoming," *Jewish Chronicle*, 25 June 1965, pp. 7, 31). Pinter's own wife Vivien Merchant played Ruth on the first night in London, but Pinter has denied that he ever writes parts for her and, publicly at least, he has not expressed any personal guilt about marrying outside the Jewish community.

43. Pinter, *Plays*, volume 3, p. 65. The apparent misprint for "bygones be bygones" appears in the text.

44. Hugh Nelson has argued this quite convincingly in "*The Homecoming*: Kith and Kin," in John Russell Brown, ed., *Modern British Dramatists: A Collection of Critical Essays* (Englewood Cliffs, 1968), pp. 145–63.

45. North London is a sufficiently vague description to include anywhere from Hackney to the outer suburbs, while the ambiguity of Hackney's social and geographical status is reflected in the differentiation between Clapton, Dalston and Stoke Newington, between local postal districts E.5, E.6 and N.16. The frustrated delusion of respectability characteristic of this situation is released in verbal abuse in much the same way in Clifford Odets' *Awake and Sing!*; indeed, Ruth is unkosher not so much in the sense Teddy married below himself (at least, that is what Max suggests Teddy is afraid of), for the family's origins do not seem much better than hers. Rather, Teddy has cheated the old man's aspirations for his rise above them: Max says he is always urging Lenny and Joey to find a decent match, while Teddy is spoken of as a "standard" and an example. Teddy loses his kinship and becomes a "stranger," while Ruth becomes kin and is adopted as the daughter-in-law ally in the family feud so typical of the Jewish novel.

46. Pinter, *Plays*, volume 3, p. 44.

47. Ibid., p. 69.

48. Pinter, *Plays*, volume 1, p. 60.

49. As Pinter stressed in G. Plimpton, ed., *Writers at Work*, p. 362.

50. Pinter, *Plays*, volume 1, p. 11.

51. Pinter, *Plays*, volume 2, p. 45.

52. Ibid., p. 82.

53. Ibid., p. 112.

54. Shaffer, *Equus* (Harmondsworth, 1977), pp. 19–20.

55. Cited in Brian Glanville, "The Man Behind the Pen (2)," *Jewish Chronicle*, 26 December 1958, p. 13.

56. Pinter, *Plays*, volume 1, p. 11.

57. *Five Finger Exercise*, in *Three Plays* (Harmondsworth, 1962), p. 80. Emphasis in the original.

58. Glanville, "The Man Behind the Pen (2)," *Jewish Chronicle*, 26 December 1958, p. 13.

59. Ibid.

60. 1963 interview cited in J. Russell Taylor, *Peter Shaffer* (London, 1974), p. 17.

NOTES TO CHAPTER 6

1. Bermant, *Troubled Eden*, p. 176.

2. Compare the description, from a non-Jewish point of view, of the pre-war Jewish financier in C. P. Snow's *The Conscience of the Rich* (1958).

3. "*The Bankrupts:* Some Defence Reactions," *Jewish Quarterly*, 6, 1 (1958), pp. 34–5.

4. Glanville, "Indirect Approach to Jewishness," *Jewish Quarterly*, 13, 1 (1965), pp. 12–13.

5. See Glanville, "The Anglo-Jewish Writer," *Encounter*, 24, 2 (1960), pp. 62–4.

6. Gerda Charles once claimed Kingsley Amis as a Jewish writer, and the author of *Lucky Jim* expressed his own affinities in his article "Anglo-Jewish Literature: The Need for Criticism," *Jewish Quarterly*, 1, 2 (1955), pp. 81–2.

7. *The Crossing Point* (London, 1960), p. 256.

8. Conversation with Terry Coleman, "Revenge is Sour," *Guardian*, 27 May 1971, p. 11. The moral perspective is not, of course, exclusively Jewish property, but it derives from a specific social situation, as in the refusal to attend synagogue at age ten by a superbright Cricklewood schoolgirl in *Favourite Nights* (1981), by Stephen Poliakoff, author of the militant anti-nuclear bomb television play, *Stronger than the Sun* (1977).

9. Gerda Charles citing her novel *The Slanting Light* in J. Vinson, ed., *Contemporary Novelists*, 2nd edition (New York: St Martin's Press, 1976), p. 248.

10. R. Winegarten, "The World of Gerda Charles," *Jewish Quarterly*, 15, 1–2 (1967), p. 37.

11. C. P. Snow, "Facing the Music," *Financial Times*, 15 April 1971.

12. Arnold Wesker, "A Crucial Question," *Jewish Quarterly* 7, 3 (1960), pp. 43–5. Similar sentiments are expressed by Alexander Baron, "Gerda Charles: A Visionary Realist," *Jewish Quarterly*, 19, 1–2 (1971), pp. 39–41.

13. Judith Vincent, "Bernice Rubens," in J. Halio, ed., *British Novelists Since 1960* (Detroit: Gale Research Co., 1983), p. 633.

14. Raphael's application of *Sprachphilosophie* is his own, though hardly novel if one thinks of literature as a linguistic search for philosophic truths, or if one thinks of Wittgenstein's own grounding in the social criticism of Karl Kraus and the Vienna Circle.

15. *The Limits of Love* (London, 1960), p. 4.

16. Ibid., p. 258.

17. Ibid., p. 231.

18. Ibid., p. 224.

19. Ibid., p. 310.

20. Ibid., p. 323.

21. Ibid., p. 317.

22. Raphael, 1963 interview in *Jewish Perspectives*, p. 77. Compare Kafka's declaration that he had nothing in common with himself.

23. Raphael quoted in J. Vinson, ed., *Contemporary Novelists*, p. 1145.

24. *The Glittering Prizes* (Harmondsworth, 1976), p. 269.

25. Interview with Raphael by William Boyd, "The Price of Glittering," *Oxford Literary Review*, 2, 1 (1977), p. 7.

26. *The Glittering Prizes*, p. 12.

27. Ibid., pp. 33–4.

28. Ibid., p. 43.

29. Raphael in J. Vinson, ed., *Contemporary Novelists*, p. 1145. Raphael stated earlier, "The problems of philosophy and the problems of Jewishness have common features" ("Sacred and Profane," *Jewish Quarterly*, 8, 1 (1961), p. 4).

30. *The Glittering Prizes*, p. 269.

31. Ibid., p. 297.

32. Ibid., p. 159.

NOTES TO CHAPTER 7

1. *Mavericks* (London: Editions Poetry and Poverty, 1957), p. 10. The Movement, if it existed beyond the convenient journalists' label invented by the *Spectator*, pursued an uninvolved, restrained verse, and the poets represented in *New Lines* were all in some way connected with the English academic world (John Holloway, Thom Gunn, Kingsley Amis, John Wain,

Donald Davie, Elizabeth Jennings), none of them alienated in the same sense as was Abse.

2. *Jewish Perspectives*, pp. 83–4.

3. Ibid., pp. 84–6.

4. *Selected Poems* (London, 1970), p. 50.

5. Ibid., p. 63.

6. Ibid., p. 49. Emanuel Litvinoff's poem "To T. S. Eliot" and Bernard Kops' play *Ezra* (1980) also ponder the enigma of the two great poets whose attitudes to the Jews define in one way the Jewishness of the Jewish writer, just as they bind Karl Shapiro to a position in his *Defense of Ignorance* (New York: Random House, 1960), p. 205.

7. *Selected Poems*, p. 68.

8. *Stand*, 24, 1 (1983), p. 4.

9. Silkin, "Cultural Survival," *Jewish Quarterly*, 3, 2 (1955), pp. 36–7.

10. Silkin, "Anglo-Jewish Poetry," *Jewish Quarterly*, 5, 3 (1958), pp. 9–11.

11. As in Glatstein's *Smoke* or Nelly Sachs' "O, the chimneys," poetic metaphor has been literalized into horrible reality; see Silkin's introduction to his anthology *Poetry of the Committed Individual* (Harmondsworth: Penguin Books, 1973), pp. 17–39.

12. Jon Silkin, "Anglo-Jewish Poetry," *Jewish Quarterly*, 5, 3 (1958), p. 9. A useful contrast might be made with Seamus Heaney as a naturalist or with Ted Hughes' image of the poet as fox or hawk.

13. *Jewish Quarterly* (Spring 1967), p. 24.

14. "The Poetry of Jon Silkin," *Jewish Quarterly*, 13, 3 (1965), pp. 10–11.

15. Silkin, "Note on 'Flower' Poems," *Nature with Man* (London, 1965), p. 54.

16. Silkin, *Selected Poems* (London, 1980), p. 89.

17. Ibid., p. 70.

18. Ibid., p. 178.

19. *The Little Time-Keeper* (New York, 1977), p. 72.

20. Ibid., p. 73.

21. *Selected Poems* (London, 1980), p. 8.

22. Steiner, *Language and Silence* (Harmondsworth: Penguin Books, 1969), p. 200.

23. *Selected Poems* (London, 1980), p. 36. Patient and tolerant, the English waited close on eight centuries until the martyrdom of York Jews was commemorated with a silent plaque in 1978. The plaque quotes Isaiah's prophetic words, "They ascribe glory to the Lord and his praise in the isles," taken exegetically to refer to the British Isles and to those who died rather than sacrifice their faith. See *The Times*, 11 October 1978 and 1 November 1978.

24. Peter Porter has pointed to the characteristic need of the Jewish poet for self-probing and self-definition in "A Survey of Anglo-Jewish Poetry," *Jewish Quarterly*, 14, 2 (1966), p. 28; this is something that Philip Larkin

does not need as he flashes past provincial railway stations in *The Whitsun Weddings*, nor, more appropriately, does Thom Gunn in *The Sense of Movement* require the Jewish poet's socioethnic adjustment, even though Gunn does seek to *become* in Nietzschean terms. Jewish poets living in England lack obvious signs of the at-homeness of Betjeman, Heath-Stubbs or Larkin; rather, their outsideness is one clue to their radicalism, as well as to their role of cultural mediators in their capacity as editors and translators (Abse, Silkin, Hamburger, Fainlight, Feinstein, Rudolf, Robson).

25. *Selected Poems* (London, 1980), p. 148. See Silkin's note on the changes he later made to this and other poems, ibid., pp. ix–x.

26. Ibid., p. 166.

27. Ibid., p. 112.

28. Howard Schwartz and Anthony Rudolf, eds., *Voices Within the Ark: The Modern Jewish Poets* (New York: Avon Books, 1980), p. 399.

29. *Selected Poems* (London, 1980), p. 54.

30. *The Psalms with their Spoils* (London, 1980), p. 11. Silkin's Jerusalem is much more than Arnold Wesker's emblem of social salvation in *I'm Talking About Jerusalem*, but, like Wesker, Silkin is clearly thinking in Blakean terms of a northerly Jerusalem, as in his poem "The Ship's Pasture," *Times Literary Supplement*, 13 November 1981, p. 1335.

31. See Abraham Joshua Heschel, *God in Search of Man: A Philosophy of Judaism* (Philadelphia: Jewish Publication Society, 1956), pp. 88–100.

32. "The Lapidary Style," *The Psalms with their Spoils* (London, 1980), p. 29.

33. "Lapidary Words," ibid., p. 28.

34. Silkin cited in Kenneth Allcott, ed., *The Penguin Book of Contemporary Verse, 1918–1960*, 2nd edition (Harmondsworth: Penguin Books, 1962), p. 382.

35. T. W. Adorno cited in George Steiner, *Language and Silence* (Harmondsworth: Penguin Books, 1969), p. 167. The frequent iconoclasm of the outsider features in much of the innovation in twentieth-century modernism and is, naturally, shared by the modern Jewish writer.

NOTES TO CHAPTER 8

1. Robert Alter, "Deformations of the Holocaust," *Commentary*, 71, 2 (1981), pp. 48–54. See also Sidra Dekoven Ezrahi, *By Words Alone: The Holocaust in Literature* (Chicago: University of Chicago Press, 1980), pp. 176–216; Bellow, Malamud and Philip Roth have been reread as post-Holocaust writers in Dorothy S. Bilik, *Immigrant-Survivors: Post Holocaust Consciousness in Recent Jewish American Fiction* (Middletown: Wesleyan University Press, 1981).

2. A storm of publicity blew up around D. M. Thomas' *White Hotel*, but it raged mainly over the legitimacy of plagiarism from Kuznetsov's *Babi Yar*, and did not center on the legitimacy of use of the Holocaust, though see P. Swinden, "D. M. Thomas and *The White Hotel*," *Critical Quarterly*, 24, 4 (1982), pp. 74–80, and compare Dannie Abse's Freudian imagery discussed in Chapter 7.

3. Hyam Maccoby, "George Steiner's 'Hitler': Of Theology and Politics," *Encounter*, 58, 5 (1982), pp. 27–34.

4. 1963 interview, *Jewish Perspectives*, pp. 80–1.

5. Ibid., p. 81.

6. Arnold Wesker, "Wanted: A New Code of Human Behaviour," *Jewish Quarterly*, 9, 1 (1962), pp. 5–6.

7. 1964 interview, *Jewish Perspectives*, p. 89.

8. "I Was Not There," *Selected Poems* (London, 1966), p. 11.

9. On this, see Karen Gershon, "A Stranger in a Strange Land," *Jewish Quarterly*, 7, 1 (1959), pp. 10–11. Of course, Joseph Conrad is a precedent for Michael Hamburger, Karen Gershon, Isaac Deutscher and Arthur Koestler.

10. Hamburger cited by Stephen Spender in his introduction to Abba Kovner and Nelly Sachs, *Selected Poems* (Harmondsworth: Penguin Books, 1971), p. 17.

11. 1964 interview, *Jewish Perspectives*, p. 88.

12. Hamburger, "In a Cold Season," *Collected Poems* (Manchester, 1984), p. 129.

13. Hamburger cited by Spender in Kovner and Sachs, *Selected Poems* (Harmondsworth: Penguin Books, 1971), p. 17.

14. Spender, ibid., pp. 16–18.

15. Nelly Sachs, "Job," *Selected Poems* (London: Jonathan Cape, 1968), p. 63. Rabbi J. Soloveitchik takes a different view in his essay *Kol dodi dofek*, included in P. Peli, ed., *Besod hayakhid vehayakhad (In Aloneness, In Togetherness: A Selection of Hebrew Writings by Rabbi J. Soloveitchik)* (Jerusalem: Orot, n.d.), pp. 331–400, and sees Job's sin as the Diaspora Jew's inability to identify with the community out of fear of dual allegiance and his failure to identify with his neighbor's suffering. For Soloveitchik the cause of evil and suffering is speculative and ultimately unknowable; the existential problem after the Holocaust is how to act *(halakha lemaase)*.

16. See A. Neher, *The Exile of the Word: From the Silence of the Bible to the Silence of Auschwitz* (Philadelphia: Jewish Publication Society, 1981). Another way of looking at the hiddenness of the Divine Presence is the khasidic parable which likens God to the little boy who plays hide-and-seek, but whose friends forget to look for him: it is man who has forgotten to discover the Presence.

17. Hamburger, *Collected Poems*, p. 133.

18. "Introduction," in Jon Silkin, ed., *Poetry of the Committed Individual: A Stand Anthology of Poetry* (Harmondsworth: Penguin Books, 1973), p. 21.

19. Communication of Jon Silkin to Kenneth Allcott, editor of *The Penguin Book of Contemporary Verse, 1918–1960*, 2nd edition (Harmondsworth: Penguin Books, 1961), p. 383.

20. See on this for example, L. Langer, *The Holocaust and the Literary Imagination* (New Haven: Yale University Press, 1975); Alvin Rosenfeld, *A Double Dying: Reflections on Holocaust Literature* (Bloomington: Indiana University Press, 1980).

21. Raphael interviewed by William Boyd, "The Price of Glittering," *Oxford Literary Review*, 2, 1 (1977), p. 7.

22. 1963 interview, *Jewish Perspectives*, pp. 66–72.

23. 1963 interview, *Jewish Perspectives*, pp. 72–5.

24. Fisch, "Nathaniel Tarn and A. M. Klein: Poets of the Hebraic Consciousness," *Judaism*, 14, 4 (1965), p. 479.

25. Dannie Abse, *Ash on a Young Man's Sleeve*, 3rd edition (London, 1971), p. 191.

26. David Daiches, "Some Aspects of Anglo-American Jewish Fiction," in *Jewish Perspectives*, p. 108.

27. Bermant, "Coming and Going," *Present Tense*, 10, 3 (1983), p. 52.

28. See Dannie Abse, "Pages from a Princeton Diary," *Jewish Quarterly*, 24, 3 (1976), pp. 10–15. Frederic Raphael, among other "Jews of June 1967," soon voiced misgivings about Israel's moral position following victory in the Six Day War ("Must We Always be on the Defensive?" *Jewish Quarterly*, 16, 2–3 (1968), pp. 3–7). But then, he, like Pinter, would claim the right of any citizen to political confusion and mixed motives (see "Intellectuals and Just Causes: A Symposium, II," *Encounter*, 29, 4 (1967), pp. 46–7). Compare Leslie Field's survey of American Jewish writers' treatment of Israel, "Israel Revisted in American Jewish Literature," *Midstream*, 28, 9 (1982), pp. 50–4.

29. Recent counterparts to Louis Golding's *Magnolia Street* series, Naomi Jacob's *Gollantz Saga* and G. B. Stern's *The Matriarch* include Chaim Bermant's *The Patriarch* (1982), Bernice Rubens' *Brothers* (1983), Jack Ronder's *The Lost Tribe* (1978), and Maisie Mosco's *Almonds and Raisins* (1979, first part of a trilogy published in the United States as *From the Bitter Land*, followed in 1980 by *The Scattered Seed* and in 1981 by *Glittering Harvest*). Their challenge to rabbinical authority and to family values comes from a basic commitment to Jewish activism and things Jewish, which differs from the wartime patriotic and assimilationist stand of Toni Block, in the play *You Must Stay to Tea*, or the equanimity toward intermarriage in Yvonne Mitchell's play *The Same Sky* (1952).

30. See Bernard Kops, "Non-Conformist Jewish Writers in Modern London," *European Judaism*, 14, 2 (1980), pp. 8–9. Michael Hastings' comedy *Gloo-Joo* (1978) hilariously combines West Indian and Jewish experiences, but it also very curiously draws on the sheeny-coon in the extinct Brixton music-hall who sang, "Oh, Rachel, my darling, come and see the silver in the silvery moon" (quoted in M. J. Landa, *The Jew in Drama* (New York:

Ktav, 1969), p. 277); the example of Al Jolson in the United States is, of course, better known.

31. A. Memmi, *The Liberation of the Jew* (New York: Orion Press, 1966), p. 180.

32. George Steiner, "A View from Without," *Jewish Quarterly*, 16, 4 (1968–1969), p. 3.

33. Nathaniel Tarn, "Portrait of a Modern Jew," *Old Savage/Young City* (London: Cape, 1964), p. 49.

34. See especially the comments of English poets Roy Fuller, John Smith and Howard Sergeant in the symposium on Anglo-Jewish poetry in the *Jewish Quarterly*, 14, 2 (1966), 24–31.

Bibliography of Contemporary Anglo-Jewish Writing

The following bibliography gives the published literary works of contemporary Jewish authors in modern British literature and concentrates on Anglo-Jewish writers who are generally regarded of serious standing in the period 1953–1983. I have not tried to be exhaustive in my coverage and I have ignored books for children, adaptation of the work of others, and reviews, though one or two longer notices of particular interest are included. I have also not given literary criticism and other specialized publications which do not specifically address the Anglo-Jewish situation. For this reason I have excluded A. Alvarez and Gabriel Josipovici, who are primarily critics, and George Steiner, the philosopher and critic, who is a very European commuter between Cambridge and Geneva. Beyond my present scope are Arthur Koestler and Isaac Deutscher; for Koestler, see R. Merrill and T. Frazier, eds., *Arthur Koestler: An International Bibliography* (Ann Arbor: Ardis, 1979).

The bibliography is divided into sections which broadly parallel the divisions in this book, although one cannot speak of organized groupings and there is some overlap between geographical areas or genres.

I. East End Writers
II. Dramatists
III. Novelists
IV. Poets
V. Refugees
VI. New Voices
VII. Anthologies
VIII. Suggested Reading

Individual pieces first published in journals and later collected have in most cases not been listed separately.

1. Bibliographic Sources

Bibliographic information is given in the Anglo-Jewish sections of the *Jewish Book Annual,* and in *Contemporary Literary Criticism.* Anglo-Jewish novelists are included in Anthony Burgess, *The Novel Now,* 2nd edition (London: Faber, 1971), and in Frederick R. Karl, *The Contemporary English Novel* (New York: Farrar, Straus and Giroux, 1962).

Additional critical sources on individual dramatists may be found in P. F. Breed and F. M. Sniderman, eds., *Dramatic Criticism Index* (Detroit: Gale Research Company, 1972), and H. H. Palmer, ed., *European Drama Criticism, 1900–1975* (Hamden, Conn.: Shoestring Press, 1977).

2. Biographical Sources

British Dramatists since World War 2. Dictionary of Literary Biography, volume 13. Ed. Stanley Weintraub. In two parts. Detroit: Gale Research Company, 1982.

British Novelists, 1930–1959. Dictionary of Literary Biography, volume 15. In two parts. Detroit: Gale Research Company, 1983.

British Novelists since 1960. Dictionary of Literary Biography, volume 14. In two parts. Detroit: Gale Research Company, 1983.

Contemporary Dramatists. Ed. James Vinson and D. L. Kirkpatrick, 3rd edition. New York: St Martin's Press, 1982.

Contemporary Novelists. Ed. James Vinson. 2nd edition. London: St James Press, and New York: St Martin's Press, 1976.

Contemporary Poets. Ed. James Vinson. 2nd edition. London: St James Press, and New York: St Martin's Press, 1976.

World Authors, 1950–1970. Ed. John Wakeman. New York: H. W. Wilson, 1975.

I. East End Writers

Bernard Kops (born 1926)

Collected Works

Four Plays. London: McGibbon & Kee, 1964. Includes *The Hamlet of Stepney Green, Enter Solly Gold, Home Sweet Honeycomb, The Lemmings.*

Novels

Awake for Morning. London: McGibbon & Kee, 1958.
Motorbike. London: New English Library, 1962.

The World is a Wedding. London: McGibbon & Kee, and New York: Coward McCann, 1964; republished London: Vallentine & Mitchell, 1973.

Yes from No Man's Land. London: McGibbon & Kee, 1965, and New York: Coward McCann, 1966.

The Dissent of Dominick Shapiro. London: McGibbon & Kee, 1966, and New York: Coward McCann, 1967.

By the Waters of Whitechapel. London: Bodley Head, 1969, and New York: Norton, 1970.

The Passionate Past of Gloria Gaye. London: Secker & Warburg, 1971, and New York: Norton, 1972.

Settle Down Simon Katz. London: Secker & Warburg, 1973: republished, London: New English Library, 1977.

Partners. London: Secker & Warburg, 1975.

Verse

Poems. London: Bell & Baker Press, 1955.

Poems & Songs. Lowestoft: Scorpion Press, 1958.

An Anemone for Antigone. Lowestoft: Scorpion Press, 1959.

Erica, I Want to Read You Something. Lowestoft: Scorpion Press, and New York: Walker, 1967.

For the Record. London: Secker & Warburg, 1971.

On Margate Sands. London: Secker & Warburg, 1978.

Drama

The Hamlet of Stepney Green. London: Evans, 1959. Republished in *Three Plays (Shaffer, Wesker, Kops).* Harmondsworth: Penguin Books, 1959. Produced Oxford, London and New York, 1958.

Goodbye World. Produced Guildford, 1959.

All Change for the Angel. Produced London, 1960.

The Dream of Peter Mann. Harmondsworth: Penguin Books, 1960. Produced Edinburgh, 1960.

Stray Cats and Empty Bottles. Produced Cambridge, 1961; television production, 1964.

Enter Solly Gold. In *Satan, Socialities and Solly Gold: Three Plays from England.* New York: Coward McCann, 1961. Produced at the Center 42 Festival, Wellingborough, 1962.

Ezra. Adam International Review, 431–2 (1980), pp. 21–62. Produced London, 1981.

Radio Plays

Born in Israel, 1963.

The Dark Ages, 1964.

Israel: The Immigrant, 1964.

Television Plays

I Want to Go Home, 1963.
The Lost Years of Brian Hooper, 1967.
Alexander the Greatest, 1971.
Just One Kid, 1974.
It's a Lovely Day Tomorrow, 1975.
Moss, 1975.
Rocky Marciano is Dead, 1976.
Night Kids, 1983.

Interview

Glanville, B. "The Man Behind the Pen (4)." *Jewish Chronicle,* 9 January 1959, p. 17.

Essays

"The Young Writer and the Theatre." *Jewish Quarterly,* 8, 3 (1961), pp. 19–20, 22.
"Non-Conformist Jewish Writer in Modern London." *European Judaism,* 14, 2 (1980), pp. 8–9.

Critical Studies

Abse, D. "Poems and Songs," *Jewish Chronicle,* 28 November 1958, supplement, p. ii.
Glanville, B. "A Writer's World," *Jewish Quarterly,* 11, 3 (1963), pp. 46–7.
Knight, G. Wilson. "The Kitchen Sink." *Encounter,* 21, 6 (1963), pp. 48–54.
Lumley, F. *New Trends in Twentieth-Century Drama.* New York: Oxford University Press, 1972, pp. 240–3.
McInnes, C. "Hamlet and the Ghetto." *Encounter,* 14, 5 (1960), pp. 62–4.
Sutton, N. "Deep Waters of Whitechapel," *Guardian,* 6 September 1969.
Taylor, John Russell. *Anger and After.* 2nd revised edition. London: Methuen, 1969.
Wellwarth, G. E. "Bernard Kops: The Jew as 'Everyman.'" In his *The Theater of Protest and Paradox: Developments in the Avant-Garde Drama.* Revised edition. New York: New York University Press, 1971, pp. 283–7.

EMANUEL LITVINOFF (BORN 1915)

Novels

The Lost Europeans. New York: Vanguard, 1959, and London: Heinemann, 1960.
The Man Next Door. London: Hodder & Stoughton, 1968, and New York: Norton, 1969.

Journey Through a Small Planet. London: Michael Joseph, 1972; republished, Harmondsworth: Penguin Books, 1976.

A Death Out of Season. London: Michael Joseph, 1975, and New York: Scribner, 1974; republished, London: Sphere Books, 1974; Harmondsworth: Penguin Books: 1979. First part of a trilogy.

Blood on the Snow. London: Michael Joseph, 1975; republished, Harmondsworth: Penguin Books, 1979. Second part of a trilogy.

Face of Terror. London: Michael Joseph, 1978; republished, Harmondsworth: Penguin Books, 1979. Concluding part of trilogy.

Falls the Shadow. London: Michael Joseph, 1983.

Drama

Magnolia Street Drama. Produced London, 1951. Adapted from Louis Golding's novel *Magnolia Street.*

Television Plays

Another Branch of the Family, 1967.
Marriage and Henry Sunday, 1967.
A Dream in the Afternoon, 1967.
A Foot in the Door, 1969.
The World is a Room, 1970.
Warm Feet, Warm Heart, 1970.

Uncollected Stories

"The Day the World Came to an End." *Jewish Quarterly,* 1, 1 (1953), pp. 25–34.

"Dance in No-Man's Land." *Jewish Quarterly,* 30, 1–2 (1982), pp. 46–51. Excerpt from a novel in progress.

Autobiography

"Children of Two Inheritances: How it Worked Itself Out." *Commentary,* 15, 3 (1953), pp. 272–9.

"They Made a Jew of Me." *Jewish Chronicle,* 14 December 1973, Literary Supplement, pp. vii–viii.

Critical Study

Abse, D. "Portrait of a Jewish Poet." *Jewish Quarterly,* 1, 4 (1954), pp. 16–22.

WOLF MANKOWITZ (BORN 1924)

Collected Works

Five One-Act Plays. London: Evans, 1955. Includes *The Bespoke Overcoat, The Baby, It Should Happen to a Dog, The Last of the Cheese Cake*, and *The Mighty Hunter*.

The Mendelman Fire and Other Stories. London: Deutsch, and Boston: Little Brown, 1957.

Expresso Bongo: A Wolf Mankowitz Reader. New York: Yoseloff, 1967.

The Penguin Wolf Mankowitz. Harmondsworth: Penguin Books, 1967.

The Blue Arabian Nights: Tales of a London Decade. London: Vallentine & Mitchell, 1973.

The Day of the Women and the Nights of the Men: Fables. London: Robson Books, 1977.

Novels

Make Me an Offer. London: Deutsch, and New York: Dutton, 1952; republished with *A Kid for Two Farthings*, London: Pan Books, 1956. Television adaptation, 1952. Screenplay, 1954. Stage production London, 1959.

A Kid for Two Farthings. London: Deutsch, 1953, and New York: Dutton, 1954; republished with *Make Me An Offer*, London: Pan Books, 1956. Screenplay, 1955.

Laugh Till You Cry: An Advertisement. New York: Dutton, 1955.

My Old Man's a Dustman. London: Deutsch, 1956, and, under the title *Old Soldiers Never Die*, Boston: Little Brown, 1956; republished, London: Vallentine & Mitchell, 1973.

Cockatrice. London: Longmans, Green & Co., and New York: Putnam, 1963; republished, London: Pan Books, 1965.

The Biggest Pig in Barbados: A Fable. London: Longmans, 1965.

Raspberry Reich. London: Macmillan, 1979; London: Pan Books, 1979.

Mazeppa. London: Muller, 1981.

Uncollected Short Stories

"The Plan." In *Focus Two*. Ed. B. Rayan and A. Pearse. London: Dobson, 1946, pp. 88–90.

"The World Saver." *Jewish Quarterly*, 14, 3 (1966), 36–7.

Verse

XII Poems. London: Workshop Press, 1971.

!Abracadabra! London: Macmillan, 1980.

Drama

The Boychik. Produced London, 1954.
It Should Happen to a Dog. London: Evans, 1955. Television production, 1955. Produced Princeton, 1967.
The Bespoke Overcoat. London: Evans, 1955, and New York: French, n.d. Stage production London, 1953. Screenplay, 1955.
The Samson Riddle: An Essay and a Play. London: Vallentine & Mitchell, 1972. Produced Dublin, 1972.
The Hebrew Lesson. London: Evans, 1977. Screenplay, 1972.

Essays

"The Truth about Orpheus." *Jewish Quarterly,* 1, 2 (1953), pp. 33–4.
"How American Can You Get?" *Jewish Quarterly,* 1, 3 (1953), pp. 35–6.
"On Being a Jewish Writer." *Jewish Quarterly,* 2, 1 (1954), p. 73.

Interviews

Glanville, B. "The Man Behind the Pen (1)." *Jewish Chronicle,* 19 December 1958, p. 19. See also the editorial in the same issue and Mankowitz' reply, *Jewish Chronicle,* 2 January 1959, pp. 20–1, in the form of a letter to a deceased great-grandfather; this letter was answered, through the medium of Rabbi Kopel Rosen, *Jewish Chronicle,* 9 February 1959, p. 22.
"On Being English and Jewish (3)." *Jewish Quarterly,* 11, 4 (1963), pp. 10–11.
Maccoby, H. *The Day God Laughed.* London: Robson Books, 1978. A Talmudic anthology which includes conversations with Wolf Mankowitz.

ARNOLD WESKER (BORN 1932)

Collected Works

The Wesker Trilogy. London: Cape, 1960, and New York: Random House, 1961; republished, Harmondsworth: Penguin Books, 1964.
Six Sundays in January. London: Cape, 1971.
Love Letters on Blue Paper: Three Stories. London: Cape, 1974, and New York: Harper & Row, 1975.
Three Plays. Harmondsworth: Penguin Books, 1976.
The Plays of Arnold Wesker. In two volumes. New York: Harper & Row, 1976–1977.
Said the Old Man to the Young Man. Cape: London, 1978.
Love Letters on Blue Paper and Other Stories. Harmondsworth: Penguin Books, 1980.
Wesker—Plays. In four volumes. Harmondsworth: Penguin Books, 1980.

Drama

The Kitchen. In *Three Plays (Shaffer, Wesker, Kops).* Harmondsworth: Penguin
Books, 1959. Published separately, Harmondsworth: Penguin Books,
1960; revised edition, London: Cape, 1961, and New York: Random
House, 1962. Produced London, 1959.

Chicken Soup with Barley. Harmondsworth: Penguin Books, 1959. Produced
Coventry, 1959.

Roots. Harmondsworth: Penguin Books, 1959. Produced Coventry, 1959.

I'm Talking About Jerusalem. Harmondsworth: Penguin Books, 1959. Produced
London, 1960.

Vaudeville (1962). Unpublished.

Chips with Everything. London: Cape, 1962, and New York: Random House,
1963; republished, Harmondsworth: Penguin Books, 1963. Produced
London, 1962, and New York, 1963.

The Nottingham Captain. Libretto for Center 42 festival, 1962. Published in
Six Sundays in January. London: Cape, 1971.

The Four Seasons. London: Cape, 1966; republished Harmondsworth: Penguin
Books, 1966. Produced Coventry, 1965; New York, 1968.

Their Very Own and Golden City. London: Cape, 1966; republished, Harmondsworth: Penguin Books, 1967. Notes for Act 2, Scene 3, with
typescript and authorial amendments published, *Quest,* 1 (1965), pp.
58–65. Produced Belgium, 1965; London, 1966.

The Friends. London: Cape, 1970. Produced Stockholm and London, 1970.

The Old Ones. London: Cape, 1973; revised edition, London: Blackie & Sons,
1974. Produced London, 1972; New York, 1974.

The Journalists. London: Writers & Readers Cooperative, 1975; republished
with notes on Wesker's "Journey into Journalism," London: Cape,
1979. Produced London, 1975.

The Wedding Feast. Plays and Players, 24, 7 (1977), pp. 45–50; 24, 8 (1977),
pp. 37–50. Produced Stockholm, 1974; revised version, Leeds, 1977.

The Merchant. London: Methuen, 1983. Critical edition with a preface by
Wesker and a commentary by Glenda Leeming. Produced Stockholm,
1976; New York, 1977; Birmingham, England, 1977.

One More Ride on the Merry-Go-Round (written pseudonymously, 1978).

Love Letters on Blue Paper. London: T. Q. Publications, with the Writers &
Readers Cooperative, 1978. Script based on the story of the same
name. Televized, 1976. Radio adaptation, 1982.

Caritas. London: Cape, 1981. Produced London, 1981.

Sullied Hands (1981). Unpublished.

Annie Wobbler. Jewish Quarterly, 30, 1–2 (1982), pp. 36–40. Produced London,
1983.

Mothers. Produced Tokyo, 1982.

Television Plays

The Menace. Jewish Quarterly, 11, 1 (1963), pp. 15–22.
Whitsun. Adapted from the story "The Visit", 1980.
Breakfast, 1981.

Uncollected Short Stories

"The Hill." *Jewish Quarterly*, 6, 1 (1958), pp. 37–9.
"A Time of Dying: A Sort of Story." *Jewish Quarterly*, 21, 1–2 (1973), pp. 134–43.

Verse

"Time Parts the Memory." *Jewish Quarterly*, 7, 1 (1959), p. 9.

Selected Essays

"Let Battle Commence" (1958). In *Encore Reader*. Ed. C. Marowitz. London: Methuen, 1965, 96–103.
"To React—to Respond." *Encore* (March-April 1959), pp. 6–8.
Labour and the Arts, or What, then, is to be Done? Oxford: Gemini, 1960.
The Modern Playwright, or "Mother, is it Worth it?" Oxford: Gemini, 1961.
"Art is Not Enough." *Twentieth Century*, 169 (1961), pp. 190–4.
"Wanted: A New Code of Human Behaviour." *Jewish Quarterly*, 9, 1 (1962), pp. 5–6.
Fears of Fragmentation. London: Cape, 1970.
"The London Diary for Stockholm." In *Six Sundays in January*. London: Cape, 1971.
Words as Definitions of Experience. London: Writers & Readers Cooperative, 1976.
Journey into Journalism. London: Writers & Readers Cooperative, 1977.
"A Zero's Death." *Jewish Quarterly*, 26, 3–4 (1978), pp. 89–94.
"Art Between Truth and Fiction." *Encounter*, 54, 1 (1980), pp. 48–57.
"Not Tea and Sympathy, Just Words of Courage." *The Times*, 9 July 1980, p. 18.
"The Playwright as Director." *Canadian Theatre Review*, 32 (1981), pp. 24–31.

Autobiography

(With John Allin.) *Say Goodbye—You May Never See them Again: Scenes from Two East End Backgrounds.* London: Cape, 1974.

Interviews

Glanville, B. "The Man Behind the Pen (5)." *Jewish Chronicle*, 9 January 1959, p. 17.

Trussler, S. 1966 interview in *Theatre at Work: Playwrights and Productions in the Modern British Theatre*. Ed. C. Marowitz and S. Trussler. London: Methuen, 1967, pp. 78–95.

Wager, W. *The Playwrights Speak*. Ed. W. Wager. New York: Dell, and London: Longmans, 1967, pp. 213–30.

See also the interviews in the studies by R. Hayman and L. Kitchin below.

Critical Studies

Alvarez, A. "The Anti-Establishment Drama." *Partisan Review*, 26 (1959), pp. 606–11.

Andereth, M. "Sartre and Wesker: Committed Playwrights." *Comment*, 5 (1964), 18–28.

Anderson, M. "Arnold Wesker: The Last Humanist." *New Theatre Magazine*, 8, 3 (1968), pp. 10–27.

Brown, John Russell. *Theatre Language: A Study of Arden, Osborne, Pinter and Wesker*. London: Allen Lane, 1972.

Brown, John Russell, ed. *Modern British Dramatists: A Collection of Critical Essays*. Englewood Cliffs, N.J.: Prentice-Hall, 1968.

Dennis, N. "What Though the Field Be Lost?" *Encounter*, 19, 2 (1962), 43–5.

Feldman, G. and Gartenburg, M., eds. *The Beat Generation and the Angry Young Man*. New York: Citadel Press, 1958, pp. 299–315.

Fraser, G. S. *The Modern Writer and his World*. Revised edition. Harmondsworth: Penguin Books, 1970.

Hayman, R. *Arnold Wesker*. London: Heinemann, 1970; 2nd edition, 1974.

Kitchin, L. *Mid-Century Drama*. 2nd revised edition. London: Faber, 1962.

Latham, J. "*Roots*: A Reassessment." *Modern Drama*, 8 (1965), pp. 192–7.

Lee, J. "Wesker's 'Centre 42.'" *Encounter*, 19, 2 (1962), pp. 95–6. A letter to the editor.

Leech, C. "Two Romantics: Arnold Wesker and Harold Pinter." *Stratford-Upon-Avon Studies*, 4 (1962); revised edition 1968, pp. 10–31.

Leeming, G. *Arnold Wesker*. Writers and Their Work, 225. London: Longmans, 1972.

Leeming, G. *Wesker: The Playwright*. New York: Methuen, 1983.

Leeming, G. and Trussler, S. *The Plays of Arnold Wesker*. London: Gollancz, 1971.

Lindemann, V. *Arnold Wesker als Gesellschaftskritiker*. Salzburg Studies in English Literature, 60. Salzburg: University of Salzburg, 1980.

Mander, J. *The Writer and Commitment*. London: Secker & Warburg, 1961, pp. 194–211.

Marland, M., ed. *Arnold Wesker*. Times Author Series, 1. London: 1970.

Marowitz, C. "Oh Mother Is It Worth It?" *Theatre Arts* (May 1962), pp. 72–3.

Maschler, T. "Knowingness and Optimism." *Jewish Quarterly*, 13, 2 (1965), pp. 5–6.

Meaker, D. *Man and Work: Literature and Culture in Industrial Society*. London: Methuen, 1976.

Ribalow, H. *Arnold Wesker*. New York: Twayne's, 1965.

Sonntag, J. "The World of Arnold Wesker." *Jewish Quarterly*, 20, 3 (1972), pp. 37–8.

Spencer, C. "Arnold Wesker as a Playwright." *Jewish Quarterly*, 7, 1 (1959), pp. 40–1.

Styan, J. *Modern Drama in Theory and Practice*. Volume 1. Cambridge, England: Cambridge University Press, 1981, pp. 156–9.

Taylor, John Russell. *Anger and After*. London: Methuen, 1962; 2nd revised edition, 1969.

Tynan, K. *Tynan Right and Left*. London: Longmans, and New York: Atheneum, 1967.

Wellwarth, G. "Arnold Wesker: 'Awake and Sing' in Whitechapel." In his *The Theater of Paradox and Protest: Developments in the Avant-Garde Drama*. Revised edition. New York: New York University Press, 1971, pp. 271–82.

Winegarten, R. "Arnold Wesker: Is Sincerity Enough?" *Jewish Observer and Middle East Review*, 19 April 1963, pp. 18–19.

II. Dramatists

Michael Hastings (born 1938)

Collected Works

Three Plays. London: W. H. Allen, 1966. Includes *Don't Destroy Me, Yes, And After, The World's Baby*.

Three Plays. Harmondsworth: Penguin Books, 1980.

Drama

Don't Destroy Me. London: Nimbus, 1956. Produced London, 1956; New York, 1957.

Yes, And After. In *New English Dramatists, 4 (Shaffer, Arden, Hastings)*. Harmondsworth: Penguin Books, 1962; republished in *Three Plays (Hall, Hastings, Lessing)*. Harmondsworth: Penguin Books, 1975. Produced London, 1956; New York, 1957.

The Silence of Lee Harvey Oswald. Harmondsworth: Penguin Books, 1966. Produced London, 1965.

The Silence of Saint-Just. London: Weidenfeld & Nicolson, 1970. Produced Brighton, 1971.

The Cutting of the Cloth. Produced London, 1973.

Gloo-Joo. Plays and Players, 25, 12 (1978), and 26, 1 (1978). Produced London, 1978.

Novels

The Game. London: W. H. Allen, 1957, and New York: McGraw Hill, 1958.

The Frauds. London: W. H. Allen, 1960, and New York: Orion Press, 1961.

Tussy is Me: A Romance. London: Weidenfeld & Nicolson, 1970, and New York: Delacorte Press, 1971.

The Nightcomers. New York: Delacorte Press, 1972; republished, London: Pan Books, 1973. Film version, 1971.

Verse

Love Me Lambeth and Other Poems. London: W. H. Allen, 1961.

Essay

"Glum Theatre, Or Killing Them With Laughter." *Plays and Players,* 26, 12 (1979), p. 12.

HAROLD PINTER (BORN 1930)

So much has been written on Pinter that this can only be a selection of the available material. I have therefore not attempted to list the plays individually and have given only a few articles not included in collections of essays.

Bibliography

Gale, S. *Harold Pinter: An Annotated Bibliography.* Boston: G. K. Hall, 1978.

Schroll, H. *Harold Pinter: A Study of his Reputation (1958–1969) and a Checklist.* Metuchen, N.J.: Scarecrow Press, 1971.

Collected Works

Plays. In four volumes. London: Eyre Methuen, and New York: Grove Press, 1977–1981. Includes plays, sketches and essays.

Poems and Prose, 1949–1977. London: Eyre Methuen, 1978.

Uncollected Drama

The Hothouse. London: Eyre Methuen, and New York: Grove Press, 1980.

Other Places: Three Plays. London: Methuen, 1982.

Screenplays

Five Screenplays. London: Methuen, 1971, and New York: Grove Press, 1974.
The Proust Screenplay. London: Eyre Methuen, 1978.

Verse

Poems. London: Enitharmon Press, 1968; revised edition, 1970.

Interviews

"Talk of the Town." *New Yorker,* 25 February 1967.
Bensky, L. "Harold Pinter." In *Writers at Work: The Paris Interviews (3rd series).* New York: Viking, 1967, pp. 347–68.
Tynan, K. "In Search of Harold Pinter." *Evening Standard,* 25 April 1968, and 26 April 1968.

Selected Critical Studies

Almansi, G. and Henderson, S. *Harold Pinter.* London: Methuen, 1983.
Andretta, R. "The Chicken that Crossed the Road: A Study of Harold Pinter's *The Birthday Party.*" *Journal of English,* 8 (1980), pp. 75–108.
Baker, W. and Tabachnick, S. *Harold Pinter.* Edinburgh: Oliver & Boyd, 1973.
Ben-Zvi, L. "Harold Pinter's *Betrayal:* The Patterns of Banality." *Modern Drama,* 23 (1980), pp. 227–37.
Bernhard, F. "Beyond Realism: The Plays of Harold Pinter." *Modern Drama,* 8 (1965–1966), pp. 185–91.
Brown, John Russell. "Mr Pinter's Shakespeare." In *Essays in the Modern Drama.* Ed. M. Freedman. Boston: Heath & Co., 1966, pp. 352–66.
Brown, John Russell. *Theatre Language: A Study of Arden, Osborne, Pinter and Wesker.* London: Allen Lane, 1972.
Burkman, K. *The Dramatic World of Harold Pinter: Its Basis in Ritual.* Columbus: Ohio State University Press, 1971.
Burton, D. *Dialogue and Discourse: A Socio-Linguistic Approach to Modern Drama and Naturally Occuring Discourse.* London: Routledge & Kegan Paul, 1980.
Cohen, M. "The Plays of Harold Pinter." *Jewish Quarterly,* 8, 3 (1961), pp. 21–2.
Colby, D. *As the Curtain Rises: On Contemporary British Drama, 1966–1976.* Cranbury, N.J.: Associated University Presses, 1978.
Dukore, B. *Harold Pinter.* New York: Macmillan, 1982.
Esslin, M. *The Peopled Wound: The Plays of Harold Pinter.* London: Methuen, 1970; revised edition published as *Pinter: A Study of His Plays.* London: Methuen, 1973.
Gale, S. *Butter's Going Up.* Durham: Duke University Press, 1977.

Ganz, A., ed. *Pinter: A Collection of Critical Essays.* Englewood Cliffs, N.J.: Prentice-Hall, 1972.

Gillen, F. "'Nowhere to Go': Society and the Individual in Harold Pinter's *The Hothouse.*" *Twentieth-Century Literature,* 29, 1 (1983), pp. 86–96.

Gordon, G. *Strategems to Cover Nakedness: The Drama of Harold Pinter.* Columbia: University of Missouri Press, 1969.

Hall, P. "Directing Pinter." *Theatre Quarterly,* 4, 16 (November 1974–January 1975), pp. 4–17.

Hayman, R. *Harold Pinter.* London: Heinemann, 1970.

Hinchcliffe, A. *Harold Pinter.* Revised edition. Boston: G. K. Hall, 1981.

Hobson, H. Review of *The Birthday Party. Sunday Times,* 25 May 1958.

Hollis, J. *Harold Pinter: The Poetics of Silence.* Carbondale: South Illinois University Press, 1970.

Kennedy, A. *Six Dramatists in Search of a Language.* Cambridge, England: Cambridge University Press, 1975, pp. 165–91.

Lahr, J., ed. *The Homecoming: Harold Pinter, A Casebook.* New York: Grove Press, 1971.

Morrison, K. *Canters and Canticles: The Use of Narrative in the Plays of Samuel Beckett and Harold Pinter.* Chicago: University of Chicago Press, 1983.

Nelson, H. "*The Homecoming:* Kith and Kin." In *Modern British Dramatists.* Ed. John Russell Brown. Englewood Cliffs, N.J.: Prentice-Hall, 1968, pp. 145–63.

Supple, B. "Pinter's Homecoming." *Jewish Chronicle,* 25 June 1965, pp. 7, 31.

Schiff, E. "Pancakes and Soap Suds: A Study of Childishness in Pinter's Plays." *Modern Drama,* 16, 1 (1973), pp. 91–101.

Spencer, C. "Pinter in Print." *Jewish Quarterly,* 16, 2–3 (1968), p. 43.

Stamm, R. "*The Hothouse:* Harold Pinter's Tribute to Anger." *English Studies,* 62, 3 (1981), pp. 290–8.

Taylor, John Russell. *Anger and After.* 2nd revised edition. London: Methuen, 1969.

Taylor, John Russell. *Harold Pinter.* Writers and their Work Series, 212. London: Longmans, 1969.

ANTHONY SHAFFER (BORN 1926)

Drama

The Savage Parade. One performance only, London, 1963.

Sleuth. London: Calder, and New York: Dodd, Mead, 1970. Produced London, 1963. Screenplay 1973.

Murderer. London and Boston: Boyars, 1979. Produced London, 1975.

The Case of the Oily Levantine. Produced London, 1979; as *Whodunit,* New York, 1982.

Novel

Absolution. London: Severn House, 1979. Screenplay, 1970.

Interview

Gow, G. "Murder Games." *Plays and Players*, 27, 1 (1979), pp. 10–13. Includes a brief comment on Anthony Shaffer's *The Savage Parade* about the "Eichmann business."

<h2 style="text-align:center">PETER SHAFFER (BORN 1926)</h2>

Bibliography

Carpenter, C., ed. In *Modern Drama*, 24, 4 (1981), pp. 550–1.

Collected Works

Five Finger Exercise, Shrivings, Equus. Harmondsworth: Penguin Books, 1976.
Four Plays. Harmondsworth: Penguin Books, 1981.
Collected Plays. New York: Crown, 1982.

Drama

Five Finger Exercise. London: Hamish Hamilton, 1958, and New York: Harcourt Brace, 1959; republished in *Three Plays (Shaffer, Wesker, Kops).* Harmondsworth: Penguin Books, 1959; in *New English Dramatists, 4 (Shaffer, Arden, Hastings).* Harmondsworth: Penguin Books, 1962. Produced London, 1958; New York, 1959.
The Private Ear and the Public Eye. London: Hamish Hamilton, 1962, and New York: Stein & Day, 1964. Produced London, 1962; New York, 1963.
The Royal Hunt of the Sun. London: Hamish Hamilton, 1964, and New York: Stein & Day, 1965. Produced Chichester, 1964; New York, 1965. Later filmed.
Black Comedy. London: French, 1967. With *White Lies*, New York: Stein & Day, 1967. Produced Chichester, 1965; New York, 1967.
A Warning Game. Produced New York, 1967.
White Lies. In *Black Comedy, Including White Lies*, New York: Stein & Day, 1967, and as *The White Liars*, London: French, 1967. Produced New York, 1967; London, 1968. Revised version produced, London and New York, 1976.
The White Liars, Black Comedy. London: Hamish Hamilton, 1968.
It's About Cinderella. Produced London, 1969.
Shrivings. London: Deutsch, 1974. Produced as *The Battle of Shrivings*, London, 1970.

Equus. London: Deutsch, 1973, and New York: Avon Books, 1975; republished
    Harmondsworth: Penguin Books, 1977. Produced London, 1973. Later
    filmed.
Equus and Shrivings. New York: Atheneum.
Amadeus. London: Deutsch, 1980.

Television Plays

The Salt Land, 1955.
Balance of Terror, 1957.

Radio Play

The Prodigal Father, 1957.

Essay

"Figure of Death." *Observer.* 4 November 1979, p. 37.

Interviews

Chambers, C. "Psychic Energy." *Plays and Players,* 27, 5 (1980), pp. 40–1.
Glanville, B. "The Man Behind the Pen (2)." *Jewish Chronicle,* 26 December
    1958, p. 13.
Pree, B. 1963 interview in *Behind the Scenes: Theatre and Film Interviews
    from the Transatlantic Review.* London, 1971.

Critical Studies

Ebner, I. "The Double Crisis of Sexuality and Worship in Shaffer's *Equus.*"
    Christianity and Literature, 31, 2 (1982), p. 29–47.
Gillespie, M. "Peter Shaffer: 'To Make Whatever God There Is.'" *Claudel
    Studies,* 9, 2 (1982), p. 61–70.
Hayman, R. "Like a Woman they Keep Going Back to." *Drama,* 98 (1970),
    pp. 57–64.
Klein, D. *Peter Shaffer.* Boston: Twayne, 1979.
Klein, D. "*Amadeus:* The Third Part of Peter Shaffer's Dramatic Trilogy."
    Modern Language Studies, 13, 1 (1983), pp. 31–8.
Scott, M. "*Amadeus:* A Glimpse of the Absolute Theatre." *Plays and Players,*
    27, 5 (1980), pp. 40–1.
Taylor, John Russell. *Anger and After.* 2nd revised edition. London: Methuen,
    1969.
Taylor, John Russell. *Peter Shaffer.* Writers and their Work Series. London:
    Longmans, 1974.

ANTHONY AND PETER SHAFFER (AS JOINT AUTHORS)

Novels

Peter Antony. *How Doth the Little Crocodile?* London: Evans, 1951.
Peter Antony. *The Woman in the Wardrobe.* London: Evans, 1952, and New York: Macmillan, 1957.
Anthony and Peter Shaffer. *Withered Murderer.* London: Gollancz, 1955, and New York: Macmillan, 1956.

Critical Studies

Glenn, J. "Twins in Disguise: A Psychoanalytic Essay on *Sleuth* and *Royal Hunt of the Sun.*" *Psychoanalytic Quarterly,* 43 (April 1974), pp. 288–302.
Glenn, J. "Anthony and Peter Shaffer's Plays: The Influence of Twinship on Creativity." *American Imago,* 31 (fall 1974), pp. 270–92.

C. P. TAYLOR (1929–1981)

Among the seventy plays written by C. P. Taylor, only *Schippel* (adapted from Carl Sternheim), *And the Nightingale Sang,* and *Good* were seen at non-fringe London theaters. His unpublished plays include *Mr David, Oil and Water, Next Year in Tel-Aviv, Goldberg, Black and White Minstrels, Walter,* and a musical, *Who's Pinkus? Where's Chelm?* It is to be hoped that posterity will posthumously accord him more attention.

Drama

Fable. Edinburgh: Edinburgh University Drama Society, 1967. Produced Glasgow, 1965.
Happy Days are Here Again. In *Radio Plays: New English Dramatists, 12.* Harmondsworth: Penguin Books, 1968. Produced Edinburgh, 1965.
Allergy. In *Traverse Plays.* Harmondsworth: Penguin Books, 1966. Produced London and Edinburgh, 1966, and New York, 1974.
Bread and Butter. In *New English Dramatists, 10.* Harmondsworth: Penguin Books, 1967. Produced Edinburgh, 1966, and Washington, D.C., 1969.
The Ballachulish Beat. London: Rapp and Carroll, 1967.
Lies About Vietnam/Truth About Sarajevo. Published under the title *The Truth About Sarajevo.* Kirknewton, Midlothian: Scottish Theatre Editions, 1970. Produced Edinburgh, 1969.
Thank You Very Much. London: Methuen, 1970. Produced Shiremore, Northumberland, 1969.
Bloch's Play. Kirknewton, Midlothian: Scottish Theatre Editions, 1971. Produced Edinburgh, 1971.
Words. In *Second Playbill 2.* Ed. A. Durband. London: Hutchinson, 1973. Televized, 1972.

Apples. In *Prompt One.* Ed. A. Durband. London: Hutchinson, 1976. Produced Newcastle-upon-Tyne, 1976.
Bandits! North Shields, Tyne and Wear: Iron Press, 1977.
And the Nightingale Sang. London: Eyre Methuen, 1979.
Good. London: Methuen, 1982. Produced London, 1981.
Happy Lies. Stand, 23, 2 (1982), pp. 8–31.

Critical Study

Nightingale, B. "C. P. Taylor." *Stand,* 23, 2 (1982), pp. 32–3.

III. NOVELISTS

ALEXANDER BARON (BORN 1917)

Novels

From the City, From the Plough. London: Cape, 1948, and New York: Washburn, 1949. Republished London: Pan Books, 1953; London: Panther Books, 1960; London: Mayflower Books, 1972; Bath: Lythway Press, 1974.
There's No Home. London: Cape, 1950. Republished Bath: Chivers, 1972.
Rosie Hogarth. London: Cape, 1951. Republished Bath: Chivers, 1972.
With Hope Farewell. London: Cape, and New York: Washburn, 1952. Republished as *The Thunder of Peace.* London: Corgi Books, 1962. Also republished Bath: Chivers, 1973.
The Golden Princess. London: Cape, 1954. Republished London: Collins, 1958.
Queen of the East. London: Collins, and New York: Washburn, 1956. Republished London: Panther Books, 1960.
Seeing Life. London: Collins, 1959.
The Lowlife. London: Collins, 1963, and New York: Yoseloff, 1964. Republished Hornchurch: Ian Henry, 1979.
Strip Jack Naked. London: Collins, 1966, and New York: Yoseloff, 1967.
King Dido. London: Macmillan, 1969.
The In-Between Time. London: Macmillan, 1971.
Gentle Folk. London: Macmillan, 1976.
Franco is Dying. London: Macmillan, 1977.

Short Stories

The Human Kind. London: Cape, 1953. Republished, London: Pan Books, 1957; Bath: Chivers, 1973. Adapted for the cinema as *The Victors.* London: Panther Books, and New York: Dell, 1963.

"My Grandmother's Hands." In *Modern Jewish Stories*. Ed. Gerda Charles. London: Faber, 1963, and Englewood Cliffs, N.J.: Prentice Hall, 1964, pp. 151–7.

Television Play

The Harsh World (about 1963).

Autobiography

"My Teachers." *Quest*, 1 (1965), pp. 30–1.

Essays

"As an Englishman and a Jew." *Jewish Quarterly*, 1, 2 (1953), pp. 10–12.
"The Anniversary." *Jewish Quarterly*, 1, 4 (1959), pp. 7–10.
"The Jew in Victorian Literature." *Jewish Quarterly*, 2, 4 (1955), pp. 10–12.
"The Jew Inside Me." *Jewish Quarterly*, 4, 2 (1956), p. 6–7.
"Louis Golding (1896–1958)." *Jewish Quarterly*, 6, 1 (1958), p. 3.
"Prelude to Tragedy: Afterthoughts on 'Incident at Vichy.'" *Jewish Quarterly*, 14, 1 (1966), pp. 11–13.

Interviews

"On Being English and Jewish (1)." *Jewish Quarterly*, 11, 1 (1963), pp. 6–10.
Glanville, B. "The Man Behind the Pen (3)." *Jewish Chronicle*, 2 January 1959, p. 15.

Critical Studies

Baker, W. "The World of Alexander Baron." *Jewish Quarterly*, 17 (Winter 1969), pp. 17–20.
Collier, J. "Live History." *Jewish Quarterly*, 2, 2 (1954), pp. 81–3.
Sonntag, J. "Harryboy's Return." *Jewish Quarterly*, 13, 4 (1966), pp. 46–7.
Winegarten, R. "Why Alexander Baron is Popular." *Jewish Observer and Middle East Review*, 1 April 1966, p. 14.

CHAIM BERMANT (BORN 1929)

Novels

Jericho Sleep Alone. London: Chapman & Hall, 1964. Republished New York: Mayflower-Dell, 1966; with *Berl Make Tea*, New York: Holt Rinehart, 1966.
Berl Make Tea. London: Chapman & Hall, 1965. Republished with *Jericho Sleep Alone*, New York: Holt Rinehart, 1966.

Ben Preserve Us. London: Chapman & Hall, 1965, and New York: Holt Rinehart, 1966.

Diary of an Old Man. London: Chapman & Hall, 1966, and New York: Holt Rinehart, 1967.

Swinging in the Rain. London: Hodder & Stoughton, 1967.

Here Endeth the Lesson. London: Eyre & Spottiswoode, 1969.

Now Dowager. London: Eyre & Spottiswoode, 1971.

Roses are Blooming in Picardy. London: Eyre Methuen, 1972.

The Last Supper. London: Eyre Methuen, 1973, and New York: St. Martin's Press, 1973.

The Second Mrs. Whitberg. London: Allen & Unwin, and New York: St. Martin's Press, 1976.

Squire of Bor Shachar. London: Allen & Unwin, and New York: St. Martin's Press, 1977.

Now Newman was Old. London: Allen & Unwin, and New York: St. Martin's Press, 1978.

Belshazzar. London: Allen & Unwin, 1979.

The Patriarch: A Jewish Family Saga. London: Weidenfeld & Nicolson, 1981; republished Feltham, Middlesex: Hamlyn, 1982.

The House of Women. London: Weidenfeld & Nicolson, 1983.

Autobiography

Coming Home. London: Allen & Unwin, 1976.

Essays

"The Writer's Universe." *Jewish Quarterly*, special edition, (Spring 1967), pp. 36–8.

"Coming and Going." *Present Tense*. 10, 3 (1983), pp. 52–4.

GERDA CHARLES (BORN 1915)

Novels

The True Voice. London: Eyre & Spottiswoode, 1959.

The Crossing Point. London: Eyre & Spottiswoode, 1960, and New York: Knopf, 1961.

A Slanting Light. London: Eyre & Spottiswoode, and New York: Knopf, 1963.

A Logical Girl. London: Eyre & Spottiswoode, and New York: Knopf, 1967.

The Destiny Waltz. London: Eyre & Spottiswoode, and New York: Scribner, 1972.

Uncollected Short Stories

"The Staircase." *Vanity Fair*, (April 1956).

"Rosh Hashana in Five Weeks." In *Pick of Today's Short Stories*, 11, London: Putnam, 1966.

"The Czechoslovakian Chandelier." In *Modern Jewish Stories.* Ed. Gerda Charles. London: Faber, 1963, and Englewood Cliffs, N.J.: Prentice-Hall, 1964, pp. 108–15.

"A Mixed Marriage." *Quest,* 1 (1965), pp. 10–14.

"The Difference." *Jewish Chronicle,* 24 November 1967.

Interviews

"On Being English and Jewish (2)." *Jewish Quarterly,* 11, 4 (1963), pp. 6–9.

Coleman, T. "Revenge is Sour." *Guardian,* 17 May 1971, p. 11.

Critical Studies

Baron, A. "Gerda Charles: A Visionary Realist." *Jewish Quarterly,* 19, 1–2 (1971), pp. 39–41.

McDowell, F. "World within World: Gerda Charles, Frederic Raphael and the Anglo-Jewish Community." *Critique,* 6, 3 (1963), pp. 143–50.

Snow, C. P. "Facing the Music." *Financial Times,* 15 April 1971.

Spencer, C. "Two Writers on a Jewish Theme." *Jewish Quarterly,* 7, 3 (1960), pp. 34–6.

Wesker, A. "A Crucial Question." *Jewish Quarterly,* 7, 3 (1960), pp. 43–5.

Winegarten, R. "The World of Gerda Charles." *Jewish Quarterly,* 15, 1–2 (1967), pp. 37–40.

BRIAN GLANVILLE (BORN 1931)

Novels

The Reluctant Dictator. London: Werner Laurie, 1952.

Henry Sows the Wind. London: Secker & Warburg, 1954.

Along the Arno. London: Secker & Warburg, 1956, and New York: Cromwell, 1957.

The Bankrupts. London: Secker & Warburg, 1956, and New York: Doubleday, 1958: republished London: Corgi Books, 1965.

After Rome, Africa. London: Secker & Warburg, 1959.

Diamond. London: Secker & Warburg, and New York: Farrar Straus, 1962.

The Rise of Gerry Logan. London: Secker & Warburg, 1963 and New York: Delacorte Press, 1965.

A Second Home. London: Secker & Warburg, 1965, and New York: Delacorte Press, 1966.

A Roman Marriage. London: Michael Joseph, 1966, and New York: Coward McCann, 1967.

The Artist Type. London: Cape, 1967, and New York: Coward McCann, 1968.

The Olympian. London: Secker & Warburg, 1969, and New York: Coward McCann, 1969. Republished New York: Dell Books, 1970.

A Cry of Crickets. London: Secker & Warburg, and New York: Coward McCann, 1970.
The Financiers. London: Secker & Warburg, 1972. Published in the U.S. as *Money is Love.* New York: Doubleday, 1972.
The Comic. London: Secker & Warburg, 1974, and New York: Stein & Day, 1975. Republished Harmondsworth: Penguin Books, 1979.
The Dying of the Light. London: Secker & Warburg, 1976.
Never Look Back. London: Michael Joseph, 1980.

Collected Stories

A Bad Streak, and Other Stories. London: Secker & Warburg, 1961.
The Director's Wife, and Other Stories. London: Secker & Warburg, 1963.
Goalkeepers are Crazy: A Collection of Football Stories. London: Secker & Warburg, 1964.
The King of Hackney Marshes, and Other Stories. London: Secker & Warburg, 1965.
A Betting Man. New York: Coward McCann, 1969.
The Thing He Loves, and Other Stories. London: Secker & Warburg, 1973.
A Bad Lot, and Other Stories. London: Severn House, 1977.

Essays

"The Bankrupts: Some Defence Reactions." *Jewish Quarterly*, 6, 1 (1958), pp. 34–5.
"Isaac Babel." *Jewish Chronicle*, 22 July 1960, Quarterly Supplement, pp. 5, 7.
"Some Notes on Writing Stories." *London Magazine*, 9, 12 (1970), pp. 7–8.

Interview

"On Being English and Jewish (2)." *Jewish Quarterly*, 11, 3 (1963), pp. 3–5.

Critical Studies

Charles, G. "Three Recent Novels." *Jewish Quarterly*, 13, 3 (1966), pp. 43–4.
Jacobson, D. "Between Hampstead and Hendon." *Commentary*, 26, 2 (1958), pp. 178–9.
Sonntag, F. "Three Generations." *Jewish Quarterly*, 9, 3 (1962), pp. 44–5.
Walsh, W. *A Human Idiom.* London: Chatto & Windus, 1965.

FREDERIC RAPHAEL (BORN 1931)

Novels

Obbligato, London: Macmillan, 1956.
The Earlsdon Way. London: Cassell, 1958.

The Limits of Love. London: Cassell, 1960, and Philadelphia: Lippincott, 1961. Republished Harmondsworth: Penguin Books, 1963.

A Wild Surmise. London: Cassell, 1961, and Philadelphia: Lippincott, 1962.

The Graduate Wife. London: Cassell, 1962. Republished with *The Trouble With England,* London: Corgi Books, 1964; Hornchurch: I. Henry, 1976.

The Trouble with England. London: Cassell, 1962. Republished with *The Graduate Wife,* London: Corgi Books, 1964; Hornchurch: I. Henry, 1976. Television script, 1964.

Lindmann. London: Cassell, 1963, and New York: Holt Rinehart, 1964. Republished London: Panther Books, 1967.

Darling. New York: New American Library, 1965.

Orchestra and Beginners. London: Cape, 1967, and New York: Viking, 1968.

Like Men Betrayed. London: Cape, 1970, and New York: Viking, 1971.

Who were You With Last Night? London: Cape, 1971, and Indianapolis: Bobbs-Merrill, 1976.

April June and November. London: Cape, 1972.

Richard's Things. London: Cape, and Indianapolis: Bobbs-Merrill, 1973.

California Time. London: Cape, and New York: Holt Rinehart, 1975.

The Glittering Prizes. Harmondsworth: Penguin Books, 1976, and New York: St. Martin's Press, 1977. Republished Baltimore: Penguin Books, 1979. Adapted for the stage as *Early Days.* Screened in Britain and the United States as a B.B.C. television serial from 1975.

Heaven and Earth. London: Cape, 1985.

Collected Stories

Sleeps Six, and Other Stories. London: Cape, 1979.

Oxbridge Blues, And Other Stories. London: Cape, 1980.

After the War. London: Cape, 1981.

Fragment

"The Diary of Paul Feldman." *Jewish Quarterly,* 11, 1 (1963), pp. 23–4. Excerpt from a novel.

Screenplays

Two for the Road. London: Cape, and New York: Holt Rinehart, 1967.

Nothing but the Best (1964).

Darling (1965).

Far From the Madding Crowd (1967).

How About Us? (1971).

A Severed Head (1971).

Daisy Miller (1974).

Original Television Scripts

The Executioners (1961).
Something's Wrong (1978).
The Best of Friends (1979).

Autobiography

Frederic Raphael: Cambridge. B.B.C. television documentary, 19 March 1980.
    Raphael revisits his *alma mater* in series on writers and places.
"The Curiousness of Anglo-Jews." *Jewish Quarterly*, 31, 2 1984, 11–16.

Essays

"Sacred and Profane." *Jewish Quarterly*, 8, 1 (1960–1961), pp. 4–5, 7.
"Intellectuals and Just Causes: A Symposium, II." *Encounter*, 29, 4 (1967),
    pp. 46–7.
"Must We Always Be on the Defensive?" *Jewish Quarterly*, 16, 2–3 (1968),
    pp. 3–7.
"Ode to a Syrian Armoured Division." *Jewish Quarterly*, 24, 4 (1976), p. 48.
    Polemical verse.
Cracks in the Ice: Views and Reviews. London: W. H. Allen, 1979. Selected
    reviews and essays.
"Leaves from a Notebook." *Jewish Quarterly*, 29, 2–3 (1981), pp. 9–12.
"The Dead Man in the Cargo." *Jewish Quarterly*, 30, 1–2 (1982), pp. 14–16.

Interviews

"On Being English and Jewish (2)." *Jewish Quarterly*, 11, 3 (1963), pp. 6–8.
Boyd, W. "The Price of Glittering." *Oxford Literary Review*, 2, 1 (1977), pp.
    4–8.
Sacks, Rabbi Jonathan. Conversation first broadcast on B.B.C. radio, 14 April
    1980.

Critical Studies

Baron, A. "A 'New Wave.'" *Jewish Quarterly*, 7, 3 (1960), p. 42.
McDowell, F. "World within World: Gerda Charles, Frederic Raphael and
    the Anglo-Jewish Community." *Critique*, 6, 3 (1963), pp. 143–50.
Spencer, C. "Two Writers on a Jewish Theme." *Jewish Quarterly*, 7, 3 (1960),
    pp. 34–6.

BERNICE RUBENS (BORN 1928)

Novels

Set on Edge. London: Eyre & Spottiswoode, 1960. Republished London:
    Vallentine & Mitchell, 1972.

Madame Souzatska. London: Eyre & Spottiswoode, 1962.

Mate in Three. London: Eyre & Spottiswoode, 1965.

The Elected Member. London: Eyre & Spottiswoode, and under the title *Chosen People,* New York: Atheneum, 1969. Republished Harmondsworth: Penguin Books, 1974; London: Sphere Books, 1980; New York: Washington Square Press, 1984.

Sunday Best. London: Eyre & Spottiswoode, 1971. Republished Harmondsworth: Penguin Books, 1974; New York: Summit, 1980.

Go Tell the Lemming. London: Cape, 1973. Republished New York: Washington Square Press, 1984.

I Sent a Letter to My Love. London: W. H. Allen, 1975, and New York: St. Martin's Press, 1978. Republished London: Sphere Books, 1980. Stage adaptation produced London, 1979.

The Ponsonby Post. London: W. H. Allen, 1977, and New York: St. Martin's Press, 1978.

A Five Year Sentence. London: W. H. Allen, and, as *Favours,* New York: Summit, 1978. Republished London: Sphere Books, 1981.

Spring Sonata: A Fable. London: W. H. Allen, 1979. Republished London: Sphere Books, 1981.

Birds of Passage. London: Hamilton, 1981. Republished New York: Washington Square Press, 1984.

Brothers. London: Hamilton, and New York: Delacorte Press, 1983.

Short Story

"The Blood of the Lamb." *Jewish Quarterly,* 21, 1–2 (1973), pp. 144–7.

Television Play

Third Party (1972).

Interview

Rose, J. "Talking to Bernice Rubens." *Jewish Chronicle,* 26 September 1979, p. 27.

IV. POETS

DANNIE ABSE (BORN 1923)

Collected Works

Three Questor Plays. London: Scorpion Press, 1967. Includes *House of Cowards, Gone* and *In the Cage.*

Collected Poems, 1948–1976. London: Hutchinson, 1977, and Pittsburgh: University of Pittsburgh Press, 1977.

Verse

After Every Green Thing. London: Hutchinson, 1949.
Walking Under Water. London: Hutchinson, 1952.
Tenants of the House. London: Hutchinson, 1957, and New York: Criterion, 1958.
Poems, Golders Green. London: Hutchinson, 1962.
Dannie Abse: A Selection. London: Studio Vista, 1963.
A Small Desperation. London: Hutchinson, 1968.
Demo. Frensham, Surrey: Sceptre Press, 1969.
Selected Poems. London: Hutchinson, and New York: Oxford University Press, 1970.
Funland. London: Hutchinson, and New York: Oxford University Press, 1973.
Pythagoras. London: Hutchinson, 1979.
Way Out in the Centre. London: Hutchinson, 1981.
One-Legged on Ice. Athens: University of Georgia Press, 1983.

Short Stories

"The Tobacconist." *Commentary*, 23, 3 (1957), pp. 250–5.
"Metamorphosis of Reg." *Twentieth Century*, 1034 (1967).

Novels

Ash on a Young Man's Sleeve. London: Hutchinson, 1954, and New York: Criterion, 1955. Republished London: Vallentine & Mitchell, 1969; Harmondsworth: Penguin Books, 1983.
Some Corner of an English Field. London: Hutchinson, 1956, and New York: Criterion, 1957.
O, Jones, O. Jones. London: Hutchinson, 1970.

Drama

Hands Around the Wall. Produced London, 1950.
Fire in Heaven. London: Hutchinson, 1956. Revised version *In the Cage* in *Three Questor Plays*. Produced London, 1948; revised as *Is the House Shut?* London, 1964.
The Eccentric, Jewish Quarterly, 7, 1 (1959), pp. 12–17, 19. In book form, London: Evans, 1961. Produced London, 1961.
The Joker. Produced London, 1962.
The Courting of Essie Glass. Jewish Quarterly, 19, 4 (1971), pp. 16–23. Radio broadcast, 1975.

The Dogs of Pavlov. London: Vallentine & Mitchell, 1973. Includes an essay
by Abse and responses by Professor Stanley Milgram. Produced London, 1969; New York, 1974.
Funland. Produced London, 1975.
Pythagoras. Produced Birmingham, England, 1976.

Radio Plays

Conform or Die (1957).
No Telegrams, No Thunder (1962).
You Can't Say Hello to Anybody (1964).
A Small Explosion (1964).

Autobiography

A Poet in the Family: An Autobiography. London: Hutchinson, 1974. Republished London: Robson Books, 1984.
A Strong Dose of Myself. London: Hutchinson, 1983.

Interviews

"On Being English and Jewish (3)." *Jewish Quarterly*, 11, 4 (1963), pp. 3–6.
Glanville, B. "The Man Behind the Pen (6)." *Jewish Chronicle*, 16 January 1959, p. 19.

Essays

"Intellectuals and Just Causes: A Symposium, I." *Encounter*, 29, 3 (1967), pp. 5–6.
"Poetry Since 1939." *Jewish Quarterly*, special edition (spring 1967), pp. 18–21, 63.
"Pages from a Princeton Diary." *Jewish Quarterly*, 24, 3 (1976), pp. 10–15.
"The Ongoing Tradition." *Jewish Quarterly*, 25, 1 (1977), pp. 43–4.
"Finding a Voice of My Own." *Jewish Quarterly*, 26, 3–4 (1978), pp. 85–8. Based on a B.B.C. radio talk.
"My Jewish Poems: New Poems with an Introduction." *European Judaism*, 14, 2 (1980–1981), pp. 2–7.

Critical Studies

Cohen, J., ed. *The Poetry of Dannie Abse: Critical Essays and Reminiscences.* London: Robson Books, 1983.
Kazin, P. "Jews in Cardiff." *Commentary*, 19 (1955), pp. 402–6.
Maccoby, D. "A Poet's Vision." *Jewish Quarterly*, 15, 3 (1977), pp. 50–1.
Mathias, R. "The Poetry of Dannie Abse." *Anglo-Welsh Review*, 16 (Winter 1967).

Zach, N. "An Israeli's View of Some Anglo-Jewish Poetry." *Jewish Quarterly*, 16, 4 (1968), pp. 31–3.

RUTH FAINLIGHT (BORN 1931)

Although American born, Fainlight lives in England with her husband, Alan Sillitoe, the English novelist.

Verse

A Forecast, A Fable. London: Outpost Publications, 1958.
Cages. London: Macmillan, 1966, and Chester Springs, Penn.: Dufour, 1967.
18 Poems from 1966. London: Turret Books, 1967.
To See the Matter Clearly, and Other Poems. London: Macmillan, 1968, and Chester Springs, Penn.: Dufour, 1969.
With Alan Sillitoe and Ted Hughes. *Poems*. London: Rainbow Press, 1971.
The Region's Violence. London: Hutchinson, 1973.
21 Poems. London: Turret Books, 1973.
Sybils. New York: Gehenna Press, 1980.
Sybils, and Others. London: Hutchinson, 1980.
Two Wind Poems. Rushden, Northamptonshire: Sceptre Press, 1980.
Fifteen to Infinity. London: Hutchinson, 1983.
Climates. Newcastle: Bloodaxe, 1983.

Short Stories

Daylife and Nightlife. London: Deutsch, 1971.

ELAINE FEINSTEIN (BORN 1930)

Although Feinstein is known equally well as a novelist, poet and translator, I have almost arbitrarily placed her among the poets, because I feel that is where she excels and because her treatment of Jewish themes has less in common with the "Golders Green" novelists.

Verse

In a Green Eye. London: Goliard Press, 1966.
The Magic Apple Tree. London: Hutchinson, 1971.
At the Edge. Rushden, Northamptonshire: Sceptre Press, 1972.
The Celebrants, and Other Poems. London: Hutchinson, 1973.
Some Unease and Angels: Selected Poems. London: Hutchinson, and University Center, Michigan, 1977.
Feast of Eurydice. London: Next Editions, 1980.

Novels

The Circle. London: Hutchinson, 1970.

The Amberstone Exit. London: Hutchinson, 1972. Republished Harmondsworth: Penguin Books, 1974.

The Glass Alembic. London: Hutchinson, 1973, and, under the title *Crystal Garden,* New York: Dutton, 1974.

The Children of the Rose. London: Hutchinson, 1975. Republished Harmondsworth: Penguin Books, 1976.

The Ecstasy of Dr. Miriam Gardner. London: Hutchinson, 1976.

The Shadow Master. London: Hutchinson, 1978, and New York: Simon & Schuster, 1979.

The Survivors. London: Hutchinson, 1982.

The Border. London: Hutchinson, 1984.

Short Stories

Matters of Chance. London: Convent Garden Press, 1972.

The Silent Areas. London: Hutchinson, 1980.

Television Plays

Breath (1975).

Lunch (1981).

PHILIP HOBSBAUM (BORN 1932)

Verse

The Place's Fault, and Other Poems. London: Macmillan, and New York: St. Martin's Press, 1964.

In Retreat. London: Macmillan, and Chester Springs, Penn.: Dufour, 1966.

Coming Out Fighting. London: Macmillan, and Chester Springs, Penn.: Dufour, 1969.

Some Lovely Glorious Nothing. Frensham, Surrey: Sceptre Press, 1969.

Women and Animals. London: Macmillan, 1972.

MICHAEL HOROVITZ (BORN 1935)

Verse

Declaration. London: New Departures, 1963.

Strangers. London: New Departures, 1965.

Nude Lines for Barking (in Present Night Soho). London: Goliard Press, 1965.

High Notes from when I Was Rolling in Moss. London: Latimer Press, 1966.

Poetry for the People: A Verse Essay in "Bop" Prosody. London: Latimer Press, 1966.

Bank Holiday: A New Testament for the Love Generation. London: Latimer Press, 1967.
The Wolverhampton Wanderer. London: Latimer Press, 1969.
Love Poems. London: New Departures, 1971.

A. C. JACOBS (BORN 1937)

Verse

The Proper Blessing. London: Menard Press, 1976.

LAURENCE LERNER (BORN 1925)

Verse

Poems. Oxford: Fantasy Press, 1955.
Domestic Interior. London: Hutchinson, 1959.
The Directions of Memory: Poems, 1958–1962. London: Chatto & Windus, 1963.
Selves. London: Routledge, 1969.
A. R. T. H. U. R.: The Life and Opinions of a Digital Computer. Hassocks, Sussex: Harvester, 1974.
A. R. T. H. U. R. & M. A. R. T. H. A., or the Loves of the Computers. London: Secker & Warburg, 1980.
Bible Poems. London: Secker & Warburg, 1983.
Selected Poems. London: Secker & Warburg, 1983.

Novels

The Englishmen. London: Hamilton, 1959.
A Free Man. London: Chatto & Windus, 1968.

JEREMY ROBSON (BORN 1939)

Verse

Penny Pamphlets. London: Writers Club, 1961.
Poems for Jazz. Leicester: L. Weston, 1963.
Thirty-Three Poems. London: Sidgwick and Jackson, 1964.
In Focus. London: Allison and Busby, 1970.
Poems out of Israel. London: Turret Books, 1970.
Travelling. Longley, Hertfordshire: Kit-Kat Press, 1979.

Miscellaneous

Letters to Israel: Summer 1967. London: Vallentine & Mitchell, 1968.

Essay

"A Survey of Anglo-Jewish Poetry: Introduction." *Jewish Quarterly*, 14, 2 (1966), pp. 5–6.

ANTHONY RUDOLF (BORN 1942)

Verse

The Manifold Circle. Manchester: Carcanet, 1971.
The Same River Twice. Manchester: Carcanet, 1976.
After the Dream: Poems, 1964–1979. St Louis: Cauldron Press, 1980.

JON SILKIN (BORN 1930)

Bibliography

Poetry Review, 69, 4 (1980), pp. 30, 75–6. Special Silkin issue.

Verse

The Portrait, and Other Poems. Ilfracombe, Devon: Stockwell, 1950.
The Peacable Kingdom. London: Chatto & Windus, 1954. Republished New York: Yorick Books, 1969; London: Heron Press, 1975.
The Re-Ordering of the Stones. London: Chatto & Windus, 1961.
The Two Freedoms. London: Chatto & Windus, 1961.
Flower Poems. Leeds: Northern House.
Nature with Man. London: Chatto & Windus, 1965.
Poems, New and Selected. London: Chatto & Windus, and Middletown, Connecticut: Wesleyan University Press, 1966.
Three Poems. Cambridge, Mass.: Pym Randall Press, 1969.
Killhope Wheel. Ashington, Northumberland: MidNAG, 1971.
Amana Grass. London: Chatto & Windus, and Middletown, Connecticut: Wesleyan University Press, 1971.
Air that Pricks Earth. Rushden, Northamptonshire: Sceptre Press, 1973.
The Principle of Water. Cheadle, Cheshire: Carcanet, and New York: Wild & Wooley, 1974.
The Little Time-Keeper. Ashington, Northumberland: MidNAG, and Manchester: Carcanet, 1976, and New York: Norton, 1977.
The Psalms with their Spoils. London: Routledge & Kegan Paul, 1980.
Selected Poems. London: Routledge & Kegan Paul, 1980.
Communal. London: Menard Press, 1980. Poem card to mark the poet's fiftieth birthday.
"The Ship's Pasture." *Times Literary Supplement*, 13 November 1981, p. 1335.
"We Were Evacuated in the War." *Stand*, 24, 1 (1983), p. 4.

Footsteps on a Downcast Path. Michigan Quarterly Review, 22, 3 (1983), pp. 352–9. Limited edition, Bath: Mammon Press, 1984.

Select Essays

"Cultural Survival . . . 1. A Writer's View." *Jewish Quarterly*, 3, 2 (1955), pp. 36–7.
"Some Reflections on Anglo-Jewish Poetry." *Jewish Quarterly*, 5, 3 (1958), pp. 9–11.
"Anglo-Jewish Poetry." *Jewish Quarterly*. Special Edition (Spring 1967), pp. 22–4.
Out of Battle: Poetry of the Great War. London and New York: Oxford University Press, 1972.
"Introduction." In *Poetry of the Committed Individual*. Ed. Jon Silkin. Harmondsworth: Penguin Books, 1973, pp. 17–39.
"Introduction." In *The Penguin Book of First World War Poetry*. Ed. Jon Silkin. Harmondsworth: Penguin Books, 1979, pp. 11–73.

Critical Studies

Abse, D. "Jon Silkin." *Jewish Quarterly*, 13, 3 (1965), pp. 10–11.
Brown, M. *Double Lyric: Divisiveness and Communal Creativity in Recent English Poetry*. New York: Columbia University Press, 1980.
Cluysenaar, A. "Alone in a Mine of Reality: A Matrix in the Poetry of Jon Silkin." In *British Poetry since 1960: A Critical Survey*. Ed. M. Schmidt and G. Lindop. Oxford: Carcanet, 1972.
Schmidt, M. *An Introduction to 50 Modern British Poets*. London: Pan Books, 1979, pp. 392–7.

V. Refugees

Eva Figes (born 1932)

Novels

Equinox. London: Secker & Warburg, 1966.
Winter Journey. London: Faber, 1967, and New York: Hill & Wang, 1968.
Konek Landing. London: Faber, 1969.
B. London: Faber, 1972.
Days. London: Faber, 1974.
Nelly's Version. London: Secker & Warburg, 1977.
Waking. London: Hamilton, 1981, and New York: Pantheon, 1982.

Autobiography

Little Eden: A Child at War. London: Faber, 1978.

KAREN GERSHON (BORN 1923)

Verse

"The Relentless Years." In *New Poets, 1959.* Ed. Edwin Muir. London: Eyre
& Spottiswoode, 1959.
Selected Poems. London: Gollancz, and New York: Harcourt Brace, 1966.
The Pulse in Stone/Hadofek shebaeven. Tel-Aviv: Eked, 1970. Bilingual text.
Legacies and Encounters: Poems, 1966-1971. London: Gollancz, 1972.
My Daughters, My Sisters. London: Gollancz, 1974.
Coming Back from Babylon. London: Gollancz, 1979.

Novel

Burn Helen. Brighton: Harvester, 1980.

Short Story

"Old Hesse." *Quest,* 2 (1967), pp. 62-4.

Miscellaneous

We Came as Children. Ed. Karen Gershon. London: Gollancz, 1966. Anthology
of the experiences of Jewish refugees from Germany.
*Postscript: A Collective Account of the Lives of Jews in West Germany since the
Second World War.* Ed. Karen Gershon. London: Gollancz, 1969.

Essays

"A Stranger in a Strange Land." *Jewish Quarterly,* 7, 1 (1959), pp. 10-11.
"Reliving the Past." *Jewish Quarterly,* Special Edition (Spring 1967), pp. 33-5.

MICHAEL HAMBURGER (BORN 1924)

Collected Works

Collected Poems. Manchester: Carcanet, 1984.

Verse

Later Hogarth. London: Cope & Fenwick, 1945.
Flowering Cactus: Poems, 1942-1949. Aldington, Kent: Hand & Flower Press,
1950.
Poems, 1950-1951. Aldington, Kent: Hand & Flower Press, 1952.

The Dual Site, Poems. New York: Poetry London-New York Editions, 1957, and London: Routledge, 1958.

Weather and Season: New Poems. London: Longmans, and New York: Atheneum, 1963.

In Flashlight. Leeds: Northern House, 1965.

Zwischen den Sprachen: Essays und Gedichte. Frankfurt am Main: S. Fischer, 1966. German and English texts.

In Massachusetts. Mnemonie, Wisconsin: Ox Head Press, 1967.

Feeding the Chickadees. London: Turret Books, 1968.

Travelling: Poems, 1963–1968. London: Fulcrum Press, 1969.

Home. Frensham, Surrey: Sceptre Press, 1969.

Travelling I–IV. London: Agenda Editions, 1973. Limited edition.

Ownerless Earth: New and Selected Poems, 1950–1972. Cheadle, Cheshire: Carcanet Press, and New York: Dutton, 1973.

Conversations with Charwomen. Rushden, Northamptonshire: Sceptre Press, 1973.

Real Estate. Manchester: Carcanet, 1977.

Variations. Manchester: Carcanet, 1981.

Autobiography

A Mug's Game: Intermittent Memoirs. Cheadle, Cheshire: Carcanet, 1973.

Interview

"On Being English and Jewish (4)." *Jewish Quarterly,* 12, 1 (1964), pp. 6–8.

Critical Studies

Crick, J. "The Chronicler and the Poet: Michael Hamburger at Fifty." *Poetry Nation,* 3 (1974), pp. 102–8.

Schmidt, M. *An Introduction to 50 Modern British Poets.* London: Pan Books, 1979, pp. 339–45.

LOTTE KRAMER

Verse

Ice-Break. Peterborough: Annakin Fine Arts, 1980.

Family Arrivals. Pinner, Middlesex: Poet & Printer, 1981.

A Lifelong House. Sutton, Surrey: Hippopotamus Press, 1984.

RUDOLF NASSAUER (BORN 1924)

Novels

The Hooligans. London: Owen, 1960.

The Cuckoo. London: Owen, 1962

The Examination. London: Cape, 1973.
The Unveiling. London: Cape, 1975.
The Agents of Love. London: Cape, 1976.
Midlife Feasts. London: Cape, 1977.
Reparations. London: Cape, 1981.

Verse

Poems. London: Methuen, 1947.

VI. NEW VOICES

STEPHEN POLIAKOFF (BORN 1952)

Drama

Granny. Produced London, 1969
Bambi Ramm. Produced London, 1970.
Day with my Sister. Produced Edinburgh, 1971.
Pretty Boy. Produced London, 1972.
Theatre Outside. Produced London, 1973.
Berlin Days. Produced London, 1973.
Carnation Gang. Produced London, 1973.
Clever Soldiers. Produced London, 1974.
Heroes. Produced London, 1975.
Join the Dance. Produced New York, 1975.
Hitting Town. London: French, 1977. Produced London, 1975, and New York, 1979.
Hitting Town and City Sugar. London: Eyre Methuen, 1976. *City Sugar* produced New York, 1978, and London, 1979.
Strawberry Fields. London: Eyre Methuen, 1977. Produced London, 1976, and New York, 1978.
Shout Across the Fields. London: Eyre Methuen, 1977. Produced London, 1978, and New York, 1980.
American Days. London: Eyre Methuen, 1979. Produced London, 1979, and New York, 1980.
The Summer Party. London: Eyre Methuen, 1980. Produced Sheffield, 1980.
Favourite Nights. Produced London, 1981.

Television Plays

Stronger than the Sun (1977).
Caught on a Train. (1980).

Critical Studies

Hayman, R. *British Theatre since 1955.* Oxford: Oxford University Press, 1979, pp. 118–25.

Kerensky, O. *The New British Drama.* London: Hamilton, 1977, pp. 245–68.

CLIVE SINCLAIR (BORN 1945)

Short Stories

Bibliosexuality. London: Allison & Busby, 1973.

Hearts of Gold. London: Allison & Busby, 1979, and New York: Schocken, 1982. Republished Harmondsworth: Penguin Books, 1983.

Bedbugs. London: Allison & Busby, and New York: Schocken, 1982. Republished Harmondsworth: Penguin Books, 1983.

"Scriptophobia." In *London Tales.* Ed. J. Evans. London: Hamilton, 1983.

VII. ANTHOLOGIES

Charles, Gerda, ed. *Modern Jewish Stories.* London: Faber, 1963, and Englewood Cliffs, N. J.: Prentice-Hall, 1964.

Dor, Moshe, ed. *Otam panim: Meshorerim yehudiim bney zmanenu beangliya.* Tel-Aviv: Eked, 1981.

Frankel, William, ed. *Friday Nights: A Jewish Chronicle Anthology, 1841–1971.* London: Jewish Chronicle Publications, 1973.

Goldman, William, ed. '. . . *In England and in English': A Collection of Modern Stories by Jewish Writers.* London: Art and Educational, 1947.

Leftwich, Joseph, ed. *Yisrōel: The Jewish Omnibus,* London: James Clerke, 1933; revised edition, 1945.

Litvinoff, Emanuel, ed. *The Penguin Book of Jewish Short Stories,* Harmondsworth: Penguin Books, 1979.

Schwartz, Howard and Rudolf, Anthony, eds. *Voices within the Ark: The Modern Jewish Poets.* New York: Avon Books, 1980.

Sonntag, Jacob, ed. *Caravan: A Jewish Quarterly Omnibus.* New York: Yoseloff, 1962.

Sonntag, Jacob, ed. *Jewish Perspectives: 25 Years of Modern Jewish Writing (A Jewish Quarterly Anthology).* London: Secker and Warburg, 1980.

VIII. SUGGESTED READING

1. CRITICAL STUDIES

Abse, D., Kershaw, J. and Hamburger, M. "Anglo-Jewish Poetry: The Poets About Themselves." *Jewish Quarterly*, 14, 2 (1966), pp. 33–6.

Amis, Kingsley. "Anglo-Jewish Literature: The Need for Criticism." *Jewish Quarterly*, 1, 2 (1955), pp. 81–2.

Baker, W. "Reflections on Anglo-Jewish Poetry." *Jewish Quarterly*, 26, 3–4 (1978), pp. 73–84.

Baker, W. and Tabachnick, S. "Reflections on Ethnicity in Anglo-Jewish Writing." *Jewish Quarterly*, 21, 1–2 (1973), pp. 94–7.

Bartov, Hanoch. *An Israeli at the Court of St. James's*. London: Vallentine and Mitchell, 1971.

Charles, Gerda. "East and West." *Jewish Quarterly*, 8, 1 (1961), pp. 5–7.

Charles, Gerda. "Elizabethan Age of Modern Jewish Literature, 1950–1960: Decade of the Great Breakthrough." *World Jewry* (September 1961), pp. 15–17.

Charles, Gerda. "Trends in Anglo-Jewish Writing." *Jewish Quarterly*, 11, 1 (1963), pp. 11–13.

Charles, Gerda. "Three Recent Novels." *Jewish Quarterly*, 14, 3 (1966), p. 43.

Daiches, David. "The Possibilities of an Anglo-Jewish Culture." *Jewish Quarterly*, 3, 1 (1955), pp. 37–9.

Daiches, David. "Some Aspects of Anglo-American Fiction." *Jewish Quarterly*, 21, 1–2 (1973), pp. 88–93. Republished in *Jewish Perpectives*.

Fisch, H. *The Dual Image: A Study of the Jew in English Literature*. New York: Lincolns-Prager, 1959; revised edition, London: World Jewish Congress, and New York: Ktav, 1971.

Fuller, R. "Anglo-Jewish Poetry: What is Different about it? (2)." *Jewish Quarterly*, 14, 2 (1966), p. 26.

Fyvel, T. "The Jewish New Wave." *Jewish Chronicle*, 13 September 1963, New Year Section, pp. 37, 44.

Glanville, Brian. "The Anglo-Jewish Writer." *Encounter*, 24, 2 (1960), pp. 62–4.

Hill, D. "Anglo-Jewish Poetry: What is Different about it? (4)" *Jewish Quarterly*, 14, 2 (1966), pp. 29–30.

Hobsbaum, P. "A Peep into the Mirror: Problems of the Anglo-Jewish Writer." *Jewish Chronicle*, 8 December 1967, Literary Supplement, pp. vii–viii.

Jackson, F. "The Outlook for New Playwrights." *Jewish Quarterly*, 1, 1 (1953), pp. 79–82.

Jacobs, L., Rayner, J., Ellinson, G., and Finestein, I. "What is the Answer?" *Jewish Chronicle*, 23 January 1959, p. 17.

Jacobson, D. "Jewish Writing in England." *Commentary*, 28 (1964), pp. 46–50.

Landa, M. *The Jew in Drama*. London: P. S. King, 1926; reprinted New York: Ktav, 1969.

Leftwich, J. "Anglo-Jewish Literature." *Jewish Quarterly*, 1, 1 (1953), pp. 14–24.

Pollins, H. "Sociological Aspects of Anglo-Jewish Literature." *Jewish Journal of Sociology*, 2 (1962), pp. 25–41.

Popkin, H. "Jewish Writers in England." *Commentary* (February 1961), pp. 135–41.

Porter, P. "Anglo-Jewish Poetry: What is Different about it? (3)" *Jewish Quarterly*, 14, 2 (1966), pp. 27–8.

Rabin, C. "English, Hebrew or Yiddish?" *Jewish Quarterly*, 3, 1 (1955), pp. 35–7.

Rabin, C. "Cultural Survival . . . 2. A Scholar's View." *Jewish Quarterly*, 3, 2 (1955), p. 37.

Reid-Banks, L. "Why Must They Indulge in Self-Flagellation?" *Jewish Observer and Middle East Review*, 17 February 1977.

Reid-Banks, L. "Why I Feel Compelled to Write about Israel." *Jewish Quarterly*, 25, 1 (1977), pp. 16–20, 40.

Roback, A. "Can we Have a Jewish Culture in English?" *Jewish Quarterly*, 3, 1 (1955), pp. 31–4.

Roditi, E., Rudolf, A. and Josipovici, G. "What is a Jewish Poem?" *Jewish Quarterly*, 29, 2 (1981), pp. 56–7.

Ross, V. "What, Why and Who?" *Jewish Quarterly*, 2, 1 (1954), pp. 74–5.

Roston, M. "Introduction." In M. Landa, *The Jew in Drama*. New York: Ktav, 1969, ix–xxx.

Schiff, E. *From Stereotype to Metaphor: The Jew in Contemporary Drama*. Albany: State University of New York Press, 1982.

Sergeant, H. "Anglo-Jewish Poetry: What is Different about it? (5)" *Jewish Quarterly*, 14, 2 (1966), pp. 30–1.

Smith, J. "Anglo-Jewish Poetry: What is Different about it? (1)" *Jewish Quarterly*, 14, 2 (1966), pp. 24–5.

Sonntag, J., and others. "Writing about Jews: A Symposium." *Jewish Quarterly*, 13, 2 (1965), pp. 12–16.

Spencer, C. "Jews in Publishing." *Jewish Quarterly*, 6, 2 (1958–1959), pp. 45–50.

Spencer, C. "The New Generation of Anglo-Jewish Playwrights." *Jewish Book Annual*, 22 (1964), pp. 42–50.

Spencer, C. "Towards a Definition of Jewish Art." *Jewish Quarterly*, 26, 4 (1978), pp. 55–60.

Trewin, J. "A Desire to Act (Yvonne Mitchell)." *Plays and Players*, 27, 3 (1979), pp. 14–15.

Winegarten, R. "The Anglo-Jewish Dramatist in Search of his Soul." *Midstream*, 12, 6 (1966), pp. 40–52.

Yudkin, L. *Jewish Writing and Identity in the Twentieth Century*. London: Croom Helm, 1982.

Croom Helm, 1982.

Zatlin, L. *The Nineteenth-Century Anglo-Jewish Novel*. New York: Twayne's, 1982.

Zucker, D. "Who Cares? Who Listens? A Rabbi's Complaint." *Jewish Quarterly*, 27, 1 (1979), pp. 27–30.

2. SOCIOLOGY, SOCIAL HISTORY, MEMOIRS

Alderman, G. *The Jewish Community in British Politics*. Oxford: Clarendon Press, 1982.

Angoff, C. "The Future of European Jewry: The Need for an Enquiry (An American Writer's View of Anglo-Jewry)." *Jewish Quarterly*, 8, 4 (1961), pp. 8–12.

Aris, S. *The Jews in Business*. London: Cape, 1970. Republished Harmondsworth: Penguin Books, 1973.

Bermant, Chaim. *Troubled Eden: An Anatomy of British Jewry*. London: Vallentine and Mitchell, 1969, and New York: Basic Books, 1970.

Bermant, Chaim. *The Cousinhood: The Anglo-Jewish Gentry*, London: Eyre and Spottiswoode, 1971, and New York: Macmillan, 1972.

Bermant, Chaim. *The Walled Garden: The Saga of Jewish Family Life and Tradition*. London: Weidenfeld & Nicholson, 1974.

Bermant, Chaim. *Point of Arrival: A Study of London's East End*. London: Eyre Methuen, and New York: Macmillan, 1975.

Bermant, Chaim. *The Jews*. London: Weidenfeld & Nicolson, 1971.

Blacker, Harry ("Nero"). *Just Like It Was: Memoirs of the Mittel East*. London: Vallentine & Mitchell, 1974.

Brotz, H. "The Position of the Jews in English Society." *Jewish Journal of Sociology*, 1, 1 (1959), pp. 94–113.

Camberton, R. "Hessel Street: Reminiscences of the East End." *Jewish Quarterly*, 3, 1 (1955), pp. 20–2.

Canetti, Elias. *The Tongue Set Free: Remembrances of a European Childhood*. New York: Seabury Press, 1979.

Daiches, David. *Two Worlds: An Edinburgh Jewish Childhood*, London, 1957. Republished Brighton: Sussex University Press, 1971.

Fishman, W. *East End Jewish Radicals, 1875–1914*. London: Duckworth, 1975.

Fishman, W. *The Streets of East London*. London: Duckworth, 1979. With photographs by Nicholas Breach.

Freedman, M., ed. *A Minority in Britain: Social History of the Anglo-Jewish Community*. London: Vallentine & Mitchell, 1955.

Gartner, L. *The Jewish Immigrant in England, 1870–1914*. London: Allen & Unwin, 1960.

Gould, J. and Esh, S. eds. *Jewish Life in Modern Britain*. London: Routledge & Kegan Paul, 1964.

Krausz, E. "Occupational and Social Advancement in Anglo-Jewry." *Jewish Journal of Sociology*, 4, 1 (1962), pp. 82–90.

Lewis, C. *A Soho Address.* London: Gollancz, 1965.

Lipman, V. *Social History of the Jews in England, 1850–1950.* London: Watts & Co., 1954.

Lipman, V. "Trends in Anglo-Jewish Occupations." *Jewish Journal of Sociology*, 2 (1960), pp. 201–18.

Litvinoff, B. *A Peculiar People: Inside the Jewish World Today.* London: Weidenfeld & Nicolson, 1969.

Mindlin, M. and Bermant, C., eds. *Explorations: An Annual on Jewish Themes.* London: Barrie and Rockliff, 1967.

Pollins, H. *Economic History of the Jews in England.* London: Associated University Presses, and Rutherford: Fairleigh Dickinson, 1983.

Prais, S. and Schmool, M. "Statistics of Jewish Marriages in Great Britain, 1901–1965." *Jewish Journal of Sociology*, 9, 2 (1967), pp. 149–174.

Prais, S. and Schmool, M. "The Size and Structure of the Anglo-Jewish Population, 1960–65." *Jewish Journal of Sociology*, 10, 1 (1968), pp. 5–34.

Prais, S. and Schmool, M. "The Social-Class Structure of Anglo-Jewry, 1961." *Jewish Journal of Sociology*, 17 (1975), pp. 5–15.

Roth, C. *A History of the Jews in England.* 3rd edition. Oxford: Oxford University Press, 1978.

Sharot, S. *Judaism: A Sociology.* Newton Abbot: David and Charles, 1976.

White, J. *Rothschild Buildings: Life in an East End Tenement Block, 1887–1920.* London: Routledge & Kegan Paul, 1980.

Index